Income and Asset Disclosure

Stolen Asset Recovery (StAR) Series

StAR—the Stolen Asset Recovery Initiative—is a partnership between the World Bank Group and the United Nations Office on Drugs and Crime (UNODC) that supports international efforts to end safe havens for corrupt funds. StAR works with developing countries and financial centers to prevent the laundering of the proceeds of corruption and to facilitate more systematic and timely return of stolen assets.

The Stolen Asset Recovery (StAR) Series supports the efforts of StAR and UNODC by providing practitioners with knowledge and policy tools that consolidate international good practice and wide-ranging practical experience on cutting edge issues related to anticorruption and asset recovery efforts. For more information, visit www.worldbank.org/star.

Titles in the Stolen Asset Recovery (StAR) Series

Stolen Asset Recovery: A Good Practices Guide for Non-Conviction Based Asset Forfeiture (2009) by Theodore S. Greenberg, Linda M. Samuel, Wingate Grant, and Larissa Gray

Politically Exposed Persons: Preventive Measures for the Banking Sector (2010) by Theodore S. Greenberg, Larissa Gray, Delphine Schantz, Carolin Gardner, and Michael Latham

Asset Recovery Handbook: A Guide for Practitioners (2011) by Jean-Pierre Brun, Larissa Gray, Clive Scott, and Kevin Stephenson

Barriers to Asset Recovery: An Analysis of the Key Barriers and Recommendations for Action (2011) by Kevin Stephenson, Larissa Gray, and Ric Power

The Puppet Masters: How the Corrupt Use Legal Structures to Hide Stolen Assets and What to Do About It (2011) by Emile van der Does de Willebois, J.C. Sharman, Robert Harrison, Ji Won Park, and Emily Halter

Public Office, Private Interests: Accountability through Income and Asset Disclosure (2012)

Income and Asset Disclosure: Case Study Illustrations (2013)

DIRECTIONS IN DEVELOPMENT
Finance

Income and Asset Disclosure

Case Study Illustrations

A companion volume to
Public Office, Private Interests:
Accountability through Income and
Asset Disclosure

StAR Stolen Asset Recovery Initiative

The World Bank • UNODC

Library of Congress Cataloging-in-Publication Data

Income and asset disclosure : case study illustrations.
    pages cm
    Includes bibliographical references.
    ISBN 978-0-8213-9796-1 — ISBN 978-0-8213-9797-8 (electronic)
    1. Political corruption—Prevention—Case studies. 2. Financial disclosure—Case studies. 3. Financial disclosure—Law and legislation—Case studies. I. World Bank.
    JF1081.I53 2013
    364.4'04563—dc23   2012051382

Contents

Boxes

Figures

Tables

Acknowledgments

This volume is the result of a project undertaken by a team from the World Bank (WB) and the Stolen Assets Recovery Initiative (StAR) that included Daniel W. Barnes, Tammar Berger, Ruxandra Burdescu, Stuart Gilman, Alexandra Habershon, Gary J. Reid, and Stephanie E. Trapnell. The case studies in this volume were prepared by the following World Bank and StAR team: Aisuluu Aitbaeva, Daniel W. Barnes, Tammar Berger, Lissa Betzieche, Ruxandra Burdescu, Alexandra Habershon, Thomas Iverson, Modest Kwapinski, Massimo Mastruzzi, Hari Mulukutla, Yousef Nasrallah, Chiara Rocha, Susana Simonyan, and Stephanie E. Trapnell.

The team gratefully acknowledges the expert guidance and advice of peer reviewers Janos Bertok (Head of the Integrity Unit, Public Governance and Territorial Development Directorate, Organisation for Economic Co-operation and Development), Drago Kos (Chair of the Council of Europe's Group of States against Corruption), Martin Kreutner (Chair of the Steering Committee, International Anti-Corruption Academy), Veronica Zavala Lombardi (Manager, Public Sector, Latin America and the Caribbean Region, the World Bank), Rick Messick (Senior Operations Specialist, Integrity Vice Presidency, the World Bank), Roberto de Michele (Principal Policy Officer, Office of Institutional Integrity, the Inter-American Development Bank), and Oliver Stolpe (Acting Country Representative, Country Office Nigeria, United Nations Office on Drugs and Crime [UNODC]).

Debbie Wetzel and Randi Ryterman (WB); Dimitri Vlassis (UNODC); Ted Greenberg (WB); Mark Vlasic (Georgetown University); Frank Anthony Fariello (WB); Ranjana Mukherjee (WB); Sanja Madzarevic-Sujster (WB); Anna Walters and Piers Harrison (DFID); Hatem Aly (UNODC); Olga Savran, Francisco Cardona, and Inese Gaika (OECD); Sahr Kpundeh (WB); James Anderson (WB); and Christiaan Poortman and Tinatin Ninua (Transparency International) have also provided expert guidance or peer review at different stages of the project. Many thanks to our colleagues from the World Bank who took time to offer advice to the team at different stages of the project: Vikram K. Chand, Chris Parel, Massimo Mastruzzi, Rob Gaylard, Felipe Saez, Gregory Kisunko, Amitabha Mukherjee, Natalia Pisareva, Matija Laco, Dubravka Jerman, Christine de Mariz Rozeira, Kathrin A. Plangemann, Zahid Hasnain, Christopher Finch, Arshad Sayed, Otgonbayar Yadmaa, Fernando Paredes, Anabela Abreu, Antonio Blasco, Karla Maria Gonzalez, Anupama Dokeniya, Brian Levy, Colum Garrity, Verena Fritz, Victor Dumas (PRMPS), Larissa Gray (FFSFI), Ivana Rossi (FPD), and

Laura Pop (FPD). We extend special thanks to Barbara Fredericks, Pamela Smith, and Catherine Newcombe (USDOJ). Ladan Cherenegar, Lark Grier, Maksat Kobonbaev, Teresa Marchiori, Sabina Dyussekeyeva, and Claudia Oriolo (WB) have also provided support at different stages of the project.

The team also wishes to thank the following colleagues for their guidance and support in the completion of this project: Linda Van Gelder (Sector Director, Governance & Public Sector, PRMPS), Jean Pesme (Manager, Financial Market Integrity, FFSFI, and Coordinator, StAR), Jim Brumby (Sector Manager, PRMPS), Francesca Recanatini (Senior Economist, PRMPS), Tim Steele (Senior Governance Specialist, StAR), Adrian Fozzard (Lead Public Sector Specialist, PRMPS), and other StAR and World Bank colleagues, including, from StAR, Eli Bielasiak-Robinson, Michelle Morales, and Zita Lichtenberg, and, from PRMPS, Monica Bascon, Marie Charity Quiroz, Humaira Qureshi, Max Jira, Khady Fall Lo, and Ayompe Ayompe. Thanks also to Diane Stamm for her editorial assistance with both volumes.

About the Contributors

Aisuluu Aitbaeva works at the International Finance Corporation (IFC), where she is part of the organization's Integrity and Anti-Money Laundering and Counter Financing of Terrorism efforts. Prior to joining the IFC, she worked for the World Bank's Governance & Public Sector Management Unit. She graduated from Georgetown University Law Center.

Daniel W. Barnes is a consultant with the Governance & Public Sector Management Unit of the World Bank, where he is advancing research on governance, anticorruption, and accountability mechanisms. Previously, he was an aide to a U.S. Member of Congress. He is a PhD candidate at Johns Hopkins University, School of Advanced International Studies (SAIS) and he holds a BA from Harvard University.

Tammar Berger is a consultant with the Stolen Asset Recovery (StAR) Initiative, where she focuses on anticorruption and asset recovery efforts. She has also worked with the World Bank's Governance & Public Sector Management Unit on transparency and accountability mechanisms. She holds a JD from Georgetown University Law Center and an MA in international relations from Johns Hopkins University, School of Advanced International Studies (SAIS).

Alexandra Habershon is the team leader on financial disclosure for the Stolen Asset Recovery (StAR) Initiative and the coordinator of the International Corruption Hunters Alliance for the World Bank's Integrity Vice Presidency Unit (INT). She has worked for over 12 years as a consultant for the World Bank and other donors on anticorruption and public sector reform. She has a PhD in cultural studies from Georgetown University.

Massimo Mastruzzi joined the World Bank Institute in 2000 and joined Global Programs in 2002. While at the World Bank, his work has focused on statistical and econometric analysis, with particular emphasis on issues related to governance and corruption. He is currently working on governance and anticorruption technical assistance projects in Latin America. He received an MA in economics and an MA in European studies from Georgetown University.

Hari Mulukutla has implemented anticorruption capacity-building programs in Africa and Asia for over seven years, with a focus on data management for income and asset disclosure mechanisms, anonymous whistleblowing, open source intelligence for financial investigations and asset recovery, reducing trade barriers in West Africa, and strengthening anticorruption commissions. He is a contributing author of *Tracing Stolen Assets*.

Yousef Nasrallah was a prosecutor in Bethlehem and chief prosecutor at the Attorney General's office in Ramallah, West Bank, from 1999 until 2005. He served as an adviser to the chief justice and, later, as a UNDP consultant on judicial reform in Palestine. Since 2008, he has worked as a Rule of Law contractor at the United States Institute of Peace and a consultant at the World Bank.

Stephanie E. Trapnell is a consultant with the Governance & Public Sector Management Unit of the World Bank, where she is leading research on transparency and accountability mechanisms and the design of actionable governance indicators. She is pursuing a PhD in sociology at George Mason University and holds an MA in international relations from Johns Hopkins University, School of Advanced International Studies (SAIS).

Abbreviations

AD	Asset Declaration
ADU	Asset Declaration Unit (Argentina)
AGI	Actionable Governance Indicator
AO	Anti-Corruption Office (Argentina)
CGC	Comptroller General's Office (Contraloría General de Cuentas) (Guatemala)
CIS	Commonwealth of Independent States
COI	conflict of interest
CPD	Corruption Prevention Department (Hong Kong SAR, China)
CSB	Civil Service Bureau (Hong Kong SAR, China)
CSR	Civil Service Regulation (Hong Kong SAR, China)
DAEO	designated agency ethics official (United States)
DAVIP	Department for Verification, Analysis and Investigation of Income and Assets (Departamento de Análisis, Verificación e Investigación Patrimonial) (Guatemala)
DDJP	Income and Asset Declaration Department (Departamento de Declaración Jurada Patrimonial) (Guatemala)
FRG	Guatemalan Republican Front (Frente Republicano Guatemalteco)
GDP	gross domestic product
GRECO	Group of States against Corruption
HR	human resources
HZMO	Croatian Pension Insurance Fund
HZZO	Croatian Health Insurance Fund
IAAC	Independent Agency against Corruption (Mongolia)
IACAC	Inter-American Convention against Corruption
IAD	income and asset disclosure
IADB	Inter-American Development Bank
ICAC	Independent Commission against Corruption (Hong Kong SAR, China)

ID	Investigations Department of the Anti-Corruption Office (Argentina)
IT	information technology
KPK	Corruption Eradication Commission (Indonesia)
LHKPN	Department for the Wealth Reports of State Officers, or Wealth-Reporting Department (Indonesia)
MenPAN	Ministry for Administrative Reform (Indonesia)
MoJ	Ministry of Justice and Human Rights (Argentina)
NGO	nongovernmental organization
OGE	Office of Government Ethics (United States)
PAM	Public Accountability Mechanisms Initiative
PAS	presidential appointment with Senate confirmation (PAS) positions (United States)
POBO	Prevention of Bribery Ordinance (Hong Kong SAR, China)
PSD	Program Services Division (United States)
SAR	special administrative region
StAR	Stolen Asset Recovery Initiative (World Bank/UNODC)
UNCAC	United Nations Convention against Corruption
UNODC	United Nations Office on Drugs and Crime
URNG	National Guatemalan Revolutionary Unity (Unidad Revolucionaria Nacional Guatemalteca)
USKOK	Office for the Suppression of Corruption and Organized Crime (Croatia)

Currency

HK$	Hong Kong dollars
HRK	Croatian kunas
JD	Jordanian dinars
Q	Guatemalan quetzales
RF	Rwandan francs
Rp	Indonesian rupiah
€	euros

Introduction

The requirement that public officials declare their income and assets can help deter the use of public office for private gain. Income and asset disclosure (IAD) systems can provide a means to detect and manage potential conflicts of interest, and can assist in the prevention, detection, and prosecution of illicit enrichment by public officials. Growing attention to anticorruption policies, institutions, and practices has led to increased interest in financial disclosure systems and the role they can play in supporting national anticorruption strategies and in helping to instill an expectation of ethical conduct for individuals in public office. IAD systems are also a key element in the implementation and enforcement of provisions of the United Nations Convention against Corruption and other international anticorruption agreements. This attention has sparked interest among policy makers and practitioners in the design features and implementation practices that make for effective financial disclosure administration. The case studies collected in this volume are intended to profile a range of systems and practices to help respond to this growing interest.

Background to the Case Studies

This publication is a companion volume to *Public Office, Private Interests: Accountability through Income and Asset Disclosure,* which provides an overview of the common questions faced by policy makers and practitioners and which illustrates approaches and key considerations for effectively responding to them. This volume of case studies profiles the financial disclosure systems in 10 countries and a single special administrative region: Argentina; Croatia;

This volume is the result of a joint project of the Stolen Asset Recovery (StAR) Initiative and the Public Accountability Mechanisms (PAM) initiative in the Governance & Public Sector Management Unit of the World Bank. The findings in these case studies are based on desk research and interviews with financial disclosure system administrators, policy makers, civil society representatives, and academics. The methodology and indicators that guided this research are provided in appendix A, appendix B provides a table of key characteristics of selected IAD systems, and Appendix C provides a list of the people and agencies consulted in the drafting of the case studies.

Guatemala; Hong Kong SAR, China; Indonesia; Jordan; the Kyrgyz Republic; Mongolia; Rwanda; Slovenia; and the United States.

This project was undertaken to help answer questions often posed by practitioners and policy makers working in the area of income and asset disclosure. These include:

- How do other economies manage and administer their IAD systems?
- What type of agency is responsible for administering each economy's system?
- What is the mandate of those agencies?
- What resources do those agencies have at their disposal?

Beyond institutional arrangements and implementation capacity, a great deal of interest also arises around the areas of data management, the use of information technology, sanctions, and public access to declarations. This interest is usually driven by such questions as:

- What is the scope and coverage of the IAD system in other economies?
- How does the IAD agency manage and monitor submission compliance?
- Do they verify the accuracy of declarations, and, if so, how?
- To what kinds of information do they provide public access, and how do they do so?
- What sanctions do they apply in cases of noncompliance, and how are these enforced?

Structure of the Case Studies

Each case study is introduced with a box that provides a summary of the key characteristics of the financial disclosure system and the main findings of the case study. The case studies are structured as follows: a brief overview of the system; a background section describing the relevant legislation (this includes a profile of the in-law provisions that define which officials are subject to the disclosure requirement, the content of declarations, filing frequency, submission compliance and content verification, sanctions, public access, and investigations); the mandate and structure of the implementing agency; and the resources and procedures of the system (this includes facilities and information technology resources, human resources, budget, regulatory function, and practices related to managing submission compliance, content verification, investigations, interagency collaboration, public access, reporting, and outreach). A conclusion summarizes the main findings.

This volume does not seek to answer the question "What works best?" Instead, and intentionally, it describes experiences in different contexts, and the approaches taken to address challenges particular to each jurisdiction, in the hope that these experiences can provide valuable insights to assist policy makers and practitioners in thinking through appropriate strategies for meeting the objectives of their financial disclosure regime. Although not emphasizing a best-practice approach, this volume highlights approaches that have been effective in different contexts and the challenges faced in implementing those approaches. The case studies do not examine the broader applications of financial disclosure systems in combating corruption, nor do they consider any results achieved that lie beyond the mandate of the implementing agency (such as successful prosecutions for corruption in which declarations may have assisted). However, where applicable, the case studies do describe the relationship between the implementing agency and other institutions and actors responsible for enforcing sanctions provided for in the financial disclosure legislation.

The findings from these case studies have contributed to the drafting of a guide on financial disclosure system design and implementation, the companion volume to this one: *Public Office, Private Interests: Accountability through Income and Asset Disclosure*, published in 2012 by the World Bank and StAR (see box I.1). The analysis and findings from that volume can be summarized by the following key considerations.

Box I.1 Key Takeaways from *Public Office, Private Interests: Accountability through Income and Asset Disclosure*

1. ***Understanding the context.*** The effectiveness of a financial disclosure system is, to a large extent, dependent on elements of the local context (including elements of the institutional, cultural, and political environment in which it operates). An assessment of these factors prior to designing or upgrading an IAD system is important to ensure a good fit between the agency's role, functions, and procedures and the local environment. The key principle here is that *context matters*.

2. ***Building capacity incrementally.*** Although there is no single or standardized approach that will work in every context, systems that begin with too many requirements—such as too large a pool of filers—and with inadequate institutional capacities to manage and enforce compliance are more likely to fail than those that start with modest, manageable objectives. Building capacity incrementally can be achieved by, for example, gradually expanding the submission requirement to a widening pool of filers, beginning with the highest-ranking officials; by putting in place the capacities and procedures for managing submission compliance before introducing verification procedures; or by limiting costly functions, such as verification, to a fraction of total declarations through systematic random sampling and risk-based selection of declarations for verification.

3. ***Managing expectations: establishing the credibility of the system with stakeholders.*** The credibility of government efforts to establish and enforce financial disclosure requirements goes a long way toward establishing a "culture of integrity" that instills behavioral norms of ethics in government. Fostering confidence in an IAD system's ability to enhance transparency can positively shift perceptions of corruption, which, in turn, influences behaviors. The process of developing IAD systems is often highly politicized, however, and managing expectations during what can be a lengthy process of debate and gradual implementation can be vital to its success.

Key Considerations in Designing and Implementing a Financial Disclosure System

What needs or behaviors is the system intended to address? Decisions about the design of an IAD system should be determined by the behaviors the system is intended to address and by consideration of the environment (institutional or political) in which it will operate. For example, for countries where perceptions of corruption are high, a system designed to detect illicit enrichment might be important. Assisting officials in detecting and managing potential conflicts of interest acquires greater significance—and becomes a greater challenge for a financial disclosure framework—if conflict-of-interest oversight mechanisms are not embedded in public service administrative mechanisms and/or codes of ethics.

How many filers should be obligated to declare, how much information, and how frequently? This question relates to the coverage and scope of an IAD system. The first hurdle for an IAD system is to ensure that all officials obligated to submit a financial disclosure form have done so. An excessively ambitious extent of coverage can compromise an agency's ability to meet that standard and can undermine the system's credibility. Keeping the filing population to a manageable size—by requiring disclosure from high-ranking and high-risk positions, for example—is one way of ensuring this.

The scope of the system (how much information is declared and how frequently) requires a similar consideration of capacity and scale. The type of information declared will largely be determined by the mandate of the system. Although there are universal elements—such as income, movable and immovable assets, and liabilities—in practice, the information required on declaration forms varies widely, even between systems with similar mandates.

What kind of budgetary and resource support is required? It is difficult to generalize about the budgetary needs for implementing an IAD system or to compare practices among different economies. This is because of the limitations of available data and the variations in practice resulting from the different mandates and contexts of country systems. The scope and coverage of the system and decisions about technology use will also have important implications for the system's workload and budget. A key consideration is that the budget be sufficient, stable, and predictable to ensure the proper staffing and functioning of the system according to its mandate.

Should the content of declarations be verified and, if so, how? As a general principle, if an IAD system is to establish *a credible threat of detection* of illicit enrichment and conflicts of interest, then some sort of scrutiny of declarations is required. Beyond reviewing declarations to ensure that they are complete when submitted, there are various possible approaches to reviewing declarations to ensure that the information is accurate. An agency's ability to cross-check the content of declarations for accuracy depends on the existence and accessibility of external sources of data against which to compare the income and assets declared by officials (for example, banking and tax information; land; auto insurance; and other registries). If these data sources are available (particularly online), or if there is effective collaboration among agencies, then it may be possible for the agency to verify a relatively large number of declarations for the accuracy of certain categories of income or assets. However, in many economies the availability and reliability of such data sources are mixed. In these contexts, developing strategies and determining risk factors for targeting the verification of declarations of high-risk individuals becomes important. Detecting irregularities between a filer's declarations over time is another strategy. For some agencies, conducting lifestyle checks provides a means—albeit a costly one—to detect potential inconsistencies between a filer's declared income and assets and his or her actual ones. In other agencies, when the declarations are publicly available, wholly or partially, civil society and the media assist in providing that additional layer of scrutiny.

Should public access to information about the content of declarations be provided and, if so, how? Public disclosure of financial disclosure information can contribute to the effectiveness and credibility of the system by enabling civil society to assist in the detection of violations of financial disclosure requirements. Although public access is a valuable complement to verification, it is not a substitute; effective verification is a specialized task, even more so in systems geared toward identifying conflicts of interest, requiring legal knowledge usually beyond the abilities (or budgets) of most civil society organizations. However, in countries with independent media and a vibrant civil society, complaints or concerns raised by civil society can provide a valuable source of red flags, leading to more effective detection and investigation of violations of the financial disclosure requirement.

Enabling public access to financial disclosure information reinforces the message that a public official's duty to accountability is to the public at large and is in the public interest. Whatever the approach taken, balancing privacy issues with the public's right to know is an important consideration. An additional but often overlooked element of the public access question is the importance of providing public access to data and statistics on compliance rates, data on investigation outcomes, and data on the enforcement of sanctions. This can help reinforce public perceptions of the agency's commitment to enforcement, and can serve as an additional inducement to compliance among public officials.

What kinds of sanctions should be applied in cases of noncompliance? If the necessary conditions are in place for an IAD system to detect irregularities, the final test of a financial disclosure regime lies in its ability to establish *a credible threat of consequences for violations of the disclosure requirement.* It is important that economies craft appropriate and proportionate sanctions and that these be consistently enforced. Sufficient political and leadership support for the IAD system is fundamental in this regard, to ensure that the implementing agency has the necessary authority to enforce the provisions of the IAD regulations.

It is particularly important for the credibility of the system that proportionate sanctions be imposed for false disclosures and for late filing or nonsubmission of a declaration. In determining what kinds of sanctions to apply for different kinds of violations, consideration should be given to the enforceability of the sanctions and their perceived impact on compliance. For example, if the courts are slow to enforce criminal sanctions for filing violations, then a prison term, if deemed unlikely to be enforced, could prove as ineffective a deterrent as a small fine, with consequent erosion in public confidence in the system. In such cases, administrative sanctions, such as suspension or barring from public office, depending on the nature of the violation, could prove to be more effective. The severity of sanctions needs to be calibrated both to their enforceability and to their potential for deterring noncompliance.

CHAPTER 1

Argentina

Alexandra Habershon and Tammar Berger

Overview

Argentina's income and asset disclosure (IAD) system (see box 1.1) is based on Public Ethics Law No. 25.188 of 1999, which, at the time of passage, envisioned a bold and comprehensive framework for a system capable of monitoring the income and asset declarations of public officials of the three branches of government under the aegis of a single oversight body. The law also invested the system with a combined mandate of both detecting and prosecuting illicit enrichment and preventing conflicts of interest. In practice, the implementation of the system has been more modest in scope. The new IAD system applies only to the executive branch and is administered by the Ministry of Justice and Human Rights' (MoJ's) Anti-Corruption Office, rather than by a national commission, as originally envisioned. IAD for the legislative and judicial branches continues to be administered according to former procedures. The IAD system for the executive is administered with rigor and zeal—although, as yet, without significant enforcement of sanctions. However, it has achieved considerable success in implementing the objectives of the 1999 law. Despite a limited track record in enforcing sanctions—attributed by practitioners and others interviewed for this study to bottlenecks in the courts and to the difficulty of proving willful omission in cases of incomplete or false filing—the IAD system has been cited by other practitioners in the region as an example of good practice in the management of submission compliance and IAD administration.

This case study focuses on the institutional and operational arrangements for the IAD regime for public officials of the executive branch at the federal level in Argentina.

This report is based on desk research and the findings of a visit to Argentina in August 2009 undertaken on behalf of the Stolen Asset Recovery (StAR) Initiative and the Governance & Public Sector Management Unit of the World Bank to examine the country's IAD system for the executive branch. Special thanks to Ruxandra Burdescu for her advice and guidance in completing this study, and to Chiara Rocha and Modest Kwapinski for their help with research on the legal framework for IAD in Argentina. The authors are very grateful to the staff of the Ministry of Justice and others interviewed for this study. A list of people consulted is provided in appendix C.

Box 1.1 Snapshot of the Income and Asset Disclosure System in Argentina

The legal framework for income and asset disclosure (IAD) in Argentina is far-reaching and one of the most ambitious among the case studies examined. When passed in 1999, the country's Public Ethics Law sought to cover the three branches of government under the aegis of a single national commission. In practice, the implementation of the system has achieved a more modest scope: it covers the executive branch and is managed by the Ministry of Justice and Human Rights' Anti-Corruption Office. The IAD requirements for the legislative and judicial branches retain the principles and procedures of the former disclosure system. Argentina's IAD administration for the executive branch is a useful example of an IAD system, the procedures of which have been adjusted and honed over time in an effort to enhance its effectiveness.

   Key elements of the system include:

- **A combined model designed for the detection and prosecution of illicit enrichment and the prevention of conflicts of interest.** Argentina's IAD unit allocates the bulk of its resources to detecting illicit enrichment by monitoring irregularities or changes in income and asset declarations over time. Conflicts of interest are also monitored, although the emphasis is on prevention by educating and advising officials.
- **Separate bodies for the receipt and review of declarations, and for investigations.** The Asset Declaration Unit (ADU) is responsible for ensuring compliance with the requirement to file and with the receipt and review of declarations. The Investigations Department of the Ministry of Justice and Human Rights investigates irregularities and may use declarations to build a case for a corruption prosecution.
- **Centrally managed oversight system with decentralized functions.** Oversight of the system is partially delegated to the approximately 190 human resources offices of the entities in which officials are employed. This model permits the monitoring of the filing compliance of 36,000 officials by an ADU staff of only 12 in the central office.
- **Electronic submission and verification processes.** Declarations are submitted electronically and in hard copy. Hard copies are stored locally by human resources offices, except for those of the most senior 5 percent of officials, which are sent to the Asset Declaration Unit. The introduction of user-friendly electronic submission has significantly reduced the incidence of noncompliance caused by incorrect filing. It also enabled electronic verification and targeted audits of disclosures based on categories of risk, which established a greater threat of detection for the 36,000 filers. The top 5 percent (1,600 in 2009) of declarations are systematically verified. The other 95 percent are verified according to categories of risk. The Asset Declaration Unit is able to verify around 2,500 declarations a year.
- **Public access to declarations, but limited by the dual public-private submission process.** Officials submit both a public and a private declaration. The private declaration (*anexo privado*) is kept under seal except by court order. Access to a hard copy of the public annex (*anexo público*) is given in situ in the premises of the Asset Declaration Unit. There are penalties for the misuse of information. The dual-submission system is designed to reduce the anxiety of officials about public access to sensitive information, and enables the IAD system to collect more information where sensitive data (addresses, bank account numbers, copy of tax declaration, and so forth) are kept private. Newspapers routinely publish the public disclosures of prominent politicians.
- **Severe criminal penalties for nonsubmission and for false declarations.** There are criminal penalties for nonsubmission and for false declarations, but judicial delay has made enforcement difficult. Administrative sanctions might be more effective, since they are potentially more likely to be enforced.

Background

Although Argentina's current IAD system is only about 12 years old, asset disclosure as a principle has existed in the country since the 1950s. The genesis of asset disclosure in Argentina was the Registro de Declaraciones Juradas Patrimoniales del Personal de la Administración Pública, created by Decree No. 7.843 in 1953. Its purpose was not explicitly to ensure the accountability of political leaders, but rather to provide a means of control over ordinary civil servants by their superiors.[1] As such, its scope did not include the highest ranks of government officialdom or provide for public disclosure. Later amendments to the law extended the obligation to file income and asset declarations to ministers and state secretaries,[2] as well as to federal government employees located in regional offices.[3] Sanctions were increased in 1957, adding income withholding for late filing and dismissal from office for refusal to submit a declaration or falsification or omission of its contents.[4]

Even though authority over the IAD system was transferred to the Federal Office of the Notary General (an agency of the MoJ) in 1975,[5] no government authority to investigate allegations of corruption existed until 1989. That year, Decree 614 granted authority to the Office of the Prosecutor for the National Treasury to demand justifications for asset acquisitions by public officials, and Decree 1639 granted authority to the Office of the Prosecutor for the National Treasury to ensure submission of a declaration, under penalty of dismissal. Decree 1639 also authorized the Secretary of Public Function to issue interpretations, clarifications, and additional regulations related to asset disclosure, and decentralized the function of the Notary Office in regard to submission verification. In addition, the requirement to submit subsequent declarations upon "substantial changes to one's assets" was amended to a fixed, three-year period.

Further reforms in 1995 reduced the time for submission from 30 days to 48 hours and obliged additional submissions upon departure from office.[6] Despite these reforms, the absence of public access, when coupled with little regard in practice for the verification of assets declared, resulted in a system that failed to meaningfully detect or deter corruption.

Argentina's ratification of the Inter-American Convention against Corruption (IACAC) in 1996 encouraged further progress in asset declaration requirements and administration.[7] In 1997, the President's National Office of Public Ethics was created. One of its objectives was to "create and develop a program of control and monitoring of the asset situation of all agents of the National Public Administration, beginning with asset declarations of the same."[8] With the passage of the Code of Ethics of the Public Function in 1999,[9] asset declarations were made available to the public and became obligatory on an annual basis and upon both taking up and leaving a public sector post.[10]

In an effort to both fulfill its mandate as outlined in the Constitution and comply with its obligations under the IACAC,[11] the Argentine Congress passed, in October 1999, the progressive Public Ethics Law No. 25.188. Among other things, this law established new ethical guidelines and obligations related to asset disclosure, created sanctions for violation of the Penal Code, and called for the creation of the National Commission of Public Ethics under the auspices of the Congress. The National Commission of Public Ethics has yet to be established, however, a fact that has been highlighted by an Organization of American States commission in its assessment of compliance with the implementation of the IACAC. In its absence, the Anti-Corruption Office (AO) of the MoJ is administering the provisions of the law that concern the executive branch. The Organization of American States compliance commission noted in 2003 that, "unlike other branches of government, the executive branch through the Anticorruption Office is fully complying with the obligation to collect and publicize sworn declarations of property and finances from its public employees."[12]

The AO was created in 1999 under the auspices of the MoJ with the objective of elaborating and coordinating programs in the fight against corruption in the national public sector.[13] Its principal mission is to enforce the provisions of the IACAC.[14] The AO has the authority to evaluate and monitor the contents of asset declarations of public officials *within the executive branch* of the federal government. The AO is divided into two functionally independent but complementary areas. The Investigations Department deals with allegations of corruption in public administration. If there is evidence of wrongdoing, it can bring charges and request prosecution. The Department for Transparency Policies is responsible for designing policies to enhance transparency and deter corrupt practices. The Asset Declaration Unit (ADU) reports to the Department for Transparency Policies and responds to requests for information from the Investigations Department.

The IAD Legal Framework in Argentina

The legal framework for the IAD system in Argentina is based on Public Ethics Law No. 25.188 and Decree No. 164/99 (Regulation of the Public Ethics Law), both passed in the latter half of 1999. The Public Ethics Law also amended the Penal Code, criminalizing the nonsubmission of a declaration or the omission or falsification of information provided in a declaration. Although the Public Ethics Law covers all three branches of government, Decree 164/99 covers only the executive branch. Although the discussion below focuses on the executive branch, other laws exist that regulate the judicial and legislative branches.[15]

The objective of Argentine IAD law is to prevent conflicts of interest and illicit enrichment, an indication of the intended robustness of the IAD system. These objectives are suggested by the dual requirement of providing, in the declaration, information related to asset value (used to investigate enrichment) and also the sources of assets (used for conflict-of-interest purposes). Indeed, Article 12 of the Public Ethics Law requires civil servants to provide, on the declaration, information *related to their prior employment* for "the sole purpose of facilitating a better control regarding possible conflicts of interests that may develop."[16]

Coverage of Officials

Article 5 of the Public Ethics Law prescribes coverage of the asset disclosure law over a broad range of public officials (table 1.1). Coverage is based on dual criteria: (1) public officials obligated because of their position (that is, president, ministers, and so forth), and (2) public officials obligated because of their function (that is, those who grant permits, those who are responsible for administrating public or private assets or for controlling or supervising public revenues, and those who are members of commissions that oversee the issue of tenders or the purchase or receipt of assets).

Content of Declarations

Article 6 of the Public Ethics Law provides comprehensive and detailed requirements regarding the content of income and asset declarations (table 1.2). Submissions must include information on property both in Argentina and abroad that is held by the official, his or her spouse, and any minor children.

Regarding the assets listed in declarations, the official must also indicate the value and date of acquisition of such assets and the origin of funds used for each acquisition.

Filing Frequency

Declarations must be submitted within 30 days after taking office, 30 days after leaving office, and on an annual basis prior to December 31.[17] Declarations are maintained for 10 years from the date of departure from office, or as otherwise determined by judicial or administrative authorities.[18] Because of the relatively large institutional capacity of the AO and the exclusion of lower-ranking civil servants from the law's purview, the frequency of the filing requirement can provide investigators with useful information to detect unjustified changes in wealth without overburdening the IAD system.

Submission Compliance and Content Verification

The declarations of the most senior 5 percent of officials are submitted directly to the Asset Declaration Unit of the AO. Submission-compliance functions for

Table 1.1 Positions Covered by IAD Filing Obligations (Article 5), Argentina

Functionaries	Senior civil servants	Managers
President and vice president	Ombudsman's Office and deputy	Public agencies
Senators and members of Parliament	ombudsman	Public institutes
Judges	Ambassadors and consuls	Public funds
Ministers, secretaries, and deputy secretaries of the executive branch	Heads of ministerial departments	Directors and managers of the entities subject to the law
Members of the Council	Directors or secretaries of municipalities	External National Congress in accordance with Article 120 of Law No. 24.156
Magistrates and prosecutors		
Attorney General		
Comptroller General		

Source: Authors' compilation, based on unofficial translation of the Public Ethics Law, Article 5.

Table 1.2 Contents of the IAD Form, Argentina

Personal data

Name

Date of birth

Marital status and name of spouse, if applicable

Assets

Real estate (commercial and private) and improvements thereto

Registered movable assets

Nonregistered movable assets (must be individualized when their value exceeds 5,000 pesos)

Cash and investments

Cash (both in foreign and domestic bank accounts)

Shares in companies or cooperatives (whether publicly traded or not)

Liabilities

Loans and mortgages

Income

Annual income and expenses

Source: Authors' compilation, based on unofficial translation of declaration form.

all other officials covered by the law are delegated to the office of administration or human resources (HR) within the agency for which the officials work.[19] Once the date for submission passes, the registry within each agency is required to forward all submitted declarations within 30 days to the AO and the National Commission of Public Ethics (in practice, they are sent to the Asset Declaration Unit of the AO, since the commission has not been established). Each agency must also include a list of their employees who have and have not submitted a declaration within the required period.[20] Employees who fail to submit a declaration must also be notified in a reliable manner of their noncompliance.[21]

The AO is charged with verifying that each declaration has been correctly completed.[22] If the declaration is found to omit information or contain errors, the AO shall require the employee to correct the submission within five days. Failure to comply by the deadline is considered serious misconduct. Article 13 of Decree 164/99 authorizes the AO to effect any necessary controls and request any clarifications it deems pertinent.

Sanctions

Argentine law provides for strong sanctions for violations of asset disclosure obligations. Article 10 of Decree 164/99 explicitly provides for the suspension of pay during the period of noncompliance as a sanction for nonsubmission of the asset declaration. Moreover, Article 268(3) of the Penal Code provides for a prison sentence of 15 days to two years for maliciously failing to submit a declaration or maliciously omitting or falsifying information therein. In addition, officials convicted under this law may be barred for life from public service.

Public Access
Asset declarations are deemed to be public records. As such, a list indicating the names and posts of officials who have submitted or not submitted declarations must be published on the Internet and in the official government publication (*Boletín Oficial*) within 90 days of receipt by the AO.[23] Parties interested in viewing or obtaining a copy of a declaration may submit a written request to the AO. Importantly, the request must be addressed by the AO within three business days.[24] The legal regime does not address the applicability of fees for obtaining access to declarations.

Although the law provides for broad public access to the content of the declarations, it also takes into consideration the potential for abuse of the sensitive information they contain. Article 10 of the Public Ethics Law requires the requesting party to provide certain basic information related to the request. For example, a requesting party must furnish some information on his or her identity (name, occupation, address) and the intended use of the declaration. On its face, this would not appear to hinder any legitimate requests. In addition, use of the declaration for illegal, commercial (except for the media), or exploitive purposes carries a fine of up to 10,000 pesos. This provision ensures that asset disclosure does not become unreasonably detrimental to public officials, thereby both undermining the IAD system and potentially discouraging qualified people from entering the public sector.

Another important privacy consideration is the prohibition on disclosing sensitive information, such as the name of a bank or financial institution, account numbers, information identifying the location of real estate, or identifying information related to movable assets. By law, this information remains accessible by judicial authorities (under court order), by the National Commission of Public Ethics (which, as mentioned, has not yet been established), and the Administrative Oversight Prosecutor (Fiscal de Control Administrativo) (in the latter case, the information is accessible only on the decision by the MoJ, with notice given to the investigated individual).[25] To enable this dual disclosure, declarations consist of a sealed private annex and a public annex. This approach appears to strike a reasonable balance between the privacy concerns of public officials and the objective of comprehensive disclosure, although practitioners point out that the sealed annex is accessible only with a court order and, therefore, limits the agency's verification powers.

Investigations
As noted, the objective of Argentine IAD law is to prevent conflicts of interest and illicit enrichment. Article 19 of the Public Ethics Law authorizes the commencement of an investigation by the National Commission of Public Ethics (and, by extension, the AO) for both "unjustified enrichment" and "violations . . .

Income and Asset Disclosure • http://dx.doi.org/10.1596/978-0-8213-9796-1

of the asset declaration and conflict of interest regime." Investigations can be initiated (1) by the superiors of the official in question, (2) by the commission, or (3) upon the filing of a complaint.[26] Investigations are conducted by the Investigations Department of the AO. The official under investigation maintains his or her due process rights, the right to offer evidence, and the right to be informed of the initiation of the investigation.[27]

Mandate and Structure of the IAD Agency

Argentina's IAD system for the executive branch is administered by the AO of the MoJ. The AO was created for the purpose of preventing and investigating conduct defined as corrupt under the IACAC. Its purview encompasses the national public administration, businesses, associations, and any other private or public entity whose chief source of funding is the state. The AO is led by an administrative oversight prosecutor (Fiscal de Control Administrativo), nominated by the MoJ and appointed by the president, with a rank of secretary of state. The mandate of the Asset Declaration Unit within the MoJ consists of the following:

- Managing submission compliance
- Verifying declarations for indicators of illicit enrichment
- Verifying declarations for potential conflicts of interest and advising filers on how to avoid conflicts of interest
- Managing public access to information about declarations.

These functions are split among separate offices within the unit.

A dedicated Asset Declaration Unit within the AO, the Unit for Monitoring and Follow-up of Income and Asset Declarations (Unidad de Control y Seguimiento de las Declaraciones Juradas), is responsible for asset declarations of all public officials covered by the law (around 36,000). It receives, and arranges for the safe storage of, the hardcopy declarations of the most senior 5 percent of public officials (approximately 1,600), and monitors filing compliance and conducts targeted audits (approximately 2,500) of the declarations of all other officials obligated to file. For that purpose, the Asset Declaration Unit has an oversight role with respect to the HR offices of the approximately 190 agencies or entities that employ individuals obligated to submit a declaration under the Public Ethics Law (see figure 1.1). The system prioritizes the verification of the declarations of the most senior 5 percent of officials, whose declarations are reviewed as a matter of course. The Asset Declaration Unit performs a formal review of these declarations and, if irregularities are detected, a preliminary investigation. For the remainder of the declarations—to which the unit has access in electronic copy—the unit conducts both targeted and random reviews of the declarations, as described below. If, after a formal review, the IAD unit deems that a full investigation is warranted, the case is handed over to the AO's Investigations Department.

Figure 1.1 Delegated Submission System Using Paper and Online Declarations, Argentina

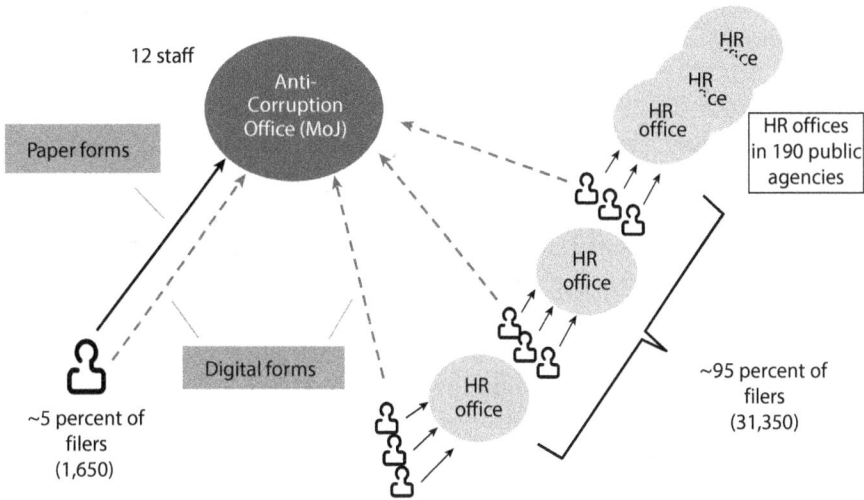

Resources and Procedures of the IAD System

Facilities and Use of Technology

The Anti-Corruption Offices are located in two buildings that house various MoJ departments. The Department for Transparency Policies and the Investigations Department together occupy three floors of one building, and the Asset Declaration Unit occupies one floor of another. The space available is fairly cramped, with boxes of paperwork lining corridors and taking up floor space, and multiple workstations in close proximity in offices and hallways. Investigators mentioned the lack of storage capacity as a concern because of the limited space available and the accumulation of case files since the department was created.

The Asset Declaration Unit has a team of 12 who occupy four offices on one floor in a separate building. It also has limited storage capacity, with two lockable, walk-in storage closets set aside for storing departmental records and boxes of hard copies of asset declaration envelopes undergoing review. Although, in principle, the declaration envelopes of the top 5 percent of officials are stored in the MoJ vault (the vault is a vestige of the building's former use as a bank), these are kept in the Asset Declaration Unit during and after the formal review phase. The system's transition in 2002 to the electronic filing of declarations for 95 percent of filers addressed a pressing challenge in terms of storage capacity at the MoJ (hard copies with the original signature of filers are stored remotely by HR offices). Nonetheless, the unit does have storage constraints for the paper declarations of the 5 percent of filers it handles every year. Practitioners have suggested that amending the law that requires an original signature on the declaration would be beneficial. Electronic signatures are increasingly the norm in systems that use online submission. Every ADU staff member has the use of a computer; however, the hardware predates the inception of the office

(1999–2000), and although the software has been updated, most recently in 2003, staff reported that very slow processor speeds hamper the unit's management of its IAD database.

Human Resources

The AO is mostly staffed by career civil servants, although budget restrictions have meant that some functions are carried out by consultants who are hired on a contract basis and whose contracts are renewed indefinitely. The Asset Declaration Unit has a staff of 12 people, of whom seven are career civil servants and five are contractors. The number of staff is considered sufficient except for the busy period (the two or three months following the annual submission deadline), when the addition of three more staff members would be considered optimal. The unit's 12 staff members review around 4,000 asset declarations per year, beginning with the systematic review of the most-high-ranking 5 percent of officials (1,600), followed by the targeted review of an additional 2,500. ADU staff includes lawyers, accountants, and political scientists. The Investigations Department has a team of 37, a number that the AO deems sufficient, bearing in mind that the number is adjusted on the basis of available resources and other factors.

Budget

The AO is financed under the MoJ budget, with some of its funding drawn from the budgets of other government entities with which the AO cooperates in its operations (for example, the national automobile registry). At the time of research in 2009, the AO was also implementing an institutional strengthening program with financing from the United Kingdom and the United Nations Development Programme.

Regulatory Function

Neither the Asset Declaration Unit nor the Investigations Department has a regulatory function. Policy is developed in the AO by the Department for Transparency Policies. In practice, close coordination among the departments of the AO, and the fact that the Asset Declaration Unit reports to the Department for Transparency Policies, mean that policy decisions reflect the need for enhancements to the procedures of the Asset Declaration Unit and the Investigations Department.

Managing Submission Compliance

As noted, public officials covered by the Public Ethics Law are required to submit a declaration within 30 days of taking up or leaving a post, and an annual declaration that coincides with tax filing during an official's period of employment.[28] The Asset Declaration Unit is responsible for monitoring compliance with the obligation to file of all officials covered by the law. The unit creates and updates the register of officials obligated to submit a declaration and cross-checks compliance against this list. The unit publishes the compliance list on the MoJ website. Maintaining the register of obligated parties is a continuous activity and fundamental to effective submission compliance monitoring. The Asset Declaration Unit receives notification from the HR offices of line agencies about newly hired or appointed officials who are subject to the requirement to file, and about officials who have retired or left a post. Unit staff are responsible for communicating and following up with the approximately 190 agencies or entities in which public officials are employed to ensure that they have up-to-date information about obligated filers,[29] and to coordinate follow-up with late filers or nonfilers. In practice, this means that the Asset Declaration Unit has both an oversight and coordination function with regard to HR offices in government agencies as part of the IAD submission compliance process.

All declarations consist of a public and a private annex. The forms are available online on the AO website,[30] as well as in an interactive CD package provided by the AO. Once completed, officials submit both the public and private annex of their declaration online (these are sent encrypted to the Asset Declaration Unit), print and sign the hard copy of the declaration, enclose the private and public annexes in separate envelopes, then submit these to their HR office. The HR offices then deliver the envelopes of the most senior 5 percent of officials to the Asset Declaration Unit (approximately 1,600 declarations) and ensure safe storage of the remainder of the envelopes. (When this study was conducted, 33,815 annual declarations were due to be submitted online.)

The Asset Declaration Unit cross-checks the list of declarations submitted online against the database of individuals required to declare, and publishes a submission compliance list on the MoJ website that identifies who has and has not complied with the requirement to submit a declaration. The list, which is organized alphabetically by agency, identifies officials by name, though not by post or title. It also identifies whether the declaration required was a first, last, or annual declaration. Instances of noncompliance with the obligation to submit a declaration are negligible and tend to occur most frequently when individuals are leaving their post.

Box 1.2 provides more information on online submission compliance management.

Content Verification

Argentina's system is designed to detect and prevent potential conflicts of interest and to detect signs of unjustified changes in wealth for possible investigation. The system relies on the content verification of a targeted sample of declarations by agency staff, and on public allegations against officials (by individuals or the media) to trigger a review of declarations. The number of public officials required to file an asset declaration (currently approximately 36,000) is too great to permit the verification of every one. However, the system is designed to enable the systematic verification of *all* of the declarations submitted by the most senior 5 percent of public officials and for a targeted (risk-based) audit of the remainder of the declarations.

Income and Asset Disclosure • http://dx.doi.org/10.1596/978-0-8213-9796-1

Box 1.2 Online Submission Compliance Management in Argentina

By international standards, Argentina's IAD system is highly automated, employing online declaration forms; online submission and submission compliance processes; and electronic data storage, records management, and reporting. The transition to online submission and compliance management was instituted by the then-director of the Policy Department shortly after the passage of the current law and the establishment of the Asset Declaration Unit in the MoJ, when it quickly became clear that the volume of paper generated by the filing requirement would rapidly overwhelm the agency's ability to fulfill its mandate.

The submission and management of declarations for the executive branch was transformed from a paper-based system to an electronic system, thanks to the development of a software platform that is downloadable from the AO's website;[a] it is also available on a CD-ROM. The impacts were significant and rapid. The declaration submission software requires that filers complete all required fields before the form can be submitted, resulting in a significant reduction in the number of errors or incorrectly filled-in IAD forms. This contributes to an increase in compliance rates and a reduced burden on the implementing agency for contacting filers for clarification on incomplete or incorrectly filed declarations. It also enables more seamless data management processes, including the creation of a submission compliance database, and automated detection of discrepancies between a filer's declared income and changes in income and assets over time.

The system also provides added safeguards for the privacy of personal information.[b] The electronic system caters to Argentina's dual submission process (of private and public annexes).[c] Filers access the declaration form online or on the CD-ROM, and complete the form electronically. When the filer submits the declarations, the software automatically splits the data into two files, corresponding to the public and private annexes. These are then sent online to be stored on the servers of the Asset Declaration Unit in the MoJ (the private annex is encrypted). The filer then prints both files, signs them, seals the private file, and delivers them to the administrative office of the agency in which he or she is employed, where these are stored (except for the top 5 percent of officials, whose hard copies of declarations are forwarded to the Asset Declaration Unit in the MoJ).

In the year following implementation of the automated submission system, submission compliance rates increased from 67 percent to 96 percent, and the estimated cost to the government per declaration decreased from US$70 to US$8. In addition, the number of conflict-of-interest investigations increased from 40 to 331, and the number of financial disclosure information requests increased from 66 to 823.[d,e] These disclosure requests come from the media, nongovernmental organizations, and public officials. In fact, automating submission processes also facilitated the government's ability to collect and report data about the performance of the system, including these kinds of impacts. Automated submission also facilitates verification procedures, as discussed under "content verification."

a. http://www.ddjjonline.gov.ar.
b. OECD 2005, p. 66.
c. Raille 2006, p. 9; http://www.oecd.org/. Available online in English, Spanish, and Portuguese at the U.S. Office of Government Ethics website: http://www.usoge.gov/.
d. de Michele 2001, pp. 17–20.
e. OECD 2005, p. 66.

For the purpose of detecting illicit enrichment, review mechanisms are principally geared to:

- Track changes in the content of declarations over time
- Identify discrepancies between declared income and assets and data (where available) from other sources, such as automobile and property registries

Argentina's banking and tax privacy laws prevent access to these kinds of information to corroborate the accuracy of declarations from such sources. The first of these verification functions (comparison of data over time) is performed electronically. The public annexes of declarations are merged into an electronic database that the agency has developed in-house and tailored to be searchable according to a variety of parameters (official's name, ministry or agency, function, percentage of change in assets and income). This allows the rapid identification of, for example, any official working in tax and customs whose declaration shows any given percentage change in wealth from one declaration to the next or across a span of many years. Any filer whose declarations indicate an unusual or disproportionate change in wealth is then flagged for closer verification.

The second function (comparison with other databases) is more time consuming and requires a more manual kind of research. ADU staff cross-check movable and immovable assets (chiefly property and vehicles) against state registries (which are not public, but to which the agency has access) to verify that declared assets match those in the registries. Unit staff indicated that, with practice, and if no significant irregularities are detected, cross-checking an asset declaration form can be completed in about 20 minutes.

To detect potential conflicts of interest, the Asset Declaration Unit is also responsible for screening the content of declarations for possible indicators of conflicts of interest (such as membership on the board of directors of a firm in the sector in which the filer has official duties and responsibilities, or other incompatibilities between official duties and private interests).

The Asset Declaration Unit has one member—a lawyer—charged with detecting potential conflicts of interest. This function is heavily focused on prevention. If a potential conflict of interest is identified, the unit contacts the filer to request additional information and, where applicable, recommends steps to ensure that any situation in which a conflict of interest could arise is avoided. However, if an actual conflict of interest is found to exist or have existed, the case is passed on to the Investigations Department.

As noted, the Asset Declaration Unit systematically verifies only the declarations of the top 5 percent of public officials (approximately 1,600). These asset declarations all undergo an initial *formal* review to check for errors in filing, to verify consistency with previous declarations, and to cross-check the content of the declaration with data available from other sources. If an irregularity or inconsistency is detected, a formal "request for clarification" is sent to the official. If no satisfactory clarification or correction is provided, then the case is passed on to the Investigations Department.

Income and Asset Disclosure • http://dx.doi.org/10.1596/978-0-8213-9796-1

The same procedure is followed with a targeted sample of the declarations of the other 95 percent of officials (approximately 34,000). Of these, the Asset Declaration Unit conducts a risk-based review of approximately 2,500 declarations, meaning that, in one year, the unit formally reviews over 4,000 asset declarations. The criteria for targeting declarations for review include (1) the function or post held by the individual (including rank), (2) the sector in which the official works, and (3) whether his or her responsibilities include public procurement or the disbursement of public funds. In practice, the sector that is targeted by default is the Federal Administration of Public Revenues (Administración Federal de Ingresos Públicos). The Federal Administration of Public Revenues includes the tax and customs authorities and employs 30 percent of the public officials covered by the Public Ethics Law. Given the responsibility that many of its staff have for handling public revenues, it is a relevant agency for targeting verifications.

The program used by the Asset Declaration Unit to search the database of asset declarations, dubbed "LUPA" (magnifying glass), was developed in-house by a consultant. Team members report that the program is essential to enabling targeted searches, but—because the verification system postdates the development of the data management software for submission compliance—verification requires manual input of data to enable searches. Unfortunately, any such database is of limited value for cross-checking and comparing nonnumerical values in asset declaration forms (such as model and make of car, membership on a board, and so forth; this has to be done manually). The LUPA program is also used to identify individuals whose declarations show significant changes in the value of assets over time. Although tailor-made for the purpose of detecting changes in the value of declared assets over time, LUPA is hampered by the limited speed and memory of the computers available in the Asset Declaration Unit (the hardware dates from approximately 2000). It requires constant manual updates by the unit staff to integrate newly submitted asset declaration forms to the database.

The digitization of the submission of asset declarations has been critical to enabling risk-based searches of the approximately 34,000 declarations, which might otherwise be subject to review only in the case of a complaint or allegation of corruption against the individual. The verification function relies heavily on electronic searches of data available from the public annexes of the declaration forms, and on the possibility of cross-checking that data with information available from other sources (such as automobile and property registries, which are mainly limited to property owned in the capital). Although the Asset Declaration Unit does not rely on informal "lifestyle checks" carried out by individuals or nongovernmental organizations (NGOs) as part of its detection strategy, the Investigations Department does have a mandate to follow up allegations of corruption made by the media. In such cases, an investigation would be instigated by the Investigations Department, not the Asset Declaration Unit.

Box 1.3 provides details on the procedures performed by Argentina's Asset Declaration Unit.

Box 1.3 Procedures Performed by Argentina's Asset Declaration Unit in the MoJ

Managing Submission Compliance

The Asset Declaration Unit performs the following functions and procedures:

1. **Maintains an up-to-date register of officials obligated to file.** This is done in coordination with individual HR offices in the 190+ line agencies or government entities that provide the names of new or departing officials required by law to submit a declaration.

2. **Receives the envelopes of the top-tier officials** (approximately 5 percent of the filing population) whose declarations are stored centrally (initially in the unit and then in the archives of the MoJ); the declarations of all other officials are stored by the HR offices of the 190+ government agencies in which they are employed (all declarations are legally required to be stored for 10 years).

3. **Monitors whether all officials obligated to file have submitted their declaration within the required deadline** and without immediately apparent inconsistencies or omissions. This is done in coordination with the HR offices of the government entities where these officials submit their declarations in hard copy (when officials complete the form online, an encrypted electronic copy is automatically sent to the central Asset Declaration Unit). This enables the delegation of certain submission compliance functions but permits central oversight of compliance. Officials can consult the IAD unit or their local HR office for assistance in completing the form.

Content Verification

The Asset Declaration Unit:

4. **Formally reviews all of the declarations of the top-tier officials to detect any irregularities** (errors, omissions, indicators of unjustified increases in wealth), and either seeks clarification from officials or makes corrections where obvious errors are detected.

5. **Formally reviews all of the declarations of the top-tier officials to detect any potential conflicts of interest**, and seeks clarification or offers guidance to remove the conflicts in such cases.

6. **Steps 4 and 5 are then repeated with a targeted selection of all the remaining declarations** (approximately 2,500 are checked annually). These are selected on the basis of risk factors that include high-risk posts or functions (for example, targeting officials in high-risk agencies such as customs and tax administration) and a significant change in wealth from one declaration to the next. The Asset Declaration Unit has access to electronic versions of these declarations (electronic filing limits the amount of manual data entry required to create databases and thus makes data mining more manageable by a small, central unit).

7. **Refers cases of suspected illicit enrichment or conflicts of interest to the Investigations Department of the MoJ,** where a formal investigation is undertaken, potentially leading to a criminal prosecution.

8. **Receives and responds to allegations of IAD violations or of corruption from the public** (in such cases, performing steps 4 and 5 with the relevant declarations, or

box continues next page

Box 1.3 Procedures Performed by Argentina's Asset Declaration Unit in the MoJ *(continued)*

referring cases not specifically pertaining to IAD violations directly to the Investigations Department).

Managing Public Access to Declarations and Information about Compliance Rates

9. **The Asset Declaration Unit manages public access to declarations** (in person, in the offices of the Asset Declaration Unit), and publishes and maintains a list on its website of officials who have not complied with the filing requirement.

Investigatory Function

An investigation of a public official's asset declaration can be triggered as a result of the formal verification process performed by the Asset Declaration Unit (described above), as a result of an allegation of corruption, or as a result of inquiries initiated by the Investigations Department. Although preliminary investigations are carried out by the Asset Declaration Unit, the Investigations Department is responsible for full investigations when irregularities are detected. The Investigations Department's task in such cases is to determine the nature of the irregularity and to gather the necessary evidence to take the case forward for prosecution. The Investigations Department prioritizes cases according to the gravity of the offense, the profile of the offender, and the likelihood of gathering the necessary evidence for a successful prosecution. The Investigations Department does not have access to the private annex of declarations without a court order, which requires either the provision of sufficient evidence of a violation of the Public Ethics Law or proof of an act of corruption for the case to merit legal action before a court. The content of the private annex is therefore not available for preliminary investigatory purposes.

Investigations of corruption may or may not involve the review of asset declarations, although these are fundamental to determining cases of illicit enrichment or noncompliance with the Public Ethics Law. Since the "willful omission of information" from a declaration constitutes a crime, investigations can be geared to securing evidence of the existence of income or assets and demonstrating their omission from the declaration (suspected nondeclaration of foreign credit cards was cited by the Investigations Department as the subject of a number of ongoing investigations, an omission that is often difficult to prove but is a likely indicator of either undeclared foreign bank accounts or sources of funds from third parties). The Investigations Department reports that no convictions have been secured for omission of data, primarily because of the difficulty of proving that an omission was made with willful intent to conceal information.

According to the AO's 2008 Annual Report, the Investigations Department has opened over 7,000 investigations since the creation of the new filing arrangements in 2000. Although no investigation into noncompliance with the asset declaration regime has resulted in a conviction, a number of corruption cases in which asset declarations serve as evidence are currently pending trial. Investigations Department officials reported that they had 20 cases awaiting trial at the time of research, although these were unlikely to be heard within at least a year because the courts were making human rights cases from the 1970s a priority.

Interagency Collaboration

The AO can cross-check ownership of property and certain moveable assets against public registries (there is an online automobile registry and a property registry for Buenos Aires, although the property registry does not include anything outside the capital). Argentina's banking and financial privacy laws seriously limit the possibility of cross-checking the financial details of an asset declaration form, and for investigative purposes there is no collaboration between the AO and the tax authorities. Tax declarations and bank account information are made available to the AO only if a court order is issued to that effect, and a judge unseals the private annex of the asset declaration, which includes bank account numbers and a copy of the tax declaration. (The AO previously had access to tax declarations, but such access was rescinded in 2007, thus requiring the AO to amend the asset declaration requirement to mandate the inclusion of a copy of the tax declaration in the private annex.)

Public Access

Requests for access to asset declaration forms are handled by the Asset Declaration Unit. The unit receives requests on a daily basis, typically from journalists, although occasionally also from private individuals. Requests are received in person, by phone, by e-mail, and on the AO website. The individual making the request is required to personally collect a copy of the public annex of the declaration at the ADU office. Requests can be denied at the discretion of the AO if considered counter to the purpose of the law, and there are penalties for the improper use of information obtained from an IAD form, as described above.

Reporting and Outreach

The AO's website provides online access to the following:[31]

- Data on system performance (annual reports)
- Anticorruption policy and legislation
- Lists of public officials who are compliant and noncompliant with the IAD requirement
- A portal for requesting access to copies of the public annex of declarations (which are viewed at the IAD offices).

The AO has also published explanatory guides on the IAD system.

Income and Asset Disclosure • http://dx.doi.org/10.1596/978-0-8213-9796-1

Summary of Key Findings

Following the adoption of the Public Ethics Law in 2000, the Anti-Corruption Office in Argentina reconfigured the country's asset declaration system from a paper-based to a more efficient and user-friendly electronic system, with resulting increases in submission compliance. The new organizational structure and data management systems and procedures also facilitated the verification of declarations and the use of declarations as evidence in corruption investigations. The AO was also better able to publicize compliance data and report on system performance, enhancing the credibility of the system with users and the public. In the year following the implementation of the automated submission system, submission compliance rates increased from 67 percent to 96 percent, and the estimated cost to the government per declaration decreased from US$70 to US$8. In addition, the number of conflict-of-interest investigations increased from 40 to 331, and the number of financial disclosure information requests increased from 66 to 823.[32] The automation of the system also resulted in an increase in the number of requests for IAD information from the media, NGOs, and the public.

These impacts do not appear to correlate, however, with a proportionate increase in the enforcement of sanctions for violations of the IAD requirement. Such enforcement lies beyond the purview of the AO, given the system's use of criminal sanctions for violations, and thus the system's dependence on the justice system for timely processing of cases and enforcement of sanctions where applicable. Argentina's IAD system is, therefore, a good example of a system that is functionally optimal in many respects but may not necessarily be delivering on its promise of serving as a credible deterrent and anticorruption enforcement mechanism. Investigators and prosecutors agreed that, had the law envisaged a range of administrative sanctions for serious filing failures, it is conceivable that these would have fostered greater credibility in the system, because—although less severe—they would have been more likely to be enforced. The possibility of pursuing criminal sanctions for suspected underlying acts of corruption would still have been possible in addition to whatever administrative sanctions might have been applied for IAD filing violations.

Argentina's experience is a good example of an IAD system where procedures have been developed and adjusted over time to enhance the effectiveness of the system, within the constraints of what is politically possible and institutionally practicable. Specialists and practitioners have suggested that the mandate of the system was too ambitious and the sanctions too severe for the system to deliver meaningful results. Current practices do not reflect the originally ambitious scope of the Public Ethics Law (intended to cover the three branches of government under the aegis of a single national commission and to monitor declarations for both conflicts of interest and illicit enrichment). Nonetheless, in over 10 years since the system was established, Argentina's IAD system for the executive branch has forged a path through the bureaucratic and operational challenges that can beset the best intentions of asset disclosure regimes and has established administrative procedures and management practices that serve as a model for the region and elsewhere.

These improvements relate to the increased effectiveness of the IAD regime in managing and monitoring submission compliance and in detecting irregularities in the content of declarations. These improvements also relate to greater public awareness of the asset declaration system and its role in monitoring and enforcing ethical standards in government. Public confidence in the system's ability to deter or prosecute acts of corruption has been slower to materialize, however, given the difficulty of carrying through successful prosecutions and enforcement of sanctions for violations of the law (including prison terms) that could apply for noncompliance. Despite the limited enforcement of sanctions, officials and representatives of NGOs in Argentina agree that the progress achieved in implementing and institutionalizing a comprehensive declaration mechanism at the federal level has been a significant achievement.

Notes

1. Gómez 2004.
2. Decree 13.659/57.
3. Decree 4.649/63.
4. Decree 13.659/57.
5. Decree 36/75.
6. Decree 494/95.
7. Law No. 24.759/96.
8. Decree 152/97.
9. Executive Order 41/99.
10. Decree 41/99.
11. Article 36: ". . . Congress shall enact a law on public ethics which shall regulate the exercise of public office."
12. OAS 2003.
13. Law No. 25.233.
14. de Michele 2001.
15. For laws that regulate the judicial branch, see CSJN, Acordada No. 1/2000; Resolución No. 562/05 del Consejo de la Magistratura; CSJN Acordada No. 29/05. For laws that regulate the legislative branch, see Article 49 of the Reglamento de la Cámara Alta. No entity per se maintains declarations by members of the Lower House; however, members may be requested to submit a declaration if a request is made to the president of the Lower House.
16. Article 13 of Law No. 25.188 states that "The exercise of public service is incompatible with: (a) directing, administrating, sponsoring, advising, or in any other form, rendering services to one who is negotiating or has a concession or is a supplier of the State, or undertakes activities regulated by the State, where the public servant has direct jurisdiction over the contracting, obtaining, negotiating or control of said concessions, benefits or activities; (b) being a supplier, directly or through third parties, of any organ of the State in which the official carries out his duties."

17. Article 4, Decree 164/99. This was subsequently changed to May 31 to coincide with tax declaration season and thereby reduce the burden on filers, who could thus do a reckoning of their income and assets once a year instead of twice. The IAD system also requires that filers include a copy of their tax declaration in the sealed private annex to their declaration.

18. Article 14, Decree 164/99.

19. Decree 164/99, Article 5.

20. Decree 164/99, Articles 7 and 8.

21. Decree 164/99, Article 9.

22. Decree 164/99, Article 11.

23. Decree 164/99, Article 20.

24. Decree 164/99, Article 17.

25. Article 19, Decree 164/99.

26. Article 20, Law 25.188.

27. Article 20, Law 25.188.

28. The system as originally set up required individuals to file at the end of the calendar year, which was then adjusted to the end of May. Annual declarations are thus timed to coincide with the tax declaration season, to avoid adding an additional administrative burden on public officials. In practice, extensions are usually granted, meaning that the deadline for annual submissions often falls in June or July.

29. AO officials report that the number of agencies with HR offices with which they have to coordinate the asset declaration process is increasing every year (up from 184 in 2008 to 190 in 2009). The number of officials required to file is also increasing commensurately, up from around 30,000 in 2000 to approximately 36,000 in 2009.

30. http://www.ddjjonline.gov.ar.

31. http://www.anticorrupcion.gov.ar.

32. de Michele 2001; OECD 2005, p. 66.

References

de Michele, R. 2001. "The Role of the Anti-Corruption Office in Argentina." *The Journal of Public Inquiry* Fall/Winter (2001): 17–20.

Gómez, N. 2004. *Declaraciones Juradas de Funcionarios Públicos.* Buenos Aires: Oficina Anticorrupción, Ministerio de Justicia y Derechos Humanos.

OAS (Organization of American States). 2003. "Report on Implementation in Argentina of the Convention Provisions Selected for Review in the Framework of the First Round." Washington, DC: Committee of Experts of the Mechanism for Follow-up on the Implementation of the Inter-American Convention against Corruption.

OECD (Organisation for Economic Co-operation and Development). 2005. "Managing Conflicts of Interest in the Public Service," Policy Brief, Paris, OECD. http://www.oecd.org.

Raille, E. 2006. "Managing Conflicts of Interest in the Americas: A Comparative Review." Available online in English, Spanish, and Portuguese at the U.S. Office of Government Ethics website: http://www.usoge.gov/.

CHAPTER 2

Croatia

Alexandra Habershon and Tammar Berger

Overview

The income and asset disclosure (IAD) system in Croatia (see box 2.1) was established in 2003 with the adoption of the Act on the Prevention of Conflict of Interest in the Exercise of Public Office. The 2003 act created the Commission for the Prevention of Conflict of Interest to implement the regulations. The commission's role includes oversight of income and asset disclosure by public officials. Since 2005, significant amendments have been made to the act, including increasing the membership of the commission, changing the coverage of the act (including a reduction in the number of local government officials covered), and increasing the sanctions for noncompliance. The 2010–12 National Anti-Corruption Strategy has emphasized raising awareness and understanding of the concept of conflict of interest and its role within the broader anticorruption agenda.

The conflict-of-interest regime in Croatia places a strong emphasis on public access to information about officials' income and assets, but relatively little on verifying the accuracy of declarations. That is, public access is intended to allow public scrutiny. Verification is undertaken if a review has been triggered by an allegation or complaint of corruption (by an individual or in the media). Amendments to the act in 2009 have created scope for more systematic verification, however, based on internal monitoring of declarations. To date, the system has been more reactive than proactive. Public interest in conflict-of-interest issues in Croatia is typically fueled by the media's interest in the wealth of very high ranking public officials rather than the more arcane issues associated with

This report is based on desk research and the findings of a visit to Croatia undertaken in June 2009 on behalf of the Stolen Asset Recovery (StAR) Initiative and the Governance & Public Sector Management Unit of the World Bank to examine the country's IAD system. To the extent possible, the content of this report has been updated to reflect relevant changes to the legislation and institutional arrangements in the time elapsed between the date of research and publication. Special thanks for assistance in the research and preparation of this report are given to other members the World Bank team led by Ruxandra Burdescu, with Daniel Barnes and Thomas Iverson. Special thanks also to Hongjoo Hahm, World Bank Country Manager for Croatia and Sanja Madzarevic-Sujster, Senior Country Economist for their guidance in conducting and completing the case study. A list of people consulted or interviewed in the preparation of this report is provided in appendix C.

Box 2.1 Snapshot of the Income and Asset Disclosure System in Croatia

The income and asset disclosure (IAD) system in Croatia was established in 2003 with the adoption of the Act on the Prevention of Conflict of Interest in the Exercise of Public Office, which also created the Commission for the Prevention of Conflict of Interest to implement the regulations. The commission is housed within the Croatian Parliament. Croatia's IAD system places a strong emphasis on the public availability of asset declaration information. Amendments to the law in 2009 increased sanctions for violations and mandated the introduction of procedures for verifying the accuracy of declarations, either at the commission's own instigation or as the result of public allegations or reports of corruption.

Key elements of the system include:

- **A parliamentary commission tasked with the detection and prevention of conflicts of interest.** The IAD system in Croatia is a conflict-of-interest system intended to foster ethical conduct by persons in public office. The responsible body for IAD administration is a parliamentary commission. It has no independent budget and is physically housed in Parliament's facilities. Amendments to the law in 2009 have strengthened the independence of the commission from Parliament by instituting public nomination procedures for commission members.
- **Targeted coverage.** The IAD system covers approximately 1,800 positions at both the national and local levels (including ministers and mayors and their deputies, and directors of the pension fund, the health insurance fund, and the employment office). The law was amended to reduce the number of lower-ranking local government officials obligated to file.
- **Composition of the commission.** The commission has a permanent composition of eleven appointees and four administrative staff. Of the eleven appointed members, six are members of Parliament (three from the government and three from the opposition), and five are "distinguished public servants," including members of civil society organizations. Commission members are appointed for a seven-year term.
- **Appointment of commission members and staff.** Members of the commission are appointed by Parliament through a public nomination process. Permanent administrative staff are civil servants, and temporary administrative support staff are hired on an ad-hoc basis during peak submission periods (for example, after elections). Temporary staff are hired to process the declarations, to ensure they are complete, and to input their contents into the commission's website.
- **A modest sanctions regime that has been progressively strengthened.** The sanction for failure to file an income and asset declaration is suspension of payment of a net monthly salary in the amount of HRK 2,000 to HRK 20,000 (Croatian kunas, or approximately US$1,000 to US$4,000). Further administrative sanctions were introduced in 2010 for false filing, including suspension from public duty and prohibition from serving in public office for two to five years.
- **Public access.** Income and asset declarations are publicly available, both online (at http://www.sukobinteresa.hr) and in person on the premises of the commission.

conflicts of interest. A national government campaign to raise awareness about the Anti-Corruption Strategy has also focused attention on public ethics and on generating better understanding of conflict of interest as a governance concept.

Background

The IAD system for public officials is governed by the regulations and procedures implemented to prevent conflict of interest. These regulations are set out in the 2003–10 Act on the Prevention of Conflict of Interest in the Exercise of Public Office and are implemented by the Commission for the Prevention of Conflict of Interest.[1] The commission has published guidelines that identify IAD as the "basic form of control of a potential conflict of interest" (see annex A).

Over the past 10 years, the government of Croatia has led an increasingly invigorated fight against corruption. As part of this mission, the Croatian Parliament enacted the Programme for the Suppression of Corruption and the Law for the Office for the Suppression of Corruption and Organized Crime (USKOK), and adopted the Criminal Law Convention of the Council of Europe.[2] The USKOK law is harmonized with international standards,[3] and since the amendments to the Criminal Code in 2009 strengthening its mandate—which included both establishing separate prosecutors for corruption cases and enabling the confiscation of assets—USKOK has successfully brought an increasing number of prosecutions forward and has confiscated assets in corruption cases.[4]

A new civil service law was introduced in 2005, the purpose of which was to introduce merit-based recruitment processes, professionalize the civil service, and introduce measures to increase transparency and accountability in the public sector. Unfortunately, implementation of the law has been slow and incomplete because of the delayed adoption of the new salary law.[5]

In 2006, Croatia enacted the Ethics Code for civil servants. The code strengthened the regulations, sanctions, and enforcement; it also created the Ethics Committee and a hotline. In April of the same year, the independent Civil Service Council was created and given the responsibility for managing complaints against administrative decisions. State officials would now be required to disclose income and asset information before taking office, and would be subject to prosecution under the conflict-of-interest law and criminal code. The code also stipulates fines for failure to submit or for false submission. The fines are slight and not accompanied by criminal penalties or other more serious administrative sanctions.

Croatia's Criminal Code, amended in 2009 to introduce the "confiscation of pecuniary gain" or non-conviction-based forfeiture of the proceeds of crime, is a potentially powerful tool for combating illicit enrichment (although without direct application in the enforcement of a conflict-of-interest regime). In June 2008, the government of Croatia instituted a revised Anti-Corruption Strategy and Action Plan for 2008–10, with a special focus on vulnerable sectors. The implementation of the Strategy and Action Plan is managed by a directorate housed in the Ministry of Justice, and a national parliamentary commission was established to monitor its implementation. The government's new

Anti-Corruption Strategy and Action Plan for 2010–12 includes revisions and improvements to the previous program, including a monitoring mechanism.

Croatia has achieved significant improvements in the coordination and implementation of anticorruption efforts. In 2008, the Commission of the European Communities Progress Report stated that, despite their efforts, "the Croatian anticorruption mission still had much work ahead of it, with corruption still widespread, the administrative capacity of state bodies for fighting corruption still insufficient, and implementation of anticorruption efforts continuing to lack strong coordination and efficient nonpartisan monitoring."[6] In contrast, the November 2010 Progress Report noted that there has been good progress in the fight against corruption,[7] including implementation of the revised Strategy and Action Plan, the adoption of a specific anticorruption program for state-owned companies, improvements in the overall coordination of anticorruption efforts, and an increase in the number and profile of indictments issued by USKOK despite a lack of additional resources. According to the 2010 report,

> USKOK has begun to investigate possible high-level corruption involving senior political figures. Other medium and high-level cases are under investigation and prosecution, often involving state-owned companies. The number of court verdicts has increased. The first high-level cases are before the courts. The National Police Office for the Fight against Corruption and Organised Crime (PNUSKOK) was reinforced. (Commission of the European Communities 2010, p. 9)

The report also notes that some limited progress has been achieved in the prevention of corruption: "The office of the commission for the prevention of conflict of interest has been restructured to give the commission further independence from Parliament"[8]—staff of the commission are now selected by Parliament through a process of open public competition—and "legal provisions have been introduced to depoliticize appointments to supervisory boards of state-owned companies."[9] The report notes, however, that these measures are not yet operational, and the prevention of conflict of interest continues to be hampered because of weak sanctions.[10] However, in addition to strengthening procedures for the verification of assets by the commission, amendments made in July 2010 to the Act on the Prevention of Conflict of Interest introduced significant changes to the sanctions regime, including the introduction of dismissal from public duty and prohibition from holding public office for five years as sanctions for violations of the law.

The 2010 Progress Report notes that corruption is still prevalent in many areas in Croatia, however. Moreover, "recently upgraded legal and administrative structures remain to be fully tested in practice, particularly in terms of the courts' ability to handle the increased number and complexity of cases."[11] On the conflict-of-interest front, the report concludes that, despite some awareness-raising measures, "the concept of conflict of interest is still little understood in Croatia, especially at the local level." Notwithstanding recent improvements, the report highlights that there is "limited monitoring of legal compliance" with the law and points to the ineffectiveness of the sanctions regime as a continuing challenge.[12]

The IAD Legal Framework in Croatia

The Act on the Prevention of Conflict of Interest in the Exercise of Public Office was passed in 2003. The act has been amended almost annually since then, including amendments that increase the size of the commission, reduce the coverage of the system, restructure the appointments process, increase the commission's independence from Parliament, implement more systematic procedures for verifying declarations of assets, and increase the sanctions that apply for noncompliance.

Coverage of Officials

Article 2 of the act identifies those officials subject to the IAD requirement (see table 2.1). Currently, approximately 1,800 officials are covered by the act.[13]

Content of Declarations

Article 7 of the Act on the Prevention of Conflict of Interest specifies the types of assets and income to be declared (table 2.2). All covered individuals are required to declare assets and their sources, whether acquired or inherited, and to identify the source of income from professional and nonprofessional activities. All are also required to declare the assets and income of their spouses and minor children.

Filing Frequency

All covered individuals must submit an income and asset declaration within 30 days of their election or appointment and within 30 days of leaving office (Article 7).

While in office, they must also declare any "significant" change to the value of their income and assets in the year in which the change occurs. A change is deemed significant when in excess of HRK 10,000 (Croatian kunas) (approximately US$1,875). This provision is applicable from the first date of filing a declaration until six months after leaving office (Article 7). Beyond filing an exit declaration upon leaving office, there is no requirement that officials submit a declaration during a set period following their departure from public office (since only administrative sanctions apply, the provisions of the act would have little enforcement effect on individuals no longer employed in public office).

All officials covered by the act must also register income from permitted activities (other than their regular salaries) within 15 days of receiving the income by sending a copy of their tax registration to the commission (Article 12).

Sanctions for Filing Failures

Sanctions for violating the provisions of the act include the withholding of salary, official warnings, and the publication of the commission's decisions in the *Official Gazette* (at the expense of the individual). As of a 2010 amendment to the act, officials can also be dismissed from their post for false filing.

Income and Asset Disclosure • http://dx.doi.org/10.1596/978-0-8213-9796-1

Table 2.1 Positions Covered by IAD Filing Obligations, Croatia

State level	Local and regional level	Other officials
The President of the Republic of Croatia	County prefects	Director and assistant directors of the Croatian Pension Insurance Fund
President and Vice Presidents of the Croatian Parliament	Mayor of the City of Zagreb	
	Mayors, heads of municipalities, and their deputies	Director and deputy directors of the Croatian Health Insurance Fund
Representatives in the Croatian Parliament		Director and assistant directors of the Croatian Employment Commercial Office
Prime Minister and members of the Government of the Republic of Croatia		Other persons performing certain duties, appointed or confirmed by the Croatian Parliament, the Government of the Republic of Croatia, or the President if so stipulated on election, confirmation, or appointment.
President and judges of the Constitutional Court of the Republic of Croatia		
Governor, Deputy Governor, and Vice-Governor of the Croatian National Bank		
Chief State Auditor and his/her deputies		
The Ombudsman and his/her deputies		
The Ombudsman for Children and his/her deputies		
The Ombudsman for Gender Equality and his/her deputies		
The Ombudsman for Persons with Disabilities and his/her deputies		
Secretary of the Croatian Parliament		
Secretary of the Government of the Republic of Croatia		
Secretary General of the Constitutional Court of the Republic of Croatia		
Secretary of the Supreme Court of the Republic of Croatia		
Deputy Secretary of the Croatian Parliament		
State secretaries		
Heads of state administrative organizations		
President and Deputy President of the Croatian Privatization Fund		
Head and assistant heads of the Croatian Pension Insurance Fund		
Head, Deputy Head, and assistant heads of the Croatian Institute for Health Insurance		
Head and Deputy Head of the Croatian Institute for Health Insurance for Health Protection at Work		
Head and deputy heads of the Croatian Employment Institute		
Chief State Treasurer		
Chief Inspector of the State Inspectorate		
Heads of agencies and directorates of the Government of the Republic of Croatia and heads of institutes appointed by the Government of the Republic of Croatia		

table continues next page

Income and Asset Disclosure • http://dx.doi.org/10.1596/978-0-8213-9796-1

Table 2.1 Positions Covered by IAD Filing Obligations, Croatia *(continued)*

State level	Local and regional level	Other officials
Officials in the Office of the President of the Republic of Croatia, appointed by the President of the Republic of Croatia in compliance with the provisions of a special act		
Chief and deputy chiefs of the General Staff Headquarters of the Armed Forces of the Republic of Croatia		
Chief Defense Inspector		
Commanders and deputy commanders of branches of the Armed Forces of the Republic of Croatia, the Command for Logistic Support, the Head and Deputy Head of the Croatian Military Academy, and the Commander of the Coast Guard of the Republic of Croatia		
The President, Vice Presidents, and members of the State Electoral Commission of the Republic of Croatia		
Presidents and members of management of companies entirely owned by the state		

Source: Article 2, Act on the Prevention of Conflict of Interest in the Exercise of Public Office (*Official Gazette* 163/03, 94/04, 48/05, 141/06 and 60/08).

Table 2.2 Contents of the IAD Form, Croatia

Inherited assets

Details of the type and total value of inherited property and from whom it was inherited

Acquired assets

Real estate (and how it was acquired)

Movable assets (vehicles, vessels, aircraft, operating machinery, hunting weapons, art, jewelry, other personal items used)

Type and value of securities, provided that the total value exceeds HRK 10,000

Business interests and company shares

Monetary savings (exceeding one year's net salary)

Debts

Obligations and guarantees

Income

Income from secondary employment (including self-employment)

Income from property and property rights

Capital, insurance, and other sources of income

Note: HRK is Croatian kunas.

Administrative sanctions are as follows:

- Salary is withheld from any official who fails to submit an income and asset declaration within 30 days of their appointment or election (Article 7).
- A suspension of salary payment (a fine) in the amount of HRK 10,000 to HRK 20,000 (approximately US$1,875 to US$3,750) can be applied to any official who provides false information on his or her declaration, fails to declare a significant change in their income and assets, or fails to submit a declaration within 30 days of leaving office (Article 19).

  Suspension of salary is limited to a maximum period of three months and cannot exceed one-third of the monthly salary (Article 19); that is, the maximum fine is equivalent to one month's salary docked over a period of three months.
- The commission can propose dismissal from public office for an official who has filed false information with the intent to conceal assets. This sanction was introduced in July 2010 in an amendment to the act. The act does not provide for criminal sanctions. If a criminal act, such as evidence of corrupt practices, is uncovered in the course of an investigation by the commission, the case is passed on to the State Attorney's Office. Officials also have a personal obligation to report knowledge of such incidents to the relevant state bodies.

Submission Compliance and Content Verification

The Commission for the Prevention of Conflict of Interest is responsible for receiving, reviewing, and storing income and asset declarations by public officials. The commission is responsible for keeping a register of officials covered by the act and for monitoring the submission process to ensure that all officials submit their declarations within the allotted time frames and that all declarations are complete.

Declarations are submitted in hard copy, in person, or by mail. The commission does not systematically verify declarations for completeness as part of the submission process. However, if, in the process of transferring data from the hard-copy declaration to the commission's website, the administrative staff of the commission detect apparent gaps or anomalies, the commission contacts the filer for further information or clarification. The commission is not charged with verifying the accuracy of the content of income and asset declarations, unless an allegation of noncompliance with the act is lodged against an official, or if a conflict-of-interest report has been lodged. The commission institutes a review procedure when such a report is received and may, for example, request corroborating evidence from officials who declared property to have been inherited (Article 7). The commission submits an annual report to Parliament on its activities and expenditures. It also submits an annual report to the National Commission for Monitoring the Implementation of the Anti-Corruption Strategy, which addresses its performance of activities set out in the Anti-Corruption Strategy and Action Plan.

Public Access to Declarations

The act states that income and asset declarations are public information and that the commission has the obligation to provide public access to the data and documents relating to income and asset declarations (Article 17). In practice, this means that the commission transcribes lists of assets declared by officials onto a public website.[14] When a request to view a complete declaration form is made, the commission grants access to the original copy on its premises.

Mandate and Structure of the IAD Agency

The Commission for the Prevention of Conflict of Interest was created by the 2003 Act on the Prevention of Conflict of Interest in the Exercise of Public Office. The commission first met in 2004. Its mandate is to implement the provisions of the act. That is, it has the responsibility of reviewing and deciding upon cases where a conflict of interest may have arisen, and of deciding whether actions by public officials that have come to its attention are in compliance with the principles of public office, as set out in the act. Among those responsibilities are the receipt, review, publication, and storage of income and asset declarations from public officials.

The commission comprises eleven members: six members of Parliament (of which three are from the government and three from the opposition), and five from among the ranks of "distinguished public servants" (drawn from business, media, nongovernmental organizations, and academia). All members of the commission are appointed by Parliament. The appointment of distinguished public servants is initiated by means of an open call published by the Parliamentary Committee for Elections, Appointments and Administrative Affairs, which proposes candidates to Parliament on the basis of their professional experience and reputation. Once appointed, the commission elects its president who, by law, must be a member of the opposition.

Members of the commission are appointed for a seven-year term. Exceptionally, members of the commission who are members of Parliament are elected to a term that corresponds to the duration of their mandates in Parliament. A member of the commission may be reappointed only once (Article 16).

Effective implementation of the conflict-of-interest system has been hampered by the adjustments required to implement the successive amendments to the act between 2004 and 2008. In 2008, the commission's effectiveness and credibility were significantly undermined by the resignation of the commission's president due to allegations of conflict of interest—which also resulted in a delay in the commission's activities. A new president was appointed in October 2008, and between then and the end of December 2008, the commission held four sessions and reached a decision on 22 of the 55 cases pending review. The commission has the authority to enforce fines for nonfiling. Where acts of corruption are suspected or revealed in the course of the commission's deliberations, the commission refers the case to the Special Prosecutor's Office for criminal investigation and possible prosecution.

Income and Asset Disclosure • http://dx.doi.org/10.1596/978-0-8213-9796-1

Other state bodies with a direct responsibility for the administration, investigation, or enforcement of conflict-of-interest regulations are the Ministry of Administration (previously the Central State Office of Administration), responsible for the implementation of the Civil Servants Act and the Code of Ethics; the Ethics Office of the Central State Office of Administration, which provides ethical oversight and guidance for civil servants and refers allegations of conflicts of interest to the Commission for the Prevention of Conflict of Interest; the National Commission for Monitoring the Implementation of the Anti-Corruption Strategy (a parliamentary oversight body); and USKOK (generally called the Special Prosecutor's Office). The Ministry of Justice is responsible for coordinating the implementation of the national Anti-Corruption Strategy and handles income and asset declarations by members of the judiciary.

Resources and Procedures of the IAD System

Facilities and Use of Technology

The Commission for the Prevention of Conflict of Interest is housed in a government building adjacent to the Parliament. The premises have five offices that house four permanent staff (and up to an additional ten short-term staff following elections), a meeting room, and locked storage for original hard copies of declarations. The facilities are adequate for the regular functioning of the commission, though somewhat inadequate for postelection periods.

All commission members and staff have the use of a computer and access to the Internet. Disclosure forms are submitted in hard copy; thus, for IAD purposes, the information technology equipment is required chiefly to enter relevant data from disclosure forms onto the commission's public website. There have been isolated cases of officials notifying the commission of changes in their assets by e-mail, though standard practice is to submit a new form in hard copy.

Human Resources

In addition to its eleven appointed members, the commission has four full-time administrative staff, all civil servants, including two lawyers and an economist. For the busy periods after elections, ten additional staff members are hired to assist with the receipt of declarations from newly elected and departing officials. The commission views these resources as adequate for its current responsibilities. If greater investigatory burdens were placed on the commission, however, its human resources capacity might need to be reviewed. The hiring of temporary staff during peak periods has the advantage of keeping the commission's costs down. However, given that administrative staff are expected to identify possible gaps or irregularities in declarations while transferring data from hardcopy forms to the commission's website, adequate training or competencies of temporary staff is also a concern.

Budget

The commission does not have an independent administrative budget, though it does manage an annual budget for educational programs. In 2008, the commission received approximately €200,000 (approximately US$250,000) for educational programming (including seminars and publications). Its overhead and support services are provided for under Parliament's administrative budget. In interviews with local staff, Transparency International Croatia raised concerns that the commission's lack of budgetary control hampers its independence.

Regulatory Function

The commission reports annually to Parliament and to the National Commission for Monitoring the Implementation of the Anti-Corruption Strategy. In its reports, the commission can recommend changes to the IAD system. The commission's role in guiding or influencing the successive amendments to the regulations is unclear, however, and it was reported that the commission was not consulted on the draft amendments to the act governing the conflict-of-interest system. In interviews with staff of Transparency International Croatia, whose president is a member of the commission, staff members indicated that the amendments to the act had failed to address some of the key issues noted in the commission's annual reports, such as its inability to achieve a quorum—and thereby make decisions and proceed with cases—for several months during parliamentary recess.

Managing Submission Compliance

The commission's administrative staff of four is responsible for handling the declarations of the approximately 1,800 officials covered by the act.[15] As stated above, 10 additional staff members are hired after election periods to assist with the receipt of declarations by officials taking or leaving office. The commission also receives approximately 300 notifications annually of a significant change in status of assets (a change being deemed significant if it amounts to HRK 10,000 (approximately US$1,875) or more. See box 2.2 for details of the procedures performed by the commission in managing submission compliance.

Content Verification

The commission is not charged with verifying the content of income and asset declarations unless it spots an anomaly or irregularity in a disclosure form when entering the data on its public website, or it receives a report of an inaccurate declaration. Verification of the forms occurs only if an investigation is triggered. Of the 55 cases reviewed by the commission in 2008, 32 were the result of requests for guidance by officials and 23 were triggered by external allegations of conflicts of interest. Changes to the law in 2010 provided greater scope for a more systematic approach to verification of declarations, although these measures had not been implemented at the time of writing.

Income and Asset Disclosure • http://dx.doi.org/10.1596/978-0-8213-9796-1

Box 2.2 IAD Procedures Performed by Croatia's Commission for the Prevention of Conflict of Interest

The Commission for the Prevention of Conflict of Interest is responsible for the following procedures:

- **Managing submission compliance and storage of declarations.** The commission is charged with ensuring that income and asset declarations are submitted correctly and completely, and within the required time frames. When submitting asset declarations, officials are encouraged to contact the commission for clarification of filing rules or, while in office, to seek guidance from the commission if uncertain as to whether a situation constitutes a conflict of interest. The hard copies of declarations are stored at the commission for 10 years, after which they are sent to the state archive.
- **Data entry for records management and publication of declaration content on commission website.** The administrative staff of the commission is responsible for reviewing declarations when they are received to ensure that they are correctly and completely filled out. They then transfer data from the hard copies onto spreadsheets to facilitate records management and the transfer of declaration content onto the commission's website (http://www.sukobinteresa.hr) to provide public access to aggregated data on income and assets.
- **Preliminary review of allegations pertaining to asset declarations.** The commission is not charged with verifying the accuracy of the information submitted, although if anomalies or irregularities are spotted in the forms while being processed, the commission contacts the filer for clarification. The commission is empowered to trigger an investigation on the basis of internal reviews, although in practice, reviews tend to be triggered by external allegations of corruption, rather than internal monitoring.

If a form is incomplete or presents clear irregularities, or if the commission receives a report of an inaccuracy in an official's declaration, the following procedure ensues: the commission contacts the official concerned to seek clarification or correction of the reported inaccuracy. The commission then decides whether the case warrants a formal investigation. If a review procedure is undertaken, the commission may seek evidence from other state bodies (tax authorities, land registry, and so forth) and from relevant witnesses. If an official is found to have been noncompliant with the provisions of the act, the commission then decides upon the applicable sanction (a fine, an official warning, or publication of the commission's decision in the *Official Gazette*). If a criminal act of corruption is uncovered in the course of the commission's investigation, the case is passed on to USKOK.

When investigations are undertaken, the verification of income and asset declarations is made more difficult by the lack of access to accurate tax or land registry data. Current changes to the tax regime, including the introduction of unique taxpayer identification numbers, are expected to make the use of declarations in investigations a little easier. USKOK reported that they have signed a memorandum of understanding with the tax administration to receive direct access to the tax administration database, but indicated that asset declarations are insufficiently detailed to be of significant use (property addresses are not provided, for example).

Investigatory Function

Although the commission has the authority and the responsibility to trigger a review and investigation as an outcome of its internal review processes, in practice, investigations are triggered by external reports, not internal review. These reports can come from a variety of sources, including anonymous reports from the public or from officials, or they can be passed on from the Ethics Office of the Central State Office of Administration. If corruption or other criminal conduct is suspected, the commission refers the case to the Special Prosecutor's Office.

When conducting an investigation, the commission's role is to determine whether an act or omission by a public official constitutes a violation of the provisions of the act and to state the reasons for its decisions (Article 17). The commission is authorized to determine the facts in a case and to collect information and evidence from other state bodies, which are obligated to respond in a timely manner (Article 18). It can also call witnesses to give evidence to the commission. Officials who are the subject of an official review by the commission also present information or bring witnesses to the commission as part of the review process.

Interagency Collaboration

In conducting a formal review or investigation, the commission is authorized to request facts and evidence from other state bodies (tax authorities, land registry, and so forth), which are obligated to respond in a timely manner (Article 18).

If evidence of a criminal act, such as corruption, is uncovered in the course of an investigation, the commission passes the case on to the State Attorney's Office. USKOK reported that interagency collaboration has been effective in supporting criminal investigations in some cases; on the whole, however, collaboration could be greatly improved. USKOK also indicated that there have been isolated cases in which they have used income and asset declarations as evidence in investigations, where they have been able to prove a discrepancy between an official's declaration of assets and his or her tax declaration. There have also been cases where an asset declaration was used as evidence linking an individual to property with known ties to criminals or criminal activity. As noted, USKOK has signed a memorandum of understanding with the tax administration to facilitate cross-checking of declarations with tax returns.

Income and Asset Disclosure • http://dx.doi.org/10.1596/978-0-8213-9796-1

Public Access to Declarations

Article 17 of the Act on the Prevention of Conflict of Interest states that income and asset declarations are public information. The commission has the obligation to provide public access to the data and the documents relating to IAD by officials covered by the act. Information about income is public but not published (Article 7). The administrative staff of the commission transcribes lists of assets declared by officials onto a public website (http://www.sukobinteresa.hr) (see box 2.3).

The public can also request to view the hard copy of the declaration. This can be done by submitting a request (in writing, online, or by phone), and making an appointment to view the declaration at the commission's premises. The commission reports that such requests are usually made by journalists.

Reporting and Outreach

The commission reports on its activities annually to Parliament. An objective of the 2008–09 Anti-Corruption Strategy and Action Plan is for the commission to publish its decisions, including date of commencement and completion of procedures, on its website.

On the education and outreach front, the commission provides guidance to filers on a demand basis, and the permanent staff of the commission participates in training events about conflict of interest for public officials and civil servants organized by the Ethics Office of the Central State Office of Administration. Most recently, the commission has been participating in training on conflicts of interest for local officials in cooperation with Transparency International and the government of Norway.

By all accounts, the principle of conflict of interest is little understood as a concept across all levels of public administration in Croatia.[16] The Anti-Corruption Strategy and Action Plan 2008–09 recognized this deficiency and required the commission to draft and publish guidelines on conflict of interest for public officials and civil society. The guidelines were approved in June 2009 (see annex A).

Summary of Key Findings

Croatia has established a legal and institutional framework for preventing conflicts of interest, and the requirement to submit a declaration appears to have been successfully institutionalized, with the Commission for the Prevention of Conflict of Interest reporting 100 percent compliance of entry and exit filing for 2008. The enforcement of the requirement that officials submit ad-hoc declarations (upon a significant change in wealth) is an inherently challenging task, however.

Croatia's Act on the Prevention of Conflict of Interest has undergone reforms every year since its enactment in 2003 (except in 2007), as a consequence of the often inevitable adjustment process that characterizes the early

Box 2.3 Management of Online Public Access to IAD Information in Croatia

The Commission for the Prevention of Conflict of Interest transfers data from hard copies of declarations to a searchable online database (http://www.sukobinteresa.hr). These data are updated after every new filing period and when an official updates his or her declaration after a significant increase in the value of his or her income or assets (the threshold is set at approximately US$2,500).

Visitors can search the site for details of an official's declared income and assets using the following parameters:

- Last name
- Place of residence
- Office
- Political party

The major categories of information displayed on the website are shown below. Given that the form consists of a combination of fixed or required categories and sections where filers add notes or clarifications (such as about the sources of income and property), in practice, the level of detail varies widely among declarations.

Categories of IAD information to which the public has access in Croatia
Personal and professional details
Name:
Occupation:
Salary: [net and gross] A 2010 amendment to the Act on the Prevention of Conflict of Interest in the Exercise of Public Office specifies that "salary" does not include reimbursed travel and other expenses incurred in the performance of public duties [no mention is made of travel allowances]
Party affiliation:
Residence: [for example, city or town]
Marital status:
Number of children:
Professional qualification:
Duties: [for example, management board/municipal deputy mayor, and so forth]
Name of institution: [address and contact information and official e-mail address]

Details of real estate
Type: [e.g., house, apartment]
Area: [square meters]
Location: [city, not address]
Value: [specify whether market or purchase value]
The ratio of ownership: [types of responses include co-owner, sole owner]
Burden: [for example, credit, owned]

box continues next page

Income and Asset Disclosure • http://dx.doi.org/10.1596/978-0-8213-9796-1

Box 2.3 Management of Online Public Access to IAD Information in Croatia (continued)

Source of ownership: [types of responses include (a) bought with income from salary, (b) bought with income generated by sale of property, (c) inheritance, (d) bought with cash loans, or (e) bought with funds from sale of assets]

This information is repeated for every property owned.

Movable assets
Type: [for example, passenger car]
Brand:
Year built:
Value: [does not specify purchase or market value]

This is repeated for every car.

Other movable assets
The aggregated value of other movable property is also listed without specifying the type of property, which can be annotated separately [such annotations tend to include categories such as, for example, paintings, jewelry, miscellaneous]. The source of the assets is also provided [for example, inheritance, purchased with income from salary, and so forth]

Shares in companies
Company name:
% of shares/number of shares:
Location of company headquarters:
Face value of shares: The sources of the shares is also clarified: [for example, purchased with income generated from the sale of property]

Membership in the management or supervisory committees/bodies
Name of company:
Location of headquarters:
Nature and duration of membership: [for example, Director 1.1.2004–1.10.2009]
Fee: [accumulated total is given]

Revenues
Type: [for example, life insurance, dividends, and so forth]
Amount:

Savings in kuna or foreign currency savings:
Source of savings: [for example, inheritance, income from salary, and so forth]

Debts: [for example, credit debt—name of bank and total amount of credit debt are provided; if a mortgage, the date of commencement and repayment period are provided]

Spouse's income and assets
Details for the following categories are provided:
Annual salary:
Real estate:

---

box continues next page

Income and Asset Disclosure • http://dx.doi.org/10.1596/978-0-8213-9796-1

Box 2.3 Management of Online Public Access to IAD Information in Croatia *(continued)*

Movable assets:
Income:
And the sources of each of the above
Debts: [as above]

Underage children's income and assets
Details are provided for the same categories as the spouse, as applicable.

---

evolution of an IAD system, particularly if laws are initially drafted under a tight timetable. These amendments have included a reduction in the size of the filing population (eliminating less-high-ranking local government positions) to reduce the administrative burden on the commission, altering the composition and appointment process for members of the commission (mandating that the chair be a member of the opposition), and strengthening sanctions for noncompliance, (including, most recently, the possibility of dismissal from public office for false filing).

Croatia's IAD system is a key element of its corruption prevention regime. Guidelines published by the commission in 2009 identify asset declarations by officials as the "basic control for preventing conflict of interest" (see the annex to this chapter). However, for IAD systems to serve this function effectively requires the means and the opportunity for monitoring the official duties of public officials and their private interests. The conflict-of-interest regime in Croatia is not designed to provide close reviews of declarations by commission staff or systematic advice to officials to assist them in identifying and preventing potential conflicts of interest as part of the submission process. Declarations are typically reviewed once a complaint or allegation has been received. The system, thus, relies heavily on public access as its control and enforcement mechanism. The lack of detail required in the IAD form means that public scrutiny of declarations for conflicts of interest is difficult, although public allegations or complaints do trigger an investigation by the commission. The 2010 amendment to the law mandating procedures for the verification of declarations should improve the commission's ability to respond to allegations or other triggers of an investigation, with better enforcement of sanctions as a possible consequence.

Public interest and media coverage of corruption in Croatia are heavily focused on graft rather than on conflicts of interest, although the commission is working to raise awareness and understanding of conflict of interest as a concept among public officials and the broader public. Media coverage of income and asset declarations often focuses on signs of illicit enrichment (a purpose for which the system was not explicitly intended). The Act on the Prevention of Conflict of Interest does require, however, that officials report any significant changes in their assets while in office, a requirement that is difficult to monitor or enforce with any certainty. The nondisclosure of a significant change in assets by a public official leaves the door open for the media to pursue any officials who show signs of changes in wealth that are not recorded in an update to their declaration. In 2009, media coverage of the prime minister wearing different luxury wristwatches—for which he did not submit an amended declaration—contributed to a public storm of attention amid allegations of corruption that contributed to his abrupt resignation.

Although the system is designed to detect and prevent potential conflicts of interest, media attention on illicit enrichment has resulted in the IAD system being used for purposes other than those for which it was explicitly designed. This suggests a possible misalignment between the objectives conceived by the designers of the IAD system in 2003 and public expectations about the purpose the system ought to serve. What this anecdote clearly demonstrates, however, is that—regardless of the stated purpose of the system—the cost of media exposure made possible by public access to the content of declarations can be a great deal costlier to public officials than many administrative sanctions that might otherwise apply in cases of noncompliance.

Annex A: Guidelines Published by Croatia's Commission for the Prevention of Conflict of Interest on "Prohibited Conduct for Public Officials"

Published by the Commission for the Prevention of Conflict of Interest,
June 2009

(English translation provided by the Commission)

INTRODUCTION BY THE CHAIRMAN OF THE COMMISSION

Dear Public Officials,
On June 19, 2008 the Croatian Parliament (*Official Gazette* No. /08) adopted the Anti-Corruption Strategy, revising the previous strategic document, the National Program of the Fight against Corruption 2006–2008, whose objective is further *enhancement* in *fight against all forms* of *corruption*.

Point 5 of the Strategy, entitled "Preventing Corruption," reads:

Preventing corruption is a key to a successful anticorruption policy, but also a commitment of the Republic of Croatia, arising from the UN Convention against Corruption and relevant documents of the Council of Europe and the European Union. The top priority anticorruption area under the Strategy is the prevention of conflicts of interest in the exercise of public office.

By publishing these Guidelines on prohibited conducts for public officials, the Commission fulfills one of its obligations specified under the measures of the Action Plan, the bylaw of the Anti-Corruption Strategy.

The Commission for the Prevention of Conflict of Interest in the Exercise of Public (the Commission) is a body whose main task is the implementation of the Act on the Prevention of Conflict of Interest in Public Office (*Official Gazette* Nos. 163/03, 94/04, 48/05, 141/06, 60/08, and 38/09, hereinafter: the Act).

However, as also indicated in strategic documents referred to above, prevention of corruption is the basic prerequisite for a successful fight against this widespread social evil. On the other hand, a wide array of the forms of corruption encountered requires a specific defining of prohibited conducts which might be qualified as corruptive acts.

By means of this short memorandum the Commission wishes to define in a simple and understandable way the basic obligations of a public official that are related to the activities prohibited under the Act. The introduction aims to clarify the basic relation between corruption in broad terms and a conflict of interest as defined by the Act.

This memorandum is intended primarily for public officials, for whose benefit the Act was adopted in the first place. However, since the fight against corruption, in order for it to be successful, cannot and must not stop only at the implementation of regulations by those to whom it directly relates, this memorandum is also intended for the civil society and the public at large in the Republic of Croatia. Only by developing a full-scale awareness of what corruption is, what the conflict of interest is, and, accordingly, evaluation of the protection of public interest as a personal moral ground, can we, all together, minimize the risk of corruption.

CHAIRMAN OF THE COMMISSION

Mate Kačan, dipl. iur.

Among a people generally corrupt, liberty cannot long exist.

Edmund Burke (1729–1797), British political thinker and statesman

The passage of the Act on the Prevention of Conflict of Interest in the Exercise of Public Office less than five years ago entailed a need to define the legal term of the conflict of interest.

However, it is impossible to define correctly and fully this new institution in the legal system of the Republic of Croatia without explaining the concept of corruption.

Of the two concepts mentioned above, corruption is, no doubt, the more famous. It is discussed far and wide as an exceptionally detrimental social phenomenon, and it is implied that it is generally known what this concept means.

Conflict of interest as a legal term has been introduced only recently. Building on international best practices, in 2003 the Republic of Croatia introduced that concept into its legal system. Its intention is to protect the sphere of discharge of public office from the grabbing of individuals who exercise public office contrary to the principles of public interest.

The Act starts from the fact that the exercise of public office opens up possibilities of the abuse of authority.

This abuse, which the Act defines as conflict of interest, is often very subtle and does not have traits of "classical" corruption.

However, unresolved conflicts of interest are often a point of entry of corruption—an introduction into corruption and even its most difficult forms.

Income and Asset Disclosure • http://dx.doi.org/10.1596/978-0-8213-9796-1

The purpose of this short memorandum is to clarify the basic relation of corruption and conflict of interest and to define the prohibited actions of officials who, in practical terms, are in conflict of interest. It is particularly important to understand that there are no insignificant forms of corruption, nor are there insignificant situations involving conflict of interest. Only the zero tolerance of any form of corruption may enable success of the combat against corruption.

In the Republic of Croatia there are currently approximately 1,800 public officials. This relatively small number of individuals, however, has been assigned an important task of discharging public authority in public interest. Therefore, each and every act of an official, and in particular each act of the disposal of public funds, should be consistent with the principles stipulated in the Act: Officials shall act honorably, honestly, faithfully, responsibly and impartially, abiding to the principles of credibility and dignity of entrusted office and the trust of citizens.

1. WHAT IS CORRUPTION?

In broadest terms, corruption is any misuse of public authority for personal gain.

Defined like this, corruption encompasses an array of most diverse illegal acts of all those who dispose of funds and make decisions in the discharge of public duties.

Corruption is possible on all levels of discharging of public authorities and civil and public service. Expanding of the scope of the public sphere also brings a consequential increase in the number of those in direct or indirect execution of activities who come into a position that potentially creates a possibility for performing corruptive acts.

In terms of content, corruption may materialize in forms ranging from those that are seemingly marginal to those that inflict huge damage on society as a whole, which is sometimes difficult to repair. In concrete terms, it can take the form of the use of office supplies for private purposes, but also the acquisition of land envisioned as the future motorway route and its subsequent re-sale at higher prices (because of inside information that the seller possessed).

In terms of the perpetrators of corruptive acts, it can be a civil servant who took office paper home, but also a high-ranking state official who bought land under favorable conditions on the basis of classified information about the precise route of the state road, and subsequently sold the same land at a considerably higher price.

Yet, as regards any particular form of the appearance of corruption, the following should be borne in mind:

Although each separate form of corruption does not have equally detrimental immediate consequences, each form of corruption is potentially equally harmful for the society in which it occurs. Therefore, combating corruption is one of the most significant tasks of the society at large.

Income and Asset Disclosure • http://dx.doi.org/10.1596/978-0-8213-9796-1

Corruption is a social phenomenon whose prevalence is very difficult to quantify precisely ("the dark figure of corruption").

One of the available benchmarks is the Corruption Perception Index, which shows the ranking of countries according to the level of perception of corruption among civil servants and politicians.

The index reflects the views of businessmen and analysts from all over the world (including the country for which the research is carried out).

Each year the research of Corruption Perception Index for the Republic of Croatia is carried out by the NGO Transparency International Croatia. On the scale from 1 to 10, where 1 represents absolute corruptness, and 10 an absolute absence of corruption, **for the year 2008 the Republic of Croatia was rated as having index 4.4.**

Since 2005, when the index was approximately 3.35, our country has recorded a continuous growth of the perception of decreasing corruption. Nevertheless, the figure above indicates that there is still full justification for activities whose objective is decreasing corruptive practices in the public sphere.

2. WHAT IS CORRUPTION IN NARROWER TERMS (IN TERMS OF CRIMINAL LAW)?

Corruption in a narrower sense represents the instances of misuse of public office that are determined as criminal acts in terms of the Criminal Code (Kazneni zakon) of the Republic of Croatia (*Official Gazette* Nos. 110/97, 27/98, 50/00, 129/00, 51/01, 111/03, 190/03, 105/04, 84/05, 71/06, 110/07, and 152/08).

Very often, for instance, the mass media state that someone was "sanctioned for corruption."

In colloquial terms, this is to say that the person in question has been sanctioned for committing a criminal offense that is usually considered to be a corruptive act.

3. WHAT IS THE RELATION BETWEEN CORRUPTION AND CONFLICT OF INTEREST?

- The Criminal Code does not recognize the term of criminal corruptive act. The following criminal offenses are usually considered corruption in terms of the Criminal Code (KZ):
  - Giving and taking bribe (Art. 347 and 348 of KZ)
  - Giving and taking bribe in business activities (Art. 294a and 294b of KZ)
  - Illegal intercession (Art. 343 of KZ)
  - Fraud in the performance of duty (Art. 344 of KZ)
  - Embezzlement (Art. 345 of KZ)
  - Unauthorized use (Art. 346 of KZ)
  - Abuse in performing governmental duties (Art. 338 of KZ)
  - Abuse of office and official authority (Art. 337 of KZ)

Income and Asset Disclosure • http://dx.doi.org/10.1596/978-0-8213-9796-1

- Entering into a harmful contract (Art. 249 of KZ)
- Disclosure of an official secret (Art. 351 of KZ)
- Disclosure and unauthorized procurement of a business secret (Art. 295 of KZ)

- The term conflict of interest implies prohibited acts of officials, stipulated in Art. 6. of the Act on the Prevention of Conflict of Interest in the Exercise of Public Office (see item 6).
- Criminal procedure is initiated exclusively by an authorized prosecutor. Authorized prosecutors are the state attorney and USKOK. USKOK performs activities of the state attorney referred to in Art. 21 of the Act on the Office for Suppression of Corruption and Organized Crime—*Official Gazette* Nos. 88/01, 12/02, 33/05 and 48/05-correction).
- The procedure of deciding on a conflict of interest is initiated by the Commission for the Prevention of Conflict of Interest in Exercise of Public Office.
- The act that the criminal procedure begins with is passed by the court, whereas proceedings in criminal law cases are within the competence of municipal courts, county courts and the Supreme Court of the Republic of Croatia.
- The procedure of deciding on conflict of interest is initiated by the Commission, on the basis of a report submitted by an official, or on the basis of its own decision to initiate a procedure, and it can also initiate a procedure on the basis of a report of other persons. The procedure before the Commission is prescribed by the provisions of the Ordinance of the Commission for Conflict of Interest in the Exercise of Public Office on Internal Organization and Procedure (*Official Gazette* No. 86/05).
- Criminal law sanctions that can be brought against a perpetrator of criminal acts are the following: penalties (imprisonment sentence and fine), warning measures (court citation and suspended sentence), safety measures, and correctional measures.
- Sanctions that the Commission may pronounce for an official are the following: suspension of payment of a portion of monthly salary of an official, a reprimand and publishing of the decision of the Commission at the expense of the official.

4. MAY THE COMMISSION PROCEED IN CASES OF FORMS OF CORRUPTION UNDER CRIMINAL LAW?

Any form of corruption which has characteristics of a criminal act is at the same time a conflict of interest.

In principle, the Commission may also proceed in cases when prohibited actions have features of criminal conduct.

However, the Commission does not have the authority of a public prosecution body, nor does it have sanctions that would match the seriousness of a committed criminal act.

The Commission will, therefore, as a rule, forward the reports the factual basis of which indicates the existence of the possibility of a criminal offense to competent bodies for corresponding procedure.

5. WHAT IS A CONFLICT OF INTEREST?

A conflict of interest is a situation in which private interests of an official are in contravention of public interest or when a private interest affects or may affect the impartiality of an official in the discharge of public duty (Art. 1. para. 2 of the Act).

In other words, a situation of a conflict of interest requires that, on one hand, there is a *protected public interest,* and on the other, a *private interest of the official which affects or might affect the protected public interest.*

Three terms are essential for the definition of a conflict of interest:

• The term OFFICIAL
• The term PRIVATE INTEREST
• The term PUBLIC INTEREST

AN OFFICIAL is a person performing activities in the scope of public authority:

• **At the state level** (President of the Republic of Croatia, Prime Minister and members of the Government of the Republic of Croatia, Speaker and representatives of the Croatian Parliament, President and judges of the Constitutional Court of the RC, state secretaries, and other state officials)
• **At the level of local and regional self-government** (county prefects, Mayor of the City of Zagreb, mayors and heads of municipalities, and their deputies)
• **And some persons at the level of the bodies with public authorities** (director and assistant directors of the Croatian Pension Insurance Fund [HZMO], director and deputy directors of the Croatian Health Insurance Fund [HZZO], director and assistant directors of the Croatian Employment Office, etc.)

All officials are stipulated in Art. 2. paras. 1 and 2 of the Act.

NOTE: Provisions of the Act also correspondingly pertain to all other persons discharging public duties (except for the obligation to submit the "asset declaration [imovinska kartica]," registration of compensations that the officials are entitled to, and prohibiting other income pursuant to Art. 13 of the Act).

According to the practice of the Commission so far, other persons who exercise public office are members of representative and executive bodies of administrative-policy units of public authorities (members of the assembly and city authorities of the City of Zagreb, members of county assemblies and their authorities, members of city and municipal councils and their authorities).

PRIVATE INTEREST of an official represents a relation of an official toward his or her own property, toward the affairs and activities that an official performs along the exercise of public office (related to the activities in business entities, such as companies, scientific, cultural, sports, and other associations, NGOs, etc.), and personal relations of officials toward others (family, friendship, interest, etc.) which may create a situation of a conflict of interest.

PUBLIC INTEREST that is protected by law can be defined by the obligation of an official to adhere to several basic principles:

- THE PRINCIPLE OF LEGALITY is the basic obligation of an official. It consists in that the official in the discharge of duty should proceed impartially, exclusively pursuant to provisions of law or in accordance with the authorities arising from law, without any exceptions toward individuals or groups.
- THE PRINCIPLE OF PROTECTION, PURPOSEFUL, RATIONAL AND COST-EFFECTIVE DISPOSAL OF PUBLIC FUNDS presumes that the official will take particular care about the funds earmarked for public purposes within the scope of authorities in exercise of public office, ensuring that they are utilized only for earmarked purposes, in the prescribed procedure.
- THE PRINCIPLE OF TRANSPARENCY presumes that the procedures of decision making in affairs of public authorities are to the greatest possible extent open to the public, and thereby to the supervision of those in whose interest the official exercises public office.

6. WHAT IS THE CONFLICT OF INTEREST IN A CONCRETE CASE?

According to the level of concretization (certainty of existence), a conflict of interest can be divided into three kinds.

- CURRENT (CONCRETE) CONFLICT OF INTEREST

  This is a situation in which there is no doubt that there exists a situation of a conflict of interest (e.g., an official has not submitted the "asset declaration" to the Commission).

- POTENTIAL CONFLICT OF INTEREST

  There are circumstances in which, on the basis of average rational assessment of relevant facts, it is not possible with certainty to exclude the existence of a conflict of interest. So, facts are *perceived* as a conflict of interest, although an actual conflict of interest does not exist (e.g., an official co-decides in a collective body on the change of purpose of land, including a land plot of a person related to the official).

Income and Asset Disclosure • http://dx.doi.org/10.1596/978-0-8213-9796-1

In particular, officials have to take care of the circumstances that might be a potential conflict of interest.

Sometimes it is not simple to identify or be fully obvious of what the circumstances of a potential conflict of interest are (e.g., in the example provided above, the official may not even know the fact that a person related to him or her is the owner of the land at issue).

However, an official must always have in mind that a potential conflict of interest is also a situation of a conflict of interest.

- FUTURE CONFLICT OF INTEREST

Officials are obliged to discharge their duties in such a manner that a potential or current conflict of interest as such is recognized in advance (before the circumstances that constitute the conflict of interest materialize) and that such a future conflict of interest is avoided.

Sometimes it is not easy to identify the circumstances of a future conflict of interest without doubt (such as the one in the example provided above), but officials are obliged to assess all of their conduct in the exercise of public office or in relation to public office in the context of the potential conflict of interest.

First of all, it is important to prevent a conflict of interest!

Officials are therefore obliged to take care of potential future circumstances of a conflict of interest and resolve them in such a way that public interest is protected.

IN CASE OF DOUBT AS TO THE EXISTENCE OF A FUTURE CONFLICT OF INTEREST, AN OFFICIAL IS OBLIGED TO REQUEST AN OPINION OF THE COMMISSION!

Concrete circumstances of a conflict of interest are divided into two groups:

- The first group includes the facts that the Act *specifically* stipulates as a conflict of interest. The existence of facts implies the existence of a conflict of interest (e.g., if an official has failed to provide the "asset declaration," this fact constitutes a conflict of interest according to the Act).
- The second group includes PROHIBITED CONDUCTS OF OFFICIALS, stipulated in Art. 6 of the Act.

At this point the Act stipulates tentative circumstances that constitute a conflict of interest, whereas the Commission in the procedure of deciding on the conflict of interest established a factual basis that, with its very existence, indicates an actual or potential conflict of interest (e.g., the official has exercised a right by breaching the principles of equality; here, all the facts on the basis of which it can be ascertained that there is a conflict of interest should be established).

- CONFLICT OF INTEREST ACCORDING TO THE ACT

1. The fact that an official has failed to submit the "asset declaration" constitutes the basic fact of conflict of interest pursuant to the Act.

"Asset declaration" of an official is the basic form of control of a potential conflict of interest.

An official beginning to exercise their office must, by providing a report on their property (izjava o imovini), has to report objectively and fully whatever he or she possesses at the moment of beginning of the exercise of their office. The official shall also provide an "asset declaration" upon the end of the exercise of their office and in the course of the exercise of their office if a major change with regard to their property has occurred.

A comparison of the content of the "asset declaration" from the beginning and end of the exercise of the office enables control over a potential material side of the conflict of interest of the official, which will be reported as a change in the "asset declaration" of the official.

An official is obliged to submit to the Commission the "asset declaration" in three cases:

- At the beginning of exercising of his or her office (within 30 days after the day of the beginning of exercising the office)
- Upon the end of exercising his or her office (within 30 days from the day of the end of exercising the office)
- In the case of a major change in their property status (upon the expiration of the year in which in the course of the exercise of the office a major change occurred)

The "asset declaration" has to be filled truthfully and completely, in accordance with the content of the form, pursuant to Art. 7 and 7a of the Act.

Untruthful and incomplete filling of the "asset declaration" also constitutes a conflict of interest.

2. According to the Act, membership of an official on the management board of a company constitutes a conflict of interest. Members of the management boards of companies fully owned by the state are an exception.

3. According to the Act, membership of an official in more than 2 supervisory boards of companies, institutions and extra-budgetary funds of special state interest is a conflict of interest (memberships in those legal persons according to the position are an exception).

4. According to the Act, membership of officials of regional and local self-government in companies that are of special interest for the respective self-government unit is a conflict of interest.

5. According to the Act, an official's receipt of compensation for membership in supervisory boards of companies, institutions, extra-budgetary funds and foundations, NGOs, and other legal persons that perform a scientific, humanitarian, cultural, sports, and similar activity is a conflict of interest.

6. According to the Act, an official's failure to appoint a commissioner who will exercise management rights of the official in companies in which the official has 0.5 percent or more shares or business stakes is a conflict of interest.

PROHIBITED CONDUCT OF OFFICIALS (CONFLICT OF INTEREST ESTABLISHED IN THE PROCEDURE)

- **Receiving or requesting any benefits or any promise of a benefit for the exercise of their office**

The benefit at issue can be material or nonmaterial, and has to be connected with the exercise of office. In the said cases, an official is otherwise obliged to do the thing for which he is offered a benefit, or is the reason for which he receives the benefit.

For example, the procedure of the issuance of a public document (for instance, a permit in a construction procedure) lasts disproportionately long. An official is offered, and he or she accepts, using a [someone else's] vacation home in exchange for urgent issuance of a permit.

Receiving un-allowed gifts is also a concrete situation of the conflict of interest mentioned above. For example, an official must not receive money, etc., regardless of the amount.

- **Exercising or acquiring an entitlement in the case where the principle of equity before the law is violated.**

The principle of equity before the law is concretization of principles of legality in the broadest terms: it presupposes primarily that the official in the exercise of office proceeds in accordance with regulations. However, breach of this is possible also when an official proceeds in accordance with regulations that he implements, but does not apply the procedure to all in the same way (as in the example mentioned above, where one person is privileged in relation to everybody else, who have to wait far longer for the completion of the procedure).

Each violation of the prescribed procedure of deciding on the entitlements and obligations constitutes a violation of the principles of equity before the law.

- **Abusing the special rights of officials arising from or necessary for the exercise of their office.**

Such special rights are, for instance: utilization of funds earmarked for public purposes, using an official car, official cards, etc.

A very frequent and important special right is the right of discretionary assessment, i.e., authority that an official (most frequently indirectly, by providing guidance to the state employee in charge of the procedure) has in assessing concrete circumstances as the foundation (or lack of foundation) for acquiring a specific concrete right.

Another example: an official has a right to compensation of travel expenses that he or she requires for the performance of duties. The official incorrectly represents fuel consumption.

- **Receiving additional remuneration for work done in exercising public offices**

The job of an official is a job of public interest, and it is supposed that such kinds of job, more than any other kind, should be discharged impartially and in accordance with regulations. An official is entitled to a salary for duty that he discharges, but any additional benefit in addition to the salary implies a possibility that the official will proceed unequally toward the person from whom the additional benefit was received.

The term *additional benefit* here means any benefit that is not the benefit for the duty that he or she discharges.

- **Requesting, accepting, or receiving anything of value or any service for voting on any matter or exerting influence over a decision of a body or person for personal gain or gain of a related person**

This represents a special form of receiving or requesting a benefit, for which an official obligates himself or herself to vote in a certain way or exert influence on a decision of a body or person.

- **Promising employment or any other entitlement in exchange for any gift or any promise of a gift**
- **Exerting influence over contracting or public procurement**

This area of a potential conflict of interest is extremely important. Those are affairs in which public authority bodies enter into contracts on public works, on public procurement of goods, and on public services.

The material value of those procedures is very big and represents a significant share of GDP (e.g., for 2006 the share of public procurement in GDP was 11.77 percent), so control over a potential conflict of interest in spending public monies for those purposes is extremely important.

Therefore, the Act itself establishes some facts and some failures to act of the officials in relation to the public procurement context as a conflict of interest according to the Act: prohibiting membership on management boards of companies, limiting the right to membership to the one only in legal persons of special public interest, transfer of management rights, reporting to the Commission on entering into a business relation with public authority bodies, prohibiting entering into public procurement contracts with a company in which a head of a body (an official) has more than 20 percent of the shares, business stakes, etc.

- **Use for personal advantage, or for the advantage of a related person, of non-public knowledge concerning the activities of state authorities**
- **Using public office in any other way in order to exert influence over the decision-making of legislative, executive, or judicial authorities, with the aim of gaining a personal advantage or the advantage of a related person, a privilege, or an entitlement, or to conclude a legal**

transaction or in any other way to favor personal interests or the interests of a related person

Here the Act leaves other possibilities for the officials to find themselves in circumstances of a conflict of interest.

7. WHAT ARE THE BASIC OBLIGATIONS OF AN OFFICIAL?

The basic obligations of an official are the following:

- Submitting of the "asset declaration" to the Commission
- Transferring management rights that he or she has in companies in which the official is the owner of 0.5 percent or more shares or business stakes, to the commissioner and a notice to the Commission in the person of the commissioner
- Reporting to the Commission on any inappropriate influence in the course of exercise of office

Should an official be offered a gift or other advantage, and should pressure be exerted on him or her in the course of discharge of duty, the official must decline the offered gift, and inform the Commission and another competent body about the pressure or inappropriate influence.

- **Avoiding circumstances which constitute prohibited conducts of officials pursuant to the Act** (Art. 6 of the Act)

Here of particular importance is for the official to take into account that even the perception that a private interest may affect his or her impartiality also constitutes a conflict of interest.

In other words, when there are concrete circumstances which, according to rational reasoning, indicate that there might exist disallowed influence on the official's impartiality (although such influence does not exist concretely), there is also a situation of a conflict of interest.

- **Respecting the prohibition for the economic entity in which an official is the owner of a business share, shares or other rights on the basis of which he or she participates in management, or in the equity with more than 20 percent, enters into public procurement contracts with the body in which the official exercises office** (Art. 5c of the Act on the Amendments to the Public Procurement Act, *Official Gazette* No. 125/08)
- **Requesting an opinion in case of doubt as to the existence of a potential conflict of interest**

In any case when an official has doubts as to a situation as being a conflict of interest, he or she is obliged according to the Act to request an opinion of the Commission.

- **Reporting to the Commission the circumstances of a conflict of interest that the official has observed in the course of exercise of office**

Income and Asset Disclosure • http://dx.doi.org/10.1596/978-0-8213-9796-1

8. HOW TO REPORT A CONFLICT OF INTEREST?

In order for the Commission to be able to proceed based on the report of the conflict of interest, it is important that the report contain the following elements:

- Name and family name of the official against whom the report is filed
- Office that the official exercises
- Facts that, according to the person filing the report, constitute the basis for the existence of a conflict of interest
- Evidence (documents), if the person filing a report possesses them.

The person submitting a report may, but does not have to, sign the report.
The report should be sent by post to the address of the Commission:
POVJERENSTVO ZA ODLUČIVANJE O SUKOBU INTERESA
(THE COMMISSION FOR THE PREVENTION OF CONFLICT OF INTEREST)
10 000 ZAGREB, TRG SV. MARKA 3
or to the web page: sukobinteresa@sabor.hr.

Notes

1. Article 1 defines *conflict of interest* as a situation in which an official has a private interest contrary to the public interest, or his or her private interest affects or may affect his or her impartiality in the exercise of his or her public office.
2. Badun 2004, p. 144.
3. Badun 2004, p. 144.
4. These amendments were enacted after the primary research for this study was undertaken. The authors are grateful to Sanja Madzarevic, Senior Country Economist for the World Bank, for guidance on recent changes to the legal framework and its implementation.
5. Commission of the European Communities 2010, p. 8.
6. Commission of the European Communities 2010, p. 9.
7. References to the 2010 report were included after the primary research for this study was completed. The authors are grateful to Sanja Madzarevic for drawing to their attention significant developments in anticorruption in Croatia prior to publication of this volume.
8. Commission of the European Communities 2010, p. 51.
9. Commission of the European Communities 2010, p. 51.
10. Commission of the European Communities 2010, p. 51.
11. Commission of the European Communities 2010, p. 9.
12. Commission of the European Communities 2010, p. 51.
13. There are approximately 65,000 civil servants and public employees in Croatia (GRECO 2005). Of these, 1,800 public officials (those elected or appointed to the most senior positions) are covered by the Act on the Prevention of Conflict of Interest in the Exercise of Public Office.

14. http://www.sukobinteresa.hr.

15. The successive amendments to the Act have resulted in a degree of confusion among government agencies regarding the current scope of the Act's reporting requirements. The commission has reported that, under current requirements, approximately 1,800 officials are covered by the Act.

16. Commission of the European Communities 2010.

References

Badun, M. 2004. "Governance and Public Administration in the Context of Croatian Accession to the European Union." In Vol. 2 of *Croatian Accession to the European Union: Institutional Challenges*, edited by K. Ott, 131–65. Zagreb: University of Zagreb.

Commission of the European Communities. 2010. "Croatia 2008 Progress Report Accompanying the Communication from the Commission to the European Parliament and the Council Enlargement Strategy and Main Challenges 2008–2009," Brussels, Commission of the European Communities.

(GRECO) Group of States against Corruption. 2005. Directorate General I—Legal Affairs, Department of Crime Problems. Second Evaluation Round: Evaluation on Croatia. Strasboug, December 9. http://www.coe.int/t/dghl/monitoring/greco/evaluations/round2/GrecoEval2(2005)4_Croatia_EN.pdf.

CHAPTER 3

Guatemala

Massimo Mastruzzi

Overview

Guatemala's Law on Probity and Responsibilities of Public Officials (the Probity Law) was introduced in December 2002 to strengthen the existing income and asset disclosure (IAD) system. This was done in response to the widespread corruption scandals and allegations of corruption that had afflicted Guatemala during its postconflict era. The law, which established the Integrity Department (Dirección de Probidad) within the Comptroller General's Office (Contraloría General de Cuentas, CGC) as the entity responsible for the management and enforcement of the system, was originally conceived to detect and prevent cases of illicit enrichment and conflicts of interest. However, because of the limited capacity of the implementing agency to detect conflicts of interest, it serves primarily as a tool for the detection of illicit enrichment (see box 3.1).

A review of the first six years of operation reveals a mixed picture. The first four years were marred by repeated corruption scandals involving heads of the CGC and the Integrity Department; high personnel turnover, especially at high-level positions;[1] considerable budget and staffing constraints; and the absence of formal standards for the verification of declarations. Not surprisingly, between 2003 and 2006, the system was characterized by very low awareness and compliance rates.

From 2007 to 2009, however, the Integrity Department enjoyed remarkably improved stability in terms of staff turnover, which, in turn, has translated into better results. The submission compliance rate, for instance, climbed from less than 40 percent to an estimated 75 percent in 2008 as a result of intensive awareness campaigns organized by the Integrity Department to foster better responsiveness on the part of human resources directors. As a result, the size of the filing

This report is based on desk research and the findings of a visit to Guatemala undertaken in July 2009 on behalf of the Stolen Asset Recovery (StAR) Initiative and the Governance & Public Sector Management Unit of the World Bank to examine the country's IAD system. This report was produced with the help of World Bank consultants Chiara Rocha and Modest Kwapinski, and with the valuable input of Walfred Orlando Rodríguez Tórtola, Head of the Dirección de Probidad; Alex Pellecer, of the Submission Verification unit; and Luz Ofelia Aquino, Head of the Investigation and Verification unit.

Box 3.1 Snapshot of the Income and Asset Disclosure System in Guatemala

Guatemala's income and asset disclosure (IAD) system is governed by the 2002 Law on Probity and Responsibilities of Public Officials (the Probity Law), which created an Integrity Department (Dirección de Probidad) within the Comptroller General's Office (Contraloría General de Cuentas, CGC). After initial difficulties stemming from corruption scandals, high personnel turnover (especially in high-level positions), budget and staffing constraints, and a lack of standards for submission and content verification, the IAD system has made significant progress since 2008. Submission rates, for instance, climbed from less than 40 percent to an estimated 75 percent in 2008, thanks in part to awareness campaigns organized by the Integrity Department to foster better responsiveness by human resources directors of covered agencies.

Key elements of the system include:

- **A focus on the detection of illicit enrichment.** Although the Probity Law was originally designed to detect and prevent both conflicts of interest and illicit enrichment, in practice, institutional capacity and other constraints have resulted in a focus on illicit enrichment.
- **Separate bodies for compliance and verification.** Two separate departments were created within the Integrity Department to implement the IAD system: the Income and Asset Declaration Department (Departamento de Declaración Jurada Patrimonial, DDJP), which is responsible for maintaining the lists of parties obligated to submit declarations, ensuring the timely and correct submission of declarations, and managing the storage of declarations; and the Department for Verification, Analysis and Investigation of Income and Assets (Departamento de Análisis, Verificación e Investigación Patrimonial, DAVIP), which is responsible for the verification of assets disclosed and the detection of any unjustified increases in assets.
- **Submission is centralized and in hard copy.** A project to introduce online submission processes was initiated in 2004 but is still being implemented. Declarations continue to be submitted in hard copy and in person at one of several CGC offices around the country. These are sent to and stored at the central CGC archives in Guatemala City. A staff of 15, who devote substantial time to manual data entry at the DDJP, are responsible for monitoring submission of approximately 16,000 officials.
- **Content verification upon departure from office.** While officials are required to submit declarations upon taking and leaving a post, and to declare significant changes in the value of their assets, verification of the content of a small sample of IADs occurs only when officials leave office. DAVIP compares the final income and asset declaration to the employee's initial and subsequent declarations to detect any significant or unjustified increases in assets.
- **Asset declarations are confidential.** The Probity Law stipulates that declarations are protected by a guarantee of confidentiality, prohibiting release except by court order.
- **Administrative sanctions for noncompliance with submission deadlines.** The law stipulates severe fines for noncompliance with submission deadlines, which in practice are frequently reduced at the discretion of the implementing agency.

population increased from around 40 percent of public officials in 2006–07 to an estimated 80 to 90 percent in 2009. Moreover, personnel turnover has declined considerably, the declaration forms have been improved to more accurately reflect statutory requirements, efforts have been made to reduce both technological and personnel constraints, and more systematic and efficient criteria for oversight and verification functions were introduced.

However, despite these improvements, significant challenges remain. Most notably, the effectiveness of the IAD system is hindered by several limitations within the legal framework. First, there exists neither a law criminalizing illicit enrichment,[2] nor a law regulating conflicts of interest, without which there are no legal consequences to potentially corrupt acts uncovered by the IAD system. Second, the declarations are protected by a guarantee of confidentiality,[3] and although public access is not necessarily indispensable to an effective IAD system, it allows for an important level of scrutiny and oversight, particularly in systems—such as Guatemala's—where verification capacity is limited and credibility low. Guatemala's low scores against indicators for the rule of law and control of corruption would suggest that building the credibility of anticorruption mechanisms, such as the implementation and enforcement of IAD by public officials, continues to be a challenge.[4] See figure 3.1 for a presentation of

Figure 3.1 Governance Indicators for the Rule of Law and Control of Corruption, Latin America, 2008

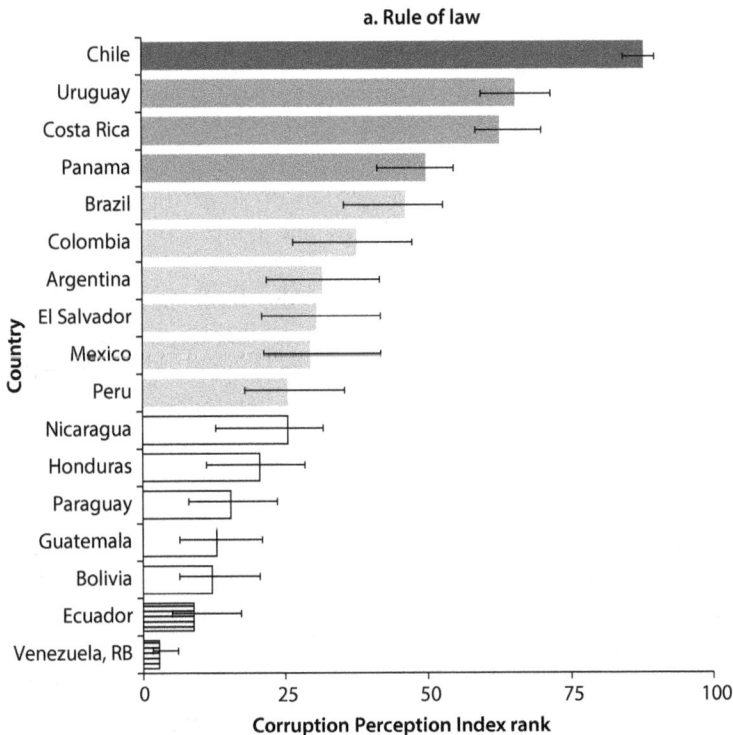

a. Rule of law

figure continues next page

Income and Asset Disclosure • http://dx.doi.org/10.1596/978-0-8213-9796-1

Figure 3.1 Governance Indicators for the Rule of Law and Control of Corruption, Latin America, 2008 *(continued)*

b. Control of corruption

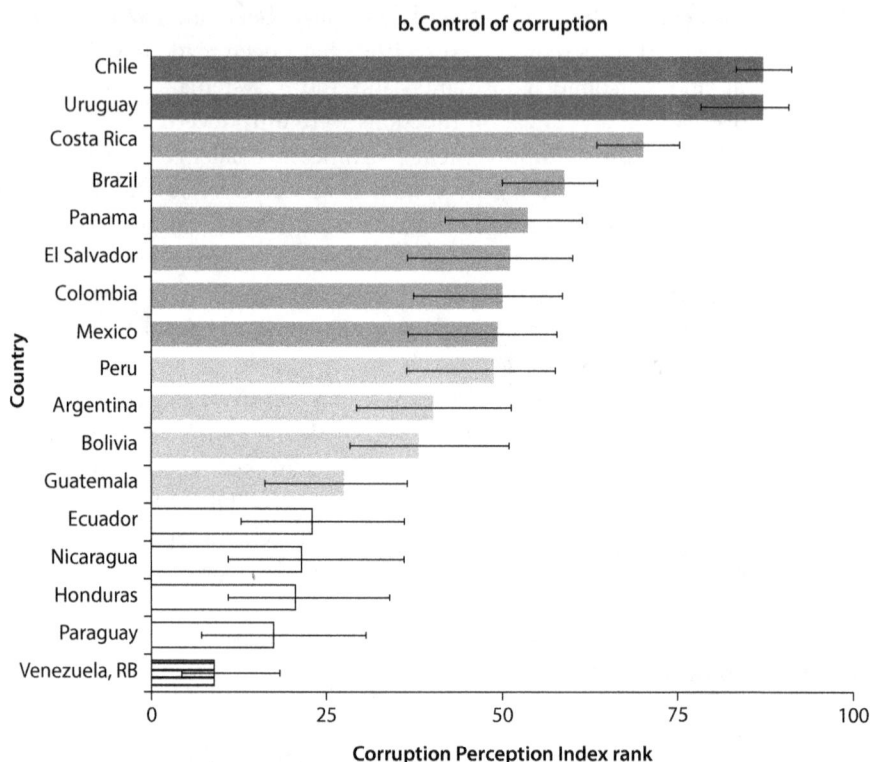

Source: Kaufmann, Kraay, and Mastruzzi 2010.
Note: For more information on Transparency International's Corruption Perception Index, see http://www.transparency.org/research/cpi/.

governance indicators for the rule of law and control of corruption in Latin America in 2008.

In addition to challenges derived from the legal and policy framework, implementation of the IAD system suffers from other important constraints. The agency remains understaffed and the budget inadequate for the broad coverage of the law. Recruitment, supervision, and other internal management processes remain anchored to a civil service law that is arguably outdated and due for an overhaul. The software used for the analysis and management of the system is not fully functional, and the application of administrative sanctions for noncompliance with the law is perceived as vulnerable to excessive discretion on the part of the comptroller. Overall, the agency lacks independence—both political and financial—needed to carry out its mandate unhindered and remains vulnerable to political shifts, which could potentially undermine its recent stability. However, despite the challenges posed by these limitations, the implementing agency has made efforts, and has achieved some success, in improving internal processes aimed at increasing compliance.

Background

Having been ruled for most of its postindependence existence by military governments, Guatemala has long suffered from poor governance and a widespread lack of transparency and accountability. Guatemala emerged from a 36-year civil war in 1996 following the signing of a United Nations–brokered peace agreement by its government and the National Guatemalan Revolutionary Unity (Unidad Revolucionaria Nacional Guatemalteca, URNG).[5] Indeed, addressing the lack of transparency was recognized in the peace accords as one of the obligations to be undertaken by the government.[6]

However, by 2002, the peace accords had been implemented only to a limited extent, which caused widespread disillusionment among Guatemalans regarding the peace process.[7] The climate of uncertainty was further exacerbated by constant press campaigns denouncing embezzlements and corruption by high-level government officials. A financial crisis caused by the misuse of resources that required a bailout of banks did little to alleviate concern.[8] Furthermore, unprecedented levels of crime, including the kidnapping of the president of the central bank, and a lack of progress on the improvement of living conditions added to disenchantment with the government just ahead of the 2003 general election.[9] International agencies such as Freedom House lowered their political rights ratings for the country "due to the continuing decay of political institutions" and "the increase of corruption and lawlessness."[10]

In response to building pressure from the international community,[11] the opposition party, and civil society to address the systemic corruption affecting all tiers and branches of government, the ruling Guatemalan Republican Front (Frente Republicano Guatemalteco, FRG) dismissed some officials who had been involved in corruption allegations and signed the Inter-American Convention against Corruption (which, in Article 3.4, requires signatories to implement an IAD mechanism). It was against this backdrop that congress passed the Law on Probity and Responsibilities of Public Officials (Reglamento de la Ley de Probidad y Responsabilidades de Empleados Públicos),[12] which formally established a new IAD system in Guatemala. Guatemala also signed the United Nations Convention against Corruption in 2008.

One reason for Guatemala's entrenched corruption and crisis of governability is rooted in the nature of its political party system.[13] Political representation is highly personalized, and support is sought on the basis of a leader's charisma and patronage rather than attachment to a party program, election platform, or ideological agenda. Political parties are, with few exceptions, subordinate to the interests of their founders or leaders, often collapsing as soon as their leader exits the political stage. Because positions and track records of individual politicians are more difficult to monitor, the short-lived political parties they establish are subject to scant accountability.

Income and Asset Disclosure • http://dx.doi.org/10.1596/978-0-8213-9796-1

In an environment where powerful business interests or individuals with close political ties play an important role in shaping public policy, legislation, and regulations affecting the business environment within which they operate, laws regulating conflicts of interest have little chance of being introduced, let alone made enforceable. It is perhaps unsurprising that, although the IAD system was originally created with the goal of detecting and preventing both conflicts of interest and illicit enrichment, the implementing agency has been given no competencies to address the former.

The IAD Legal Framework in Guatemala

The 2002 Probity Law (No. 89-2002) provides the legal framework for IAD in Guatemala and is the core piece of legislation regulating the subject. The law establishes the Integrity Department within the CGC as the entity responsible for the management of the asset declaration system. Additional regulations can be found in the Law on Probity and Responsibilities of Public Officials,[14] introduced in 2005.[15] For aspects not directly covered by the Probity Law, the implementing agency relies on the 2002 Organic Law of the Comptroller General (Ley Orgànica De La Contraloria General De Cuentas) and its Regulations of the Organic Law of the Comptroller.[16]

Coverage of Officials

Articles 3 and 4 of the Probity Law provide a general outline of officials, employees, and others subject to the submission of income and asset declarations. This includes individuals who perform public services or functions, permanently or temporarily, whether remunerated or not, in the following categories:

(a) Holders of public office, authorities, civil servants, and public employees, whom by public election, appointment, contract, or any other tie, perform their duties to the state, its organisms, municipalities, public companies, and decentralized and independent entities
(b) Members of the board of directors, managers, administrators, and other people associated with the collection, custody, management, handling, and investment of funds for associations, foundations, and other entities or companies that receive subsidy from the government, its municipalities, or companies that are in charge of public collection
(c) Managers and committee members, associations, and authorized patronage that, according to the law, collect and handle funds for public ends and social welfare and/or receive help and donations from the government, its institutions, municipalities, or entities, national or foreign, to achieve the same objective, which is the public welfare, and any other persons who are involved in the custody and handling of such funds
(d) Those who enter into a contract with the government to perform public works in which they invest or manage funds from the government, its

organisms, municipalities, and public companies, and from decentralized and independent entities

(e) Members of the board of directors, owners of companies that build, produce, install, improve, add, preserve, restore, and manage public properties or services; this provision also covers those who perform their duties to the State of Guatemala abroad, in any field

All individuals covered by Article 4 (a–e) are obligated to submit income and assets declarations, except those whose monthly salary is less than Q 8,000 (approximately US$1,000) and do not handle public funds.

According to Article 20, the following parties are also compelled to submit a declaration:

(a) All civil servants and public employees who work at Customs, Border Patrol, the Immigration Bureau, and ports and airports of the republic, even if they are working in these places temporarily

(b) Any other person not indicated in Article 4, if investigations suggest any evidence of their participation in activities that characterize misdemeanors or felonies against the public interest protected by this law

Article 28 lists the people exempt from submitting a declaration of income and assets. They are:

(a) Civil servants or public employees who perform their duties for a fixed term of no longer than one month

(b) Civil servants or public employees who are transferred to a new position in the administration, except, if they were previously exempt and because of the position change, they become obligated to submit a declaration

Overall, the coverage is extremely broad, which, given the agency's budget and personnel constraints, impinges on the efficacy of the law. In 2009, over 12,000 individuals submitted an income and asset declaration form. This figure is likely to increase over the next few years as submission compliance rates increase due to the agency's awareness campaigns (figure 3.2).

Content of Declarations

According to Article 23 of the Probity Law, a sworn declaration should be filed by the obligated party on printed forms provided by the CGC. The form requires the obligated party, per Article 8 of the Probity Law, to provide detailed information related to assets and liabilities (table 3.1).

When the system was first established, the original declaration form did not accurately reflect all the statutory requirements required in Article 23. Several diagnostics had flagged the inadequacies of the original declaration form, in particular, emphasizing how it failed to request both disclosure of the sources of an individual's liabilities, as required by Article 8 of the Probity Law, and detailed

Figure 3.2 IAD Forms Submitted, Guatemala, 2003–09

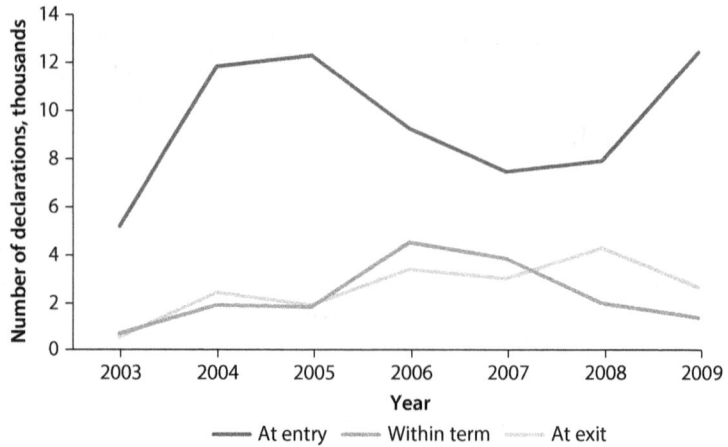

Source: CGC data, Guatemala.
Note: The spike in exit declarations in 2008 is the result of the 2007 elections and the resulting exit of officials as of January 2008.

Table 3.1 Contents of the IAD Form, Guatemala

Non–real estate assets

Promissory notes and other debt holdings (including the debtor's name, the amount of the debt, and the legal document establishing the debt)

Jewelry

Bank accounts (both domestic and foreign, including account balances)

Books of value

Other assets such as a contract for a cemetery plot, commercial stakes, domestic and international investments, equipment and workshops, and assets held in a professional capacity

Household furniture

Livestock

Vehicles

Real estate

All real estate interests held in Guatemala or abroad

Liabilities

All liabilities (and documents establishing the liability) held by banks, commercial houses, individuals, and companies

disclosure of stock ownership.[17] These studies also pointed out the subjective nature of some entries in the form that could be interpreted with arbitrariness, making the task of comparing declarations over time more difficult.

Filing Frequency

Article 22 of the Probity Law requires that a declaration be submitted within 30 days following the covered official's election or appointment, and within 30 days following departure from public office. Covered officials and public employees are also obligated to present a declaration in January of each year in the following situations:

- If they acquire real estate, regardless of its value or form of acquisition
- If they acquire movable assets worth more than Q 50,000 (approximately US$6,250)
- If they acquire credits or debts worth more than Q 50,000

This provision also applies to family members of the covered officials and public employees. In cases of noncompliance, administrative sanctions may be imposed by the CGC as established by the guidelines of the 2002 Organic Law of the Comptroller General.[18]

Sanctions for Filing Failure

Article 27 of the Probity Law outlines administrative sanctions for failure to submit a declaration on time. The only available penalties are administrative, and fines as determined by the guidelines in Article 39 that are calculated according to guidelines established in the 2002 Organic Law of the Comptroller General.[19] The law does not confer any discretion to the CGC to extend the filing time, and it is unclear whether the enforcement of exit declarations (submitted when officials leave public office) is any less efficient than the enforcement of submission while in office, given that sanctions are purely administrative (fines docked from salary).

The Probity Law does not provide for civil or criminal sanctions for irregularities detected in the course of the review of an income and asset declaration. Should the declaration of a public official suggest underlying criminal behavior, this information may be used as evidence only in ongoing criminal investigations.

Submission Compliance and Content Verification

Article 20 establishes the CGC as the depository body for the declarations of all officials covered by the law. Article 24 confers the oversight role to the CGC, including verification of the content of declarations. This verification process is mandatory every time a public employee, for any reason, returns to public office and any time a public employee ends his or her employment, but the process is only discretionary at the time of entry. According to Article 28, the CGC is also responsible for resolving questions or conflicts arising out of the obligation to submit a declaration.

If a declaration is deemed incomplete, the CGC will notify the official, who then has 15 days to rectify or clarify his or her declaration; otherwise, administrative sanctions will be imposed by the depository agency. The Probity Law does not specify the nature or the range of the sanctions, which are established according to guidelines provided by the 2002 Organic Law of the Comptroller General.

Officials and public employees who resign their duties or return to public office after an interval also submit a declaration, as mentioned above, so they can receive a release form. If, after obtaining a release form confirming the submission of a declaration, an individual wishes to take another position, he or she must request a new release form that certifies that there is no pending complaint or investigation associated with that individual (Article 30). This release form is issued by the CGC based on a comparative analysis of assets and liabilities from the declarations submitted by an official to ensure that there has not been any unjustified increase in wealth or any other action that may result in some form of legal liability.

Public Access to Declarations

Despite the passage of a freedom of information law in April 2009, public access to income and asset declarations is prohibited due to Article 30 of the constitution, which excludes personal information given under the guarantee of confidentiality from being publicly disseminated. Consequently, Article 21 of the Probity Law prohibits the public disclosure of the contents of declarations under any circumstances except when the information is part of an ongoing investigation or legal proceeding. The lack of public access to declarations calls into question the effectiveness of the IAD system or, at the very least, suggests the necessity for a more robust verification process. The absence of public access means there is no public scrutiny or oversight of the wealth of public officials by the media or interested civil society organizations, which could be perceived as depriving the CGC of potentially valuable support in its oversight functions. Moreover, social and media pressure could be an important driver for full and effective enforcement of the IAD legislation.

Mandate and Structure of the IAD Agency

As noted, the CGC is responsible for the implementation and enforcement of the IAD system. The 1985 Guatemalan constitution established the CGC as an independent technical agency with auditing authority over the monetary activities of all government organs, including persons receiving monies from the government or collecting on its behalf.[20] The CGC is headed by the comptroller general, to whom the deputy comptroller for integrity reports.

The mandate of the deputy comptroller is to ensure the transparency, honesty, and integrity of the public sector and those serving in it.[21] The under-comptroller oversees the Integrity Department, which has a director and deputy director, each of whom is statutorily required to have five years of relevant work experience. The organizational chart of the CGC is presented in figure 3.3.

The mission of the Integrity Department is to carry out the analysis, verification, and management of all files and declarations related to assets and liabilities required by law and to interpret, apply, and enforce the laws in the area of public integrity.[22] Its mandate covers the responsibility to:

- Assist in carrying out the functions assigned to it by the Organic Law of the Comptroller General and the subcontroller of integrity

- Calculate and propose fines for the failure to return declarations, as provided for by the Probity Law
- Interpret, apply, and enforce the provisions of laws in the area of integrity
- Establish a system of maintaining declarations submitted by public functionaries and employees
- Formulate the annual operational plan, including those activities requiring development as part of the Integrity Department

Accordingly, two separate departments were created within the Integrity Department to support the functions of an IAD system: the Income and Asset Declaration Department (Departamento de Declaración Jurada Patrimonial, DDJP) and the Department for Verification, Analysis and Investigation of Income and Assets (Departamento de Análisis, Verificación e Investigación Patrimonial, DAVIP). Responsibilities of the DDJP include maintaining the lists of parties obligated to submit declarations, ensuring the timely and correct submission of declarations, levying fines for noncompliance, and managing the storage of declarations. DAVIP performs investigations of the veracity of assets disclosed and conducts comparisons between declarations submitted upon entry into office and those submitted upon departure from office, checking for any unjustified increases in assets.

Resources and Procedures of the IAD System

To assess the functioning and unique characteristics of the IAD process in Guatemala, a set of processes and correlating indicators have been developed. These focus on the practical aspects of implementing an IAD system by considering physical facilities available, technology, human resources, administrative capacity, and so forth. By mapping Guatemala's structure and capabilities against this framework, this study seeks to gain a better understanding of possible strengths and weaknesses of the implementation of Guatemala's IAD system.

Facilities and Use of Technology

Although the CGC is housed in a modern building, the DDJP and DAVIP retain their offices in an old building. Notwithstanding some drawbacks, such as the lack of air-conditioning, a recent donation of new computers allows each employee to have a modern computer and workstation. This is a significant improvement over the previous 1-to-2 ratio of computers to personnel. Each computer is equipped with standard software.

Although the storage of declarations lacked organization prior to 2004, a project supported by the Inter-American Development Bank resulted in substantial improvement. The project also provided for the creation of a system of online filing of declarations called the Wealth Investigation System (Sistema de Investigación Patrimonial), which would have obviated the need for storage of hard copies and streamlined the collection of data by DDJP personnel. However, funding for the project was stalled as a consequence of a corruption scandal at

Income and Asset Disclosure • http://dx.doi.org/10.1596/978-0-8213-9796-1

Figure 3.3 Organizational Chart of the CGC, Guatemala

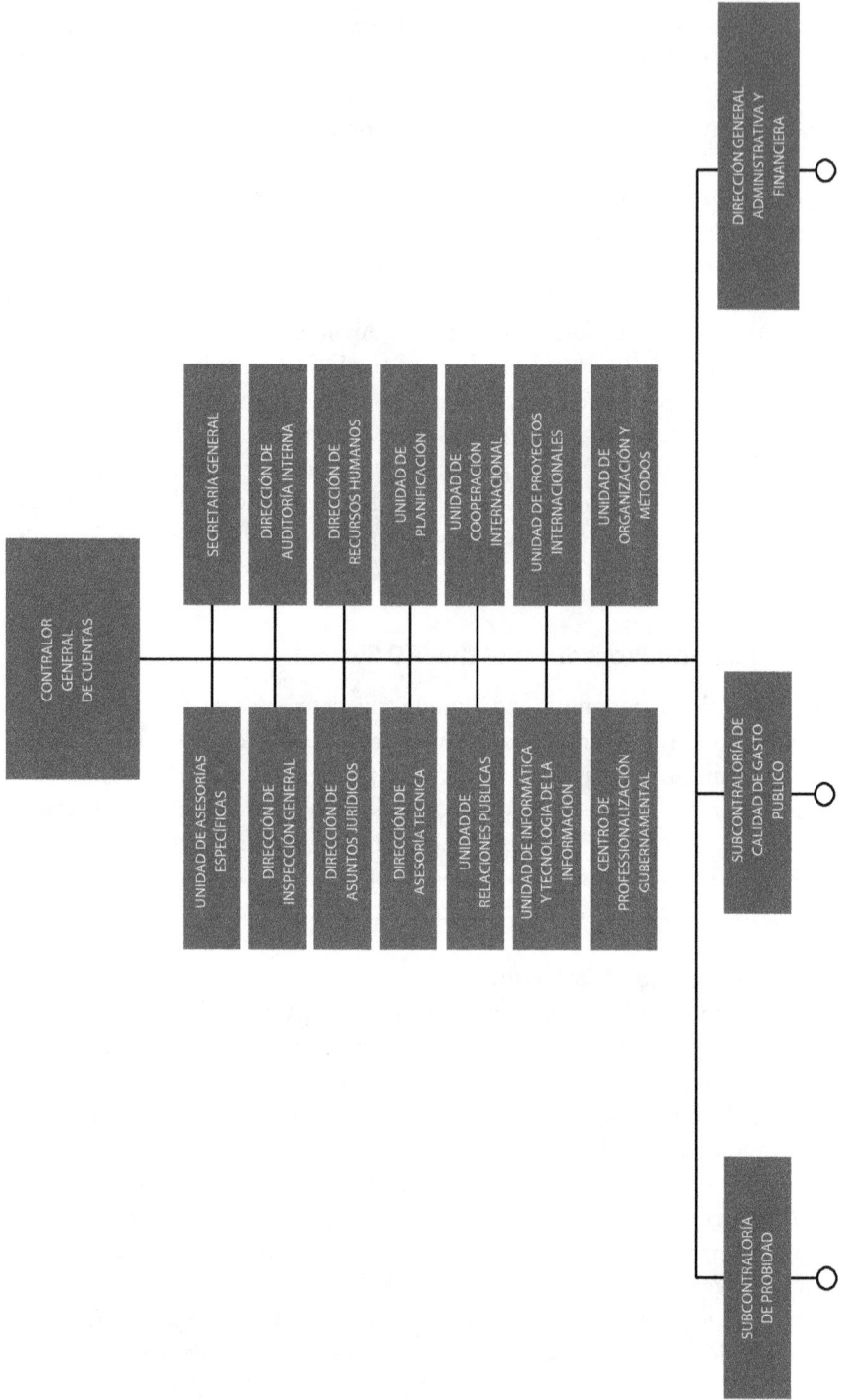

CONTRALOR GENERAL DE CUENTAS

SECRETARÍA GENERAL
DIRECCIÓN DE AUDITORÍA INTERNA
DIRECCIÓN DE RECURSOS HUMANOS
UNIDAD DE PLANIFICACIÓN
UNIDAD DE COOPERACIÓN INTERNACIONAL
UNIDAD DE PROYECTOS INTERNACIONALES
UNIDAD DE ORGANIZACIÓN Y METODOS

UNIDAD DE ASESORÍAS ESPECÍFICAS
DIRECCIÓN DE INSPECCIÓN GENERAL
DIRECCIÓN DE ASUNTOS JURÍDICOS
DIRECCIÓN DE ASESORÍA TECNICA
UNIDAD DE RELACIONES PÚBLICAS
UNIDAD DE INFORMATICA Y TECNOLOGIA DE LA INFORMACION
CENTRO DE PROFESSIONALIZACIÓN GUBERNAMENTAL

DIRECCIÓN GENERAL ADMINISTRATIVA Y FINANCIERA

SUBCONTRALORÍA DE CALIDAD DE GASTO PÚBLICO

SUBCONTRALORÍA DE PROBIDAD

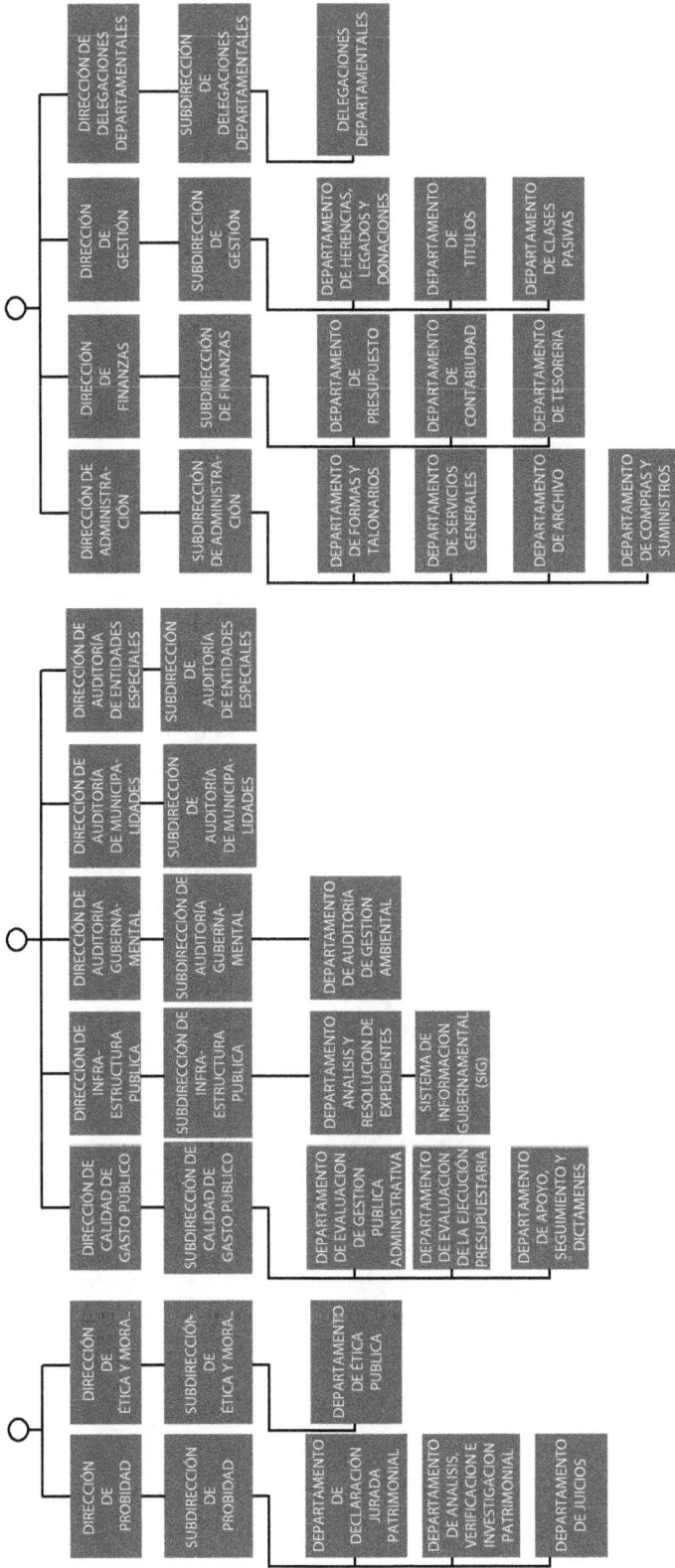

Source: CGC, Guatemala

the Integrity Department and the CGC, and the online submission system was never completed. Currently, declarations are filed in a storage room that has reached full capacity.

Moreover, because the online submission system is unfinished, DDJP personnel must manually enter data from the declarations into a partially functioning version of the Wealth Investigation System interface. Personnel must then input these data into an Excel spreadsheet, thus requiring personnel to divert limited human resources from other tasks. Completing the online submission system could potentially permit a reallocation of staff to other tasks associated with improving the enforcement of the IAD law.

Human Resources
The DDJP has 15 staff members and DAVIP has 16 staff members.[23] While an organizational chart of the CGC exists (see figure 3.3), it does not specifically outline the positions within the DDJP or DAVIP. Job descriptions of staff and operating manuals are also unavailable. Personnel thus receive most of their training "on the job." However, upon hiring, the unit staff receive some basic training in administrative processes, laws and regulations governing asset disclosure, and software and hardware operations.

The implementing agency suffers from inadequate internal management processes, ranging from an absence of periodic performance evaluations to a lack of transparent and competitive recruitment processes. These flaws are not specific to the agency but rather serve as an example of a general pattern across public administration in Guatemala, primarily attributed to an outdated civil service law. Notwithstanding these limitations, the implementing agency has reported a substantial reduction in staff turnover since 2006, in stark contrast to the high rates of turnover at its inception.

Budget
Typical of many government agencies in developing countries, the DDJP and DAVIP suffer from inadequate funding. Since no specific annual line-item budget exists for the departments, the funding they receive directly from the CGC has been and continues to be susceptible to funding shortfalls. Personnel reportedly receive a slightly lower remuneration than other similarly situated functionaries in the government.

Equally worrying is the fact that the overall budget of the CGC, which has a mandate that is much broader than just IAD, has waned over the past few years and has consistently remained below the 0.7 percent of gross domestic product mandated by law, with obvious implications in terms of the quality of operations.

Regulatory Function
Much of the operational framework related to income and asset declarations is already set out in significant detail in the Probity Law. Nevertheless, Article 33 of the Regulations of the Organic Law of the Comptroller General provides

the Integrity Department with the authority to apply and interpret laws in the area of integrity, including those related to the implementation of the IAD system.

Managing Submission Compliance

The Integrity Department is explicitly charged with the mandate to carry out the study, analysis, verification, and control of all files and declarations related to the IAD system.[24] By virtue of its power to interpret, apply, and enforce the laws in the area of public integrity, the agency has delegated the function of ensuring submission compliance to the DDJP.

The DDJP receives declarations at a window at its Guatemala City office or at other satellite offices of the CGC. Declarations are submitted at four possible stages:

- When employment begins
- If a mistake or omission has been discovered and requires correction
- If and when the value of an official's assets or liabilities has changed above the statutory threshold value of Q 50,000 (approximately US$6,250) (or any real estate acquisition)
- When the employee leaves office[25]

The obligation of notifying each covered employee of their requirement to submit a declaration lies with the agency or office of employment.[26] Each office must also submit to the DDJP a certified copy of the letter authorizing the hiring or promotion within five days of an appointment or promotion. The DDJP, therefore, maintains a register of officials obligated to file according to position and name. However, the DDJP reports that the register is probably incomplete because of underreporting by some offices and the breadth of coverage of the law, which includes, for example, public officials from all levels of government (above a threshold monthly salary of Q 8,000, or approximately US$1,000), government contractors, and all individuals handling public funds.[27] However, the Integrity Department is authorized to conduct random audits of the human resource departments within each agency to ensure the accuracy of the register of officials obligated to file a declaration.[28] Due to such audits, and the threat of such an audit, together with awareness campaigns, the Integrity Department reports that there has been considerable progress in this area.

The DDJP ensures that all declarations received have been properly and thoroughly completed, checking for lack of specificity and blank fields.[29] It provides official notices to individuals whose declarations require amendment or additional information, or have not been received within the mandated 30 days. If an obligated party fails to submit a complete declaration on time, he or she is subject to fines.[30] Article 39 of the Organic Law of the Comptroller General specifies the sanction to be calculated as a portion of a public official's monthly salary times the number of months the official is late in filing his or her declaration.

Figure 3.4 IAD Sanctions, Guatemala, 2003–06 and 2008

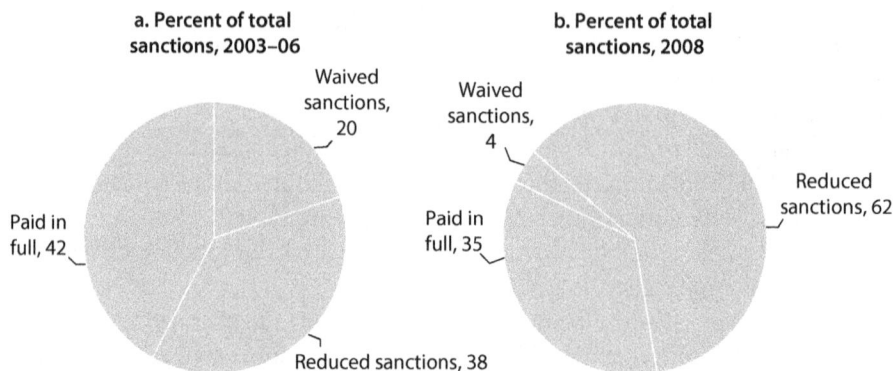

a. Percent of total sanctions, 2003–06

Waived sanctions, 20

Paid in full, 42

Reduced sanctions, 38

b. Percent of total sanctions, 2008

Waived sanctions, 4

Reduced sanctions, 62

Paid in full, 35

Source: Diagnóstico del sistema de declaraciones Juradas Patrimoniales de Guatemala, Coalición por la transparencia, 2008.

Although the language of the provision appears to ensure that fines are reasonably set, in reality, an established matrix of fines based on these criteria results in fines that are disproportionately high in relation to actual income levels. As a result, almost all fines are challenged and eventually either reduced or waived. As both the accuracy of the register and awareness of the obligation to submit a declaration have increased, so too has the number of late filers detected, resulting in an even larger number of fines and appeals against fines. While, unsurprisingly, the percentage of fines that were reduced between 2007 and 2008 was much higher than it had been in the previous four years, the percentage of fines that were completely waived decreased considerably (figure 3.4). However, there remains a strong need for legal reform to reduce CGC discretion in the enforcement of fines.

Content Verification

DAVIP is the department within the Integrity Department responsible for the verification of information submitted on the income and asset declaration forms.

Although DAVIP has been provided with broad authority to verify the accuracy of the contents of declarations, it rarely does so. Article 16 of the Probity Law allows it to solicit pertinent information regarding bank accounts from the superintendent of banks without violating bank secrecy laws. In practice, however, DAVIP staff reported that the process of confirming bank account information is slow and cumbersome—particularly because of bank secrecy laws—and therefore is often neglected as part of the investigation. DAVIP also has statutory authority to verify the accuracy of declarations with "other institutions that it deems necessary,"[31] and when verifications are performed, it cross-checks declarations against land, vehicle, and mercantile registries, and with tax agencies.

Verifications are supposed to be conducted upon the departure of an official from his or her post. Until 2007, virtually no verifications were conducted.

However, during 2007–08, DAVIP conducted verifications of approximately 1 percent of all departing officials, with priority given to high-ranking or high-risk officials, such as tax officials or border patrol agents (figure 3.5). After an employee has submitted his or her departure declaration, DAVIP compares the exit declaration to the entry declaration and all subsequent amending declarations to identify any significant increases in wealth.

The Integrity Department does not, however, carry out extensive formal content verification of declarations at entry, which is optional under the Probity Law (figure 3.6).[32] This diminishes the quality of verifications and comparisons of exit declarations. For example, because entry declarations are not verified upon receipt, the process is theoretically susceptible to the employee overstating the value of his or her assets on the initial and amending declarations in anticipation of a final comparison.

Given the capacity constraints of DAVIP, randomly auditing declarations or targeting verification on the basis of rank or risk is entirely reasonable. However, in the absence of explicit criteria for targeting verifications, this approach is susceptible to perceptions of politicization. Moreover, current procedures fall short of the mandate of the law, which stipulates verification

Figure 3.5 Verification of IAD Forms upon Exit from Office, Guatemala

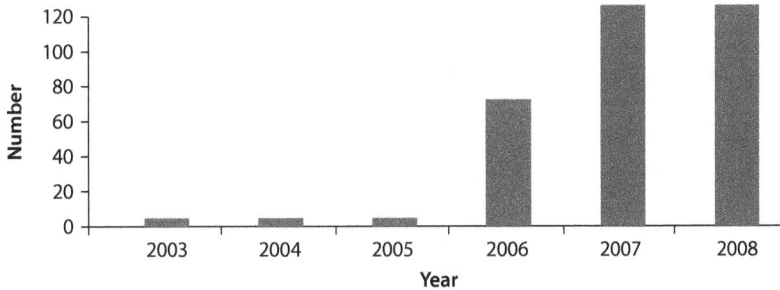

Source: Acción Ciudadana 2008.

Figure 3.6 Verification of IAD Forms upon Entry to Office, Guatemala

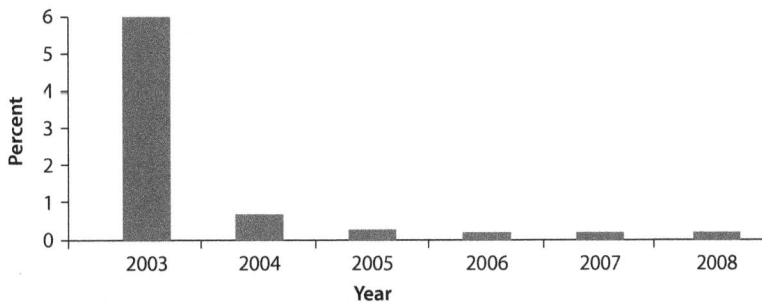

Source: Acción Ciudadana 2008.

of all declarations at exit. This mandate is clearly unrealistic, particularly given the broad coverage of the law and the budget and capacity constraints faced by DAVIP. This suggests that the effectiveness and credibility of the system would benefit from legal reform that restricts the universe of obligated parties, explicitly states procedures and criteria for the random or targeted verification of exit declarations, or both.[33]

Interagency Collaboration

As mentioned, although DAVIP has been provided with broad authority to verify the accuracy of the contents of income and asset declarations, it rarely does so. In practice, DAVIP staff report that the process of confirming bank account information is bureaucratically slow and cumbersome—in part because of bank secrecy laws that hinder the work of the unit despite provisions in Article 25 of the Probity Law[34]—and therefore is often neglected as part of the verification process. DAVIP also has statutory authority to verify the accuracy of declarations with "other institutions that it deems necessary."[35] To that end, it regularly interacts with the tax administration authorities, and with land, vehicle, and mercantile registries.

Public Access to Declarations

Due to the guarantee of confidentiality contained in Article 21 of the Probity Law, no information submitted in a declaration is open to public access.

Summary of Key Findings

The IAD system in Guatemala suffers from a combination of legal and implementation challenges that significantly limit its effectiveness. There are, nonetheless, promising indications of improvement, as illustrated by the willingness of the implementing agency to improve its internal processes aimed at maximizing compliance rates, notwithstanding the inherent challenges and limitations posed by the legal framework.

Major Achievements

The Integrity Department has significantly improved its internal administrative procedures, and has raised awareness of the Probity Law and the requirement to file a declaration, resulting in almost a doubling of the compliance rates over a relatively short period. The Integrity Department has also sought to improve its internal processes—especially with respect to personnel retention, information technology capabilities, and administrative capacity—and has established some initial criteria for more effective content verification.

Continuing Challenges

The effectiveness of the IAD system in Guatemala appears to be particularly hindered by challenges within the legal framework. The universe of obligated parties is overly broad, leaving the understaffed implementing agency with inadequate means to fulfill its mandate. In addition, filing requirements and sanctioning mechanisms require further reform to enhance the effectiveness and deterrent powers of the IAD system. Finally, declarations are protected by the guarantee of confidentiality, which excludes the possibility of leveraging public access as a potentially useful enforcement mechanism and a powerful form of oversight.

Key Lessons

The Guatemalan example highlights several key lessons for the design and implementation of an effective IAD system. These lessons include:

- It is necessary to establish clear and transparent criteria for the implementation of targeted audits.
- Manuals of operations and clear job descriptions should be introduced.
- It is necessary to perform targeted content verifications for entry declarations (particularly if public access continues to be infeasible).
- It is necessary to improve the quality and substance of annual reports of disclosure compliance statistics.

However, because improvements in implementation may continue to be impeded by deficiencies in the legal framework, lasting progress in the IAD system in Guatemala will ultimately require improvements in both law and practice.

Notes

1. During 2005 and 2006, for instance, the position of director within the Integrity Department changed five times.
2. Such a law did exist, but it was repealed in 1999 under the government of President Alvaro Arzú.
3. Guatemala is the only Latin American country where such a criterion applies.
4. Kaufmann, Kraay, and Mastruzzi 2009.
5. The URNG is a guerrilla movement founded in 1982, which became a political party in 1998 (United Nations 2002).
6. Article 20, Peace Agreement on Social and Economic Aspects and Agrarian Situation (concluded May 6, 1996), states: "In response to the population's urgent demands, the Government undertakes to: (d) Improve the administration of government resources and investments by decentralizing them and making them less concentrated and bureaucratic, reforming budget performance mechanisms by giving them autonomy in decision making and financial management to guarantee their efficiency and transparency, and strengthening supervisory and auditing mechanisms."
7. International Peace Research Institute 2002.
8. United Nations 2002.
9. International Peace Research Institute 2002.
10. Freedom House 2002.

11. For example, the Financial Action Task Force had placed Guatemala on its money-laundering blacklist; the United States decertified the country as a cooperator in the war on drugs; and the International Monetary Fund was contemplating a one-year stand-by agreement in the wake of the country's failed bond issue (United Nations 2002).

12. The law passed despite objections of opposition parties decrying the guarantee of confidentially that prohibits public disclosure of the declarations.

13. Sánchez 2008.

14. Government of Guatemala, Law on Probity and Responsibilities of Public Officials, Decree No. 89-2002, Guatemala City, Guatemala, 2002.

15. Government of Guatemala, Law on Probity and Responsibilities of Public Officials, Official Regulation No. 613-2005, Guatemala City, 2005.

16. Government of Guatemala, Reglamento de la Ley Orgànica de la Contraloría, Official Regulation No. 318-2003, Guatemala City, 2003.

17. See, for instance, Acción Ciudadana 2005, 2006.

18. Government of Guatemala, Organic Law of the Comptroller General, Decree No. 31-2002, Guatemala City, 2002.

19. Article 39 of the Organic Law of the Comptroller General.

20. The 1985 Constitution of Guatemala, Article 232.

21. Organic Law of the Comptroller General, Decree No. 31-2002, Article 15.

22. Official Regulation No. 318-2003, Regulations of the Organic Law of the Comptroller General, Article 33.

23. DAVIP is composed of eight analysts and eight auditors.

24. Regulations of the Organic Law of the Comptroller General, Article 33.

25. Regulations of the Organic Law of the Comptroller General, Article 11.

26. Law on Probity and Responsibilities of Public Officials, Article 19.

27. The agency also indicated cases of individuals submitting their income and asset declaration even though they were not supposed to present one. Fortunately, recent awareness campaigns have helped bring more clarity to defining the universe of obligated parties.

28. Law on Probity and Responsibilities of Public Officials, Article 20.

29. Law on Probity and Responsibilities of Public Officials, Article 14.

30. Law on Probity and Responsibilities of Public Officials, Article 25.

31. Law on Probity and Responsibilities of Public Officials, Article 16.

32. Despite the legal requirement that all declarations be verified upon exit, DAVIP verifies only about 1 percent. Therefore, stating that verification of declarations upon entry is optional does not implicitly suggest that legally requiring such verification would be a solution to the problem.

33. Critics of the system might indeed argue that, given the fact that the criteria for the selection of high-risk individuals are arbitrarily chosen by DAVIP, this process is vulnerable to possible manipulation and politicization of the system.

34. The Probity Law provides for close cooperation among government agencies and private entities, as well as individuals and private companies, in order to furnish required information to the CGC. In fact, Article 25 of the Probity Law foresees legal

action if any of the requested parties refuse to comply with the depository agency's request.

35. Law on Probity and Responsibilities of Public Officials, Article 16.

References

Acción Ciudadana. 2006. "Diagnóstico del sistema de declaraciones Juradas Patrimoniales de Guatemala." Guatemala: Magna Terra.

———. 2008. "Informe Independiente de Seguimiento a la Implementación de la Convención Interamericana contra la Corrupción." Guatemala City: Acción Ciudadana.

Freedom House. 2002. *Freedom in the World: Guatemala (2003)*. Washington, DC: Freedom House. http://www.unhcr.org/refworld/country,,FREEHOU,,GTM,,473c5 42b23,0.html.

International Peace Research Institute. 2002. *Guatemala: Five Years after the Peace Accords: The Challenge of Implementing Peace*. A Report for the Norwegian Ministry of Foreign Affairs, by Hilde Salvesen. PRIO: Oslo.

Kaufmann, D., A. Kraay, and M. Mastruzzi. 2009. "Governance Matters VIII: Governance Indicators for 1996–2008." Policy Research Working Paper 4978, World Bank, Washington, DC. www.govindicators.org.

———. 2010. "The Worldwide Governance Indicators: Methodology and Analytical Issues." Policy Research Working Paper 5430, World Bank, Washington, DC.

Sánchez, O. 2008. "Guatemala's Party Universe: A Case Study in Underinstitutionalization." *Latin American Politics and Society* 50 (1): 123–51. doi: 10.1111/j.1548-2456 .2008.00006.x.

United Nations. 2002. "Report of the United Nations Verification Mission in Guatemala [MINUGUA]," presented to the Consultative Group meeting in Guatemala City, January 18, 2002.

CHAPTER 4

Hong Kong SAR, China

Daniel W. Barnes

Overview

Hong Kong SAR, China, has a long history of successfully battling corruption that began with a comprehensive anticorruption system that was implemented in the 1970s. It is now regarded as one of the most effective systems in the world. Anticorruption activities, including income and asset disclosure (IAD)-related activities, are the responsibility of a number of institutions, including the Independent Commission against Corruption (ICAC), the Civil Service Bureau (CSB) of the Government Secretariat of Hong Kong SAR, China, the Parliament, and the Department of Justice (see box 4.1).

The IAD system in Hong Kong SAR, China, is focused solely on the identification and prevention of conflicts of interest for public employees and public officials. It is directed by the CSB, which is the primary human resources agency of the government, but it is implemented by designated ethics officials in each individual line agency of the government. Overlying this structure is oversight by the ICAC, which provides strategic advice to both the CSB and the individual agencies as they execute the IAD system.

Because the economy's IAD system is designed solely to prevent and detect possible conflicts of interest, it places a premium on creating a collaborative environment among the CSB, individual agencies, and individual filers. Declarations are submitted to the designated ethics official within the public official's agency; this designated ethics official follows regulations promulgated by the CSB. This ethics official then analyzes the declaration to ensure that there are no incompatibilities between the assets and interests of the filers and their official duties. Given that the system seeks to build a collaborative relationship between ethics officials and public employees, these income and asset declarations are *not* audited to verify their accuracy.

This report is based on desk research and the findings of a visit to Hong Kong SAR, China, in June 2009, undertaken on behalf of the Stolen Asset Recovery (StAR) Initiative and the Governance & Public Sector Management Unit of the World Bank to examine the IAD system. Special thanks are given to Ruxandra Burdescu and Thomas Iverson of PRMPS for their assistance with the research and preparation of this report.

Box 4.1 Snapshot of the Income and Asset Disclosure System in Hong Kong SAR, China

The IAD system in Hong Kong SAR, China, was created in 2004, but builds on a strong anticorruption framework that was first implemented in the 1970s with the creation of the Independent Commission against Corruption (ICAC). The IAD system is overseen by the Civil Service Bureau (CSB) and implemented by individual agencies within the government (while the ICAC provides advice and assistance on IAD policies to the CSB and individual agencies). Focused on conflicts of interest, the IAD system in Hong Kong SAR, China, created three tiers of public officials who must declare their income and assets to varying degrees, depending on their seniority or the sensitivity of their position. Currently, there are 24 high-level officials who must publicly declare their interests, and an additional 3,700 who file confidential declarations that are reviewed by ethics officials. Overall, there are approximately 75 or 80 ethics officials responsible for administering the IAD system throughout the government and who have been reported to achieve a 100 percent compliance rate among their filers.

Key elements of the system include:

- **Sole focus on conflicts of interest.** The IAD system in Hong Kong SAR, China, is designed solely as a conflict-of-interest prevention and detection program. As a result, the accuracy of declarations is not verified on a routine basis.
- **Tiered classification of officials obligated to file.** Government employees are categorized into three tiers. Tier I includes 24 key government positions, including permanent secretaries, the commissioner of the ICAC, the commissioner of police, and the commissioner of Customs and Excise. Tier II includes administrative assistants who support Tier I posts, all director posts, and any other posts designated by permanent secretaries according to their risk of exposure to potential conflicts of interest. Tier III posts include all other positions in the government.
- **Different levels of disclosure for different categories of official.** Tier I posts are required to disclose the greatest range of assets, including investments in companies in Hong Kong SAR, China, or abroad, and real estate, partnerships, and membership on company boards. Tier II declarations are focused on financial interests in companies. Tier III officials are not required to declare their assets on a regular basis but are required to disclose potential conflicts of interest and to avoid conflicts of interest.
- **Delegated oversight.** Individual government agencies have designated ethics officials who are responsible for receiving IAD declarations and reviewing them for completeness and conflicts of interest. Each agency is responsible for imposing administrative sanctions for noncompliance with either the requirement to disclose assets or the failure to take appropriate, prescribed action to mitigate a conflict of interest. The ICAC is responsible for investigating and pursuing criminal penalties for the failure to file or for having a conflict of interest (which, depending on the nature and severity of the conflict, can be a criminal offense).
- **Emphasis on collaboration with employees.** Although criminal penalties are available, the CSB and the ICAC place overriding emphasis on helping employees avoid conflicts of interest. Further, if a conflict of interest arises but the employee proactively declares that conflict, the employee is generally safeguarded.
- **Public access.** The declarations of individual government employees are publicly available at the CSB's headquarters, and photocopies of the declarations may be made. They are not currently available online or through the mail.

If a conflict of interest is revealed during the analysis of the declaration, depending on the nature of the conflict, the ethics official will recommend the appropriate action to be taken. This can range from divestiture to loss of position, or even to referral to the ICAC if the conflict appears to rise to the level of a criminal offense.

Indeed, the IAD system, though cast as a system designed to protect civil servants and public officials in Hong Kong SAR, China, is firmly rooted in the economy's overall anticorruption system. The ICAC is the nerve center of this anticorruption effort, and its three-pronged approach has been essential to creating the conditions for the development of the conflict-of-interest program administered by the CSB.

Background

The ICAC of Hong Kong SAR, China, was created in 1974 to fight corruption, which was pervasive and which permeated the police and other government service organizations. Relying on the Prevention of Bribery Ordinance (POBO), the ICAC began the arduous process of identifying corruption and ensuring that individual cases were referred for prosecution.

The success of this anticorruption drive and of the ICAC itself had much to do with the sweeping powers of Section 10 of the POBO. Offenses could be prosecuted under one of two subsections, 1A or 1B, of the ordinance; however, both put the burden of proof on the defendant rather than the prosecution. Under subsection 1A, it is an offense for any current or former public official to maintain a standard of living above that which is commensurate with their present or past remuneration, unless they are able to provide a satisfactory explanation as to the legitimate and legal maintenance of such a standard of living. Under subsection 1B, it is an offense for any current or former public official to be in control of pecuniary resources or property disproportionate to their present or past remuneration, unless they are able to provide a satisfactory explanation of how they legally came to control such resources or property.

The broad coverage of Section 10 is evident in its treatment of close associates. To address the possibility of an accused individual attempting to conceal assets or property by placing it under the control of a third party, Section 10.2 provides that, where there is reason to believe that a suspected individual is the beneficial owner of assets held by a close associate, and where there is insufficient evidence to the contrary, the assets are presumed to be under the control of the accused.

Although rarely, if ever, used as the basis of prosecutions today, Section 10 of the POBO played an important role in the early years of ICAC anticorruption efforts. Having achieved remarkable success by the 1990s, the ICAC, in conjunction with the CSB, continued to expand its efforts to promote ethics in public administration. One element of this expansion was the creation of comprehensive conflict-of-interest regulations, which were then supplemented with declarations of financial interests in order to help civil servants avoid these conflicts of interest.

The IAD Legal Framework in Hong Kong SAR, China

The various agencies responsible for facets of the IAD system in Hong Kong SAR, China, were established in separate laws. The two most important entities with IAD functions are the CSB and the Corruption Prevention Department of the ICAC. However, the IAD system in Hong Kong SAR, China, is a highly decentralized system that relies heavily on individual agencies to implement and administer tailored conflict-of-interest guidelines and to receive and analyze the income and asset declarations of filers working within those individual agencies.

Despite this decentralization, the CSB is the lead agency involved in the administration of the IAD system, which it refers to as a "declaration of investments system for civil servants." The principles and requirements of these declarations are outlined in CSB Circulars No. 2/2004 and No. 8/2006. The government's policy aims to strike a balance between a civil servant's right to private investment and privacy and the upholding of civil service impartiality and accountability. The economy's civil servants are free to make private investments so long as such investments do not lead to conflicts of interest with official duties and responsibilities.

Despite the robust reputation for anticorruption measures enjoyed by Hong Kong SAR, China, its IAD system is a recent creation and one that is targeted solely at identifying and preventing possible conflicts of interest for civil servants. As such, the famous anticorruption prowess of the ICAC plays a secondary role in the administration of the IAD system. That said, the Corruption Prevention Department of the ICAC played a vital role in shaping the structure of the IAD system and provides ongoing advice to the CSB on implementation of the system pursuant to its powers under the POBO (Sections 3, 4, and 10) and the Misconduct in Public Office Ordinance.

A key element of the Corruption Prevention Department's role in the IAD system is the production of guidelines for civil servants to help them complete their declarations of investments. This is particularly important because of the complexity posed by the concept of a conflict of interest; providing detailed instructions to declarers enables them to identify all covered investments that must be declared. The CSB, in turn, works closely with the ICAC to produce these guidelines, and at times serves as an intermediary between the individual agencies and the ICAC to learn from the experiences of various agencies and recommend possible changes to the structure of the declaration system or ICAC controls on corruption. However, according to the law, it is ultimately the responsibility of the individual agencies to adopt binding regulations that govern conflicts of interest within their own agency.

Coverage of Officials

Under CSB rules, public officials are designated as one of two types—Tier I or Tier II—both of which are required to declare their investments (table 4.1). Holders of public office who have access to sensitive information or who are

Table 4.1 Positions Covered by IAD Filing Obligations, Hong Kong SAR, China

Tier I posts
24 key government positions
Tier II posts
Administrative assistants and personal secretaries to Tier I posts
All director posts
Any post determined to be at heightened risk of exposure to conflicts of interest
Tier III posts
All other positions in government offices

Source: CSB Circular No. 8/2006, Hong Kong SAR, China.

exposed to a heightened risk of exposure to conflict of interest situations are designated as either Tier I or Tier II. Tier I posts are centrally designated by the government and consist of 24 key government positions, including permanent secretaries (18), the commissioner of police, the commissioner of the ICAC, the director of immigration, the commissioner of Customs and Excise, the director of audit posts (5), and the head of the Central Policy Unit. The declarations of these individuals are made publicly available.

Tier II posts include administrative assistants and personal secretaries in support of Tier I posts, all director posts other than those covered in Tier I, and nondirectorate posts that have been designated by permanent secretaries and heads of departments because of their heightened risk of exposure to potential conflict-of-interest situations. Currently, there are approximately 3,700 Tier II posts that are regularly reviewed by the CSB but not made publicly available. Beyond Tier I and Tier II lies an undesignated tier, sometimes informally referred to as *Tier III*, which includes all civil servants not included in the first two tiers. These individuals are not required to declare their investments.

Content of Declarations

Holders of Tier I and Tier II positions are required to declare any investment, shareholding, or direct or indirect interest in any company or undertaking, and any interest in land or buildings (including one's home) in Hong Kong SAR, China, and abroad. Declarations must also include the occupation of the declarer's spouse. Declarations do not include bank deposits. Both groups are required to report any single investment transaction of or exceeding HK$200,000, or the equivalent of three months' salary, whichever is less, within seven days of the transaction date. Both levels of officials must also declare their spouse's occupation. Table 4.2 provides a list of declaration contents.

Further, holders of Tier I posts are required to register additional financial interests, both domestic and international, for public inspection and requests. These interests include land and buildings (including their homes), proprietorships, partnerships or directorships of companies, and shareholdings of 1 percent or more of the issued share capital in any listed public or private company.

Table 4.2 Contents of the Income and Asset Declaration, Hong Kong SAR, China

	Tier I officials	Tier II officials	Publicly available (Tier I only)
Personal Information			
Name	✓	✓	✓
Spouse's occupation	✓	✓	n.a.
Interests			
All investments	✓	✓	n.a.
All shareholdings	✓	✓	n.a.
Investment transactions exceeding HK$200,000	✓	✓	n.a.
Assets			
Land and buildings	✓	n.a.	✓
Proprietorships, partnerships, or directorships of companies	✓	n.a.	✓
Shareholdings of 1 percent or more in any public or private company	✓	n.a.	✓

Source: CSB Circular No. 8/2006, Hong Kong SAR, China.
Note: n.a. = not applicable.

Posts designated neither Tier I nor Tier II are not required to regularly declare investments, but all civil servants are responsible for avoiding any conflict of interest between their investments and official duties, and for reporting any investments that may expose the holder to such a conflict.

In an attempt to maintain a comprehensive and dynamic IAD system, the CSB encourages the various departments and bureaus to consider their specific operational circumstances and draw up additional guidelines requiring staff to avoid or declare certain specified investment activities.

Filing Frequency

Filing frequency is the same for both the Corruption Prevention Department and CSB IAD systems. Officers holding Tier I positions are required to declare upon appointment and annually thereafter. Holders of Tier II posts are required to declare upon appointment and biennially thereafter. Between the annual or biennial declaration, both groups are required to report any single large investment transaction within seven days of the transaction date.

Content Verification

Neither the CSB nor the Corruption Prevention Department actively verifies the accuracy of submitted asset declarations. However, in situations that are part of ongoing investigations or where a complaint has been raised, verification of the information provided in asset disclosure forms will be executed. Although the declarations are not verified for accuracy, they are analyzed by the designated ethics officials in each agency to determine whether the declarer has a conflict of interest.

In an attempt to maintain an efficient IAD system, the Corruption Prevention Department recommends that departments create and publish, for internal use, examples of conflict-of-interest situations that are tailored to that specific department. Such a list, which serves only as a reference and starting point, might include business transactions and various situations that a public official within that department would commonly face. The Corruption Prevention Department also offers accounts of "best practices" for industries and sectors within Hong Kong SAR, China.

Sanctions

Where an actual or potential conflict of interest arises, management has a number of sanctions from which to choose the most appropriate. Depending on the circumstances, the individual agency may choose to:

- Ask the filer to divest himself or herself of the investments or interests that pose a conflict of interest
- Ask the filer to refrain from further acquisition or divestiture of the investments or interests
- Freeze any investment transaction for a specified period of time
- Ask the filer to place the investment in a blind trust (without the requirement to divest current investments)
- Ask the filer to refrain from handling cases with the potential for a conflict of interest with the individual's investment
- Assign duties that may create a conflict of interest to another officer

Disciplinary action is prescribed on a case-by-case basis and may be considered if there is noncompliance with the central or supplementary departmental declaration rules or investment restrictions, instructions, or management advice given to the officer, or other civil service rules and regulations on conflict of interest. Civil Service Regulation 466 describes the disciplinary measures for the failure to file a declaration.

The POBO provides administrative and criminal sanctions for violations of conflict-of-interest rules. For instance, Section 12 of that law provides for a fine of HK$100,000 (approximately US$13,000), imprisonment for up to one year, and payment of a fine equal to the amount of advantage received by a public official. Section 4 provides for a fine of HK$500,000 (approximately US$64,000), imprisonment for up to seven years, and payment of any part of the advantage received if the advantage is determined to be a bribe (an advantage becomes a bribe if the advantage is determined to have been an inducement for the public official to perform a favor for the person or entity providing the advantage). If a public official has any unexplained wealth (as defined under Section 10 of the POBO), he or she may be fined up to HK$500,000, imprisoned up to seven years, and be required to pay a sum not to exceed the amount of unexplained wealth.

Although these sanctions cover different types of advantages, they may also be interpreted to apply to any situation where a conflict of interest gives rise to monetary gain. The Misconduct in Public Office Ordinance provides for imprisonment as a disciplinary action. The aforementioned fines also apply to any unexplained wealth as covered by Section 10 of the POBO. If an income and asset declaration of a public servant reveals the existence of unexplained wealth, the declaration can be used as a tool for prosecuting the individual for the crime of illicit enrichment. However, as noted throughout this study, the IAD system in Hong Kong SAR, China, is designed primarily to detect and prevent conflicts of interest for public officials and civil servants rather than to detect bribes or illegally obtained assets.

Public Access to Declarations

Asset declarations of all Tier I officials are required to be made available to the public; declarations of Tier II officials are confidential. Requestors must come into the CSB to view the original declaration, but copies are available for a nominal copying fee. The majority of requestors are journalists. Declarations are not yet online, but the bureau is looking into making them available via the Internet.

Investigations

One of the primary tools used by the ICAC, particularly during the 1970s and 1980s, is investigations and prosecutions based on Section 10 of the POBO, which criminalized the possession of unexplained property. Specifically, the POBO makes it illegal to maintain a standard of living above that which is commensurate with official emoluments or to control resources or property disproportionate to official emoluments without a satisfactory explanation of how such a standard of living is maintained.

With the decreasing use of Section 10 prosecutions in the 1990s as systemic corruption within the public sector seemed to wane, attention turned to preventing and managing conflicts of interest for public servants. This culminated in the adoption of CSB Circulars No. 2/2004 and No. 8/2006, which created the requirement that certain tiers of civil servants make regular declarations of investments. The circulars also require all civil servants to declare a conflict of interest if one ever arises during their service.

The civil service is divided into three tiers, with the top two tiers subject to regular declarations of investments. There are currently 24 Tier I posts in Hong Kong SAR, China, including 18 permanent secretaries, 5 directors of audit posts, and the head of the Central Policy Unit. Tier I officials make public declarations of their investments upon taking office and annually thereafter. Tier II positions are officeholders with access to sensitive information or whose positions place them at higher risk of being in conflict-of-interest situations. Tier II officers make nonpublic declarations of investments upon taking office and biennially thereafter.

All declarations of investments include information on any investment, shareholding, or any interest in any company or in any land or buildings inside and outside of Hong Kong SAR, China. The declarations do not require the disclosure of bank account information, movable property such as vehicles, or debts. The declaration of investments is designed solely for preventing and managing conflicts of interest. It complements, but does not replace, the work of the ICAC aimed at uncovering and prosecuting illicit enrichment through the use of Section 10 of the POBO.

Mandate and Structure of the IAD Agency

The IAD system in Hong Kong SAR, China, is directed by the CSB, but is implemented by designated ethics officials in each individual line agency of the government who are employees of those agencies. Overlying this structure is oversight by the ICAC, which provides strategic advice for both the CSB and the individual agencies as they execute the IAD system.

The mission and operations of the ICAC are firmly rooted in clear and comprehensive laws. The agency is staffed with approximately 1,300 personnel and a yearly operating budget of HK$700 million (approximately US$90 million). With a 35-year history of combating corruption, the ICAC has developed a sophisticated array of anticorruption tools. These include prosecutions for "living beyond means" (illicit enrichment) and oversight of a conflict-of-interest declaration system administered by the CSB.

The ICAC's success, in particular, seems to be rooted in its reliance on three equal and reinforcing elements of its work: (1) prevention, (2) education, and (3) enforcement. These elements form the fundamental organizing principle of the ICAC, as reflected in its organizational chart, which lists three primary departments responsible for each of the three elements listed above (figure 4.1). These departments and their functions are as follows:

- **Operations Department:** The ICAC investigates all allegations of corruption and refers cases, as appropriate, to prosecutors. The Operations Department has a team of highly trained law enforcement officers who take care of all facets of corruption investigations, including undercover operations and financial forensic analysis.
- **Corruption Prevention Department:** This department works closely with all other public bodies and with private companies to develop and refine policies that limit the opportunity for individuals to perform corrupt acts

Figure 4.1 Organizational Chart of the ICAC, Hong Kong SAR, China

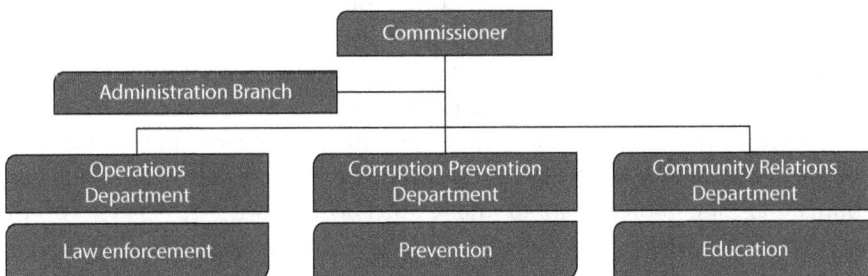

Source: ICAC, Hong Kong SAR, China.

Income and Asset Disclosure • http://dx.doi.org/10.1596/978-0-8213-9796-1

while also strengthening monitoring to detect instances of corruption quickly.

- **Community Relations Department:** The ICAC expends significant resources on education campaigns for the general public through advertising, but also through school programs and community outreach. The aim has been to build a culture of ethics and to inform citizens of their right to report corruption while assuring them that their complaints will be acted upon.

Resources and Procedures of the IAD System

The means by which Hong Kong SAR, China, has implemented its income and asset declaration system is as important as the legal framework and organization structure for understanding the overall functioning of the system. Using a set of in-practice indicators, a clear picture of the physical, budgetary, human resource, and enforcement capabilities of the system in Hong Kong SAR, China, was created. This is detailed below.

As noted throughout this report, the CSB is the primary government agency responsible for the implementation of the IAD system. The CSB, as the central administrative department of the government of Hong Kong SAR, China, maintains a large facility in Central Hong Kong SAR, China. Within the CSB, approximately three employees are in charge of monitoring the performance of the overall IAD system and the actions of each ethics official in every line agency. Civil servants are required to submit their income and asset declarations to these individual offices, rather than to the CSB, placing the primary administrative burden on the individual offices. An examination of every ethics office was beyond the scope of this study.

Facilities and Use of Technology

The ICAC, which helps the CSB and each ethics official refine their IAD procedures, has its own state-of-the-art HK$700 million (approximately US$90 million) building. In addition to offices for all personnel, there is a mess hall, a gym, detention facilities, and interrogation rooms. The Operations Department is housed on the top floors of the building, which are separated from the Corruption Prevention and Community Relations Departments by separate elevators and added security doors. The Corruption Prevention Department is the primary unit within the ICAC that handles conflict-of-interest declaration–related issues. This department has a dedicated budget, offices, and computers.

The CSB maintains a dedicated staff of information technology professionals, and the small staff dedicated to monitoring the IAD system has access to new computers, software, and technical expertise. However, income and asset declarations are submitted in hard copy to designated ethics officials within each government agency, rather than to the CSB. Furthermore, the analysis of the declarations is performed by these ethics officials and is designed solely to identify potential or current conflicts of interest. Currently, the use of technology in the submission process and analysis process is extremely limited.

The ICAC also has a dedicated staff of information technology professionals responsible for the operation of all computer and technical systems within the agency. The Corruption Prevention Department, which is responsible for providing advice that shapes the rules of the IAD system in Hong Kong SAR, China, has up-to-date software and hardware, including access to databases that track corruption statistics. However, as noted, the ICAC is not directly responsible for receiving or analyzing income and asset declarations.

Human Resources

Personnel of individual government agencies and of the CSB are hired through a competitive process according to civil service regulations and law. Those officials designated as ethics officials receive additional training pertinent to their role in receiving and analyzing the declarations of employees in their agency. Civil service rules also specify that all personnel receive periodic reviews of their performance. The ICAC has an organizational chart depicting the administrative design of the agency and provides explicit job descriptions to its staff that clearly delineate their responsibilities.

The ICAC, with its broad anticorruption mandate, has a staff of approximately 1,300. This represents a ratio of anticorruption personnel to civil population unrivaled by almost any peer anticorruption agency in the world. All staff receive extensive training upon hiring, as well as periodic reviews and ongoing training. Hiring is done on a competitive basis according to civil service hiring standards. All employees have a minimum of four years of postsecondary education, and many have advanced graduate degrees as well.

Budget

In 2009, the CSB had expenditures of HK$415 million (approximately US$53 million). However, the resources dedicated to the CSB's role in the IAD system come almost exclusively in the form of three staff members who monitor and liaise with the individual ethics officials of each of the approximately 75 line agencies.

The ICAC had an operating budget of HK$700 million (approximately US$90 million) in 2009, which accounted for approximately 0.3 percent of government spending by Hong Kong SAR, China. In fact, this funding level translates to roughly HK$15 per capita for the entire population of Hong Kong SAR, China. Such funding and staffing levels relative to overall population are unlikely to be replicable in other countries. These numbers, however, demonstrate the commitment of the economy's government to combating corruption, and reflect the fruition of over 35 years of institutional strengthening. The ICAC's mandate is, however, significantly broader than just IAD.

Regulatory Function

The ICAC, as an independent agency, has the authority to issue regulations and to investigate and refer prosecutions for all corruption-related offenses. In the case of the IAD system, however, the ICAC partners both with the CSB and the individual agencies to develop regulations that govern conflicts of interest for employees in each agency. Although the ICAC and the CSB have set certain minimum, common standards, these organizations have worked with individual agencies to adopt tailor-made guidance, as well.

Managing Submission Compliance

Verification of the submission of an asset declaration is performed by the individual ethics officials and agency within which the public employee works. When a declaration is submitted, it is the responsibility of the ethics official to examine its contents to identify potential or existing conflicts of interest based on the investments declared and the employee's duties.

The individual agencies do, however, report to the ICAC when an employee has failed to comply with the requirement to submit a declaration. The agencies are also required to report any conflicts of interest they uncover so the ICAC can then determine if any legal action is required. The individual agency is responsible for implementing any relevant administrative penalties—such as a warning, fine, or dismissal, depending on the severity of the offense—while the ICAC can pursue criminal sanctions for the failure to declare a conflict of interest, even if no personal gain occurred. According to the ICAC, there is currently a 100 percent compliance rate with the IAD requirement in Hong Kong SAR, China.

The individual agencies are required to maintain up-to-date lists of the public officials obliged to submit declarations as either Tier I or Tier II officials (those obliged to submit regular declarations). This type of decentralized system requires that significant trust be placed in the individual agencies to properly maintain these lists. The agencies send the completed declarations to the CSB for storage and archiving, where they are locked in safes and kept for five years.

Currently, there are 24 Tier I posts in the government in Hong Kong SAR, China, and approximately 3,700 Tier II posts. In addition, there are around 75 government agencies in Hong Kong SAR, China; each has a designated ethics official responsible for receiving these declarations. All civil servants are required to notify their designated ethics official if they find themselves in a conflict of interest situation. These Tier III officials do not submit asset declarations, but these notifications of conflict do increase the workload of ethics officials.

Content Verification

The system in Hong Kong SAR, China, is focused solely on identifying and preventing conflicts of interest. As a result, it places emphasis on helping civil servants to avoid conflicts of interest rather than strictly monitoring whether the declaration is accurate. Both the ICAC and the CSB emphasize that their approach is designed to protect civil servants from exposing themselves to conflict-of-interest situations rather than assuming civil servants could be engaged in illegal behavior.

As a result, the IAD system relies on a collaborative model where ethics officials, the CSB, and the ICAC work with civil servants to identify potential conflicts of interest and take steps to avoid the conflict.

However, the declaration may also be used during an investigation into underlying corrupt behavior or if a conflict of interest is suspected. In these instances, the ICAC may check the contents of the declaration. If it is determined that the civil servant failed to declare an investment or a conflict of interest, then that civil servant can be liable to criminal prosecution.

Investigatory Function

The ICAC has an extensive and sophisticated array of investigatory tools at its disposal. The Operations Department of the ICAC is the unit that performs these investigations, with teams of detectives and undercover officers. However, for the purposes of the IAD system, the primary type of investigation employed is simply an analysis of the declaration to identify possible conflicts of interest between the investments held by the civil servant and that employee's job description. This entails a desk review of the declaration and the considered judgment of the assigned ethics official.

Should a potential or existing conflict be identified, the civil servant will be advised of the action he or she must take to eliminate the conflict of interest. Such necessary actions can range from divestment of the asset presenting the conflict to temporary reassignment of duties to loss of position.

Interagency Collaboration

As noted throughout this report, the ICAC, the CSB, and individual agencies work closely together throughout the declaration process, from the formation and design of regulations to referrals for corruption investigations. However, again, since the contents of declarations are not routinely verified for accuracy, the interagency collaboration metric is somewhat less relevant than in other systems that require functioning and collaborative land registries, traffic registries, and so forth for the purpose of verifying the accuracy of an asset declaration.

During a corruption investigation, the ICAC has wide-ranging powers to access government documents, databases, and records. Further, under the law in Hong Kong SAR, China, the ICAC has the power to arrest and to refer charges to the prosecutor's office.

Public Access to Declarations

Declarations of investment for Tier I officials are made publicly available; the declarations of Tier II officials are confidential. Although the CSB has expressed an interest in making Tier I declarations available on the Internet, current policy requires interested members of the public to go to the CSB in person to request a copy. The declarations are, however, free of charge to the public, with the exception of a nominal copying fee.

Prevention and Education

A vital part of the Corruption Prevention Department's function is to produce guidelines for civil servants to help them complete their declarations of investments. This is particularly important because of the difficulty posed by the concept of a conflict of interest; providing detailed instructions to declarers enables them to identify all covered investments that must be declared. The CSB works closely with the ICAC to produce these guidelines and, at times, serves as an intermediary between the individual agencies and the ICAC to learn from the experiences of various agencies and recommend possible changes to the structure of the declaration system or ICAC controls on corruption. However, it is ultimately the responsibility of the individual agencies to adopt binding regulations that govern conflicts of interest within their agency. Although the ICAC and the CSB have created some specific requirements, the individual agencies are seen as best suited to handle the specific types of conflicts that may be peculiar to their agency.

Summary of Key Findings

The IAD system in Hong Kong SAR, China, is firmly rooted in a long-running and highly successful anticorruption effort engendered by the Independent Commission against Corruption. Because of the decades of targeted anticorruption initiatives by the ICAC and the government of Hong Kong SAR, China, the focus of the IAD system—as outlined in the CSB Circulars No. 2/2004 and No. 8/2006—is focused on reinforcing ethical conduct in public office. Therefore the system is dedicated solely to identifying and preventing conflicts of interest for government employees and officials.

To make the system as relevant as possible to all officials, it has been decentralized to the individual agencies of the government, each of which has ethics officials dedicated to tailoring the IAD system within their agency to ensure its relevance to the kinds of conflicts of interest their employees are most likely to encounter. As such, the CSB, in conjunction with advice from the ICAC, acts as the central coordinator of broad IAD procedures across the government, while providing each individual ethics official a certain latitude to tailor their own IAD system within their agency.

ICAC officials, in interviews conducted for the preparation of this report, stressed the importance of three characteristics present in Hong Kong SAR, China, that have fostered its success in combating corruption:

• An independent and uncorrupted judiciary
• An independent anticorruption agency
• A free press

The major achievements and key lessons of the IAD system of Hong Kong SAR, China, are as follows:

Hong Kong SAR, China, has achieved considerable success in the implementation of its IAD system with, for example, a 100 percent submission compliance rate. All declarations are analyzed to determine whether the assets or income sources declared present a potential conflict of interest with the official's duties. The system does not, however, routinely verify the accuracy of the information provided by the filer of the disclosure form. This is due in large measure to the robust anticorruption system already in effect under the auspices of the ICAC. In sum, the IAD system in Hong Kong SAR, China, is a finely tailored conflict-of-interest tool that complements the jurisdiction's already strong ability to fight corruption.

Because the IAD system in Hong Kong SAR, China, is designed solely for preventing and detecting possible conflicts of interest, it places a premium on creating a collaborative environment among the CSB, individual agencies, and individual filers. In interviews conducted during the research for this study, CSB officials repeatedly noted that they view the system as a form of protection for civil servants; if they declare their financial interests, then they are much more protected from accusations of having a conflict of interest, and they can work with the CSB to ensure they do not find themselves in a conflict-of-interest situation.

If a conflict of interest is revealed during the analysis of the declaration, depending on the nature of the conflict, the ethics official will recommend the appropriate action to be taken. This can range from divestiture to loss of position or even to referral to the ICAC if the conflict appears to rise to the level of a criminal (corruption) offense.

Indeed, the IAD system, though cast as a system designed to protect civil servants and public officials, is firmly rooted in the overall anticorruption system in Hong Kong SAR, China. The ICAC is the nerve center of this anticorruption effort, and its three-pronged approach has been essential to creating the conditions for the development of the conflict of interest program administered by the CSB. The ICAC's success, in particular, seems to be rooted in its reliance on three equal and reinforcing elements of its work: (1) prevention, (2) education, and (3) enforcement.

CHAPTER 5

Indonesia

Alexandra Habershon and Hari Mulukutla

Overview

Indonesia's income and asset disclosure (IAD) system (see box 5.1) is managed by its national Corruption Eradication Commission (KPK), a specialized and independent anticorruption agency with investigatory and prosecutorial powers and a broad mandate for prevention and enforcement. Indonesia's KPK has gained renown among anticorruption institutions internationally—not only for the strength of its mandate and its track record in successfully prosecuting corruption cases, but also for the level of popular recognition and support it enjoys. Since its inception, the KPK has achieved remarkable results,[1] and has successfully entrenched itself in the public imagination as a vital bulwark against rampant government corruption. Political opposition to the KPK has been fierce, however, and the institution has suffered serious setbacks. In a damaging court case in 2009, the chairman of the KPK was charged with and convicted of conspiracy to murder. In unrelated cases, two other commissioners were charged with corruption offenses. Although evidence that these charges were manufactured has come to light, a prolonged legal battle to dismiss the cases has hampered the KPK's ability to function.[2] The KPK has thus suffered numerous setbacks that, although serious, have so far hindered but not derailed the institution.

The IAD system in Indonesia, which is managed by the KPK's Department for the Wealth Reports of State Officers (the Wealth-Reporting Department, or LHKPN), is a relatively small element of the KPK's broad mandate. For an anticorruption agency with extraordinary corruption-fighting powers, income and asset declarations are one among many oversight mechanisms; in the KPK, these

This report is based on desk research and the findings of a visit to Indonesia undertaken in June 2009 on behalf of the Stolen Asset Recovery (StAR) Initiative and the Governance & Public Sector Management Unit of the World Bank to examine the country's IAD system. The content of this report reflects current legislation and institutions at the time of writing. To the extent possible, the data and findings have been updated to reflect relevant changes to the legislation and institutional arrangements in the time elapsed between the date of research and publication. Special thanks for assistance in the research and preparation of this report are given to Amien Sunaryadi and Francesca Recanatini. A list of people consulted or interviewed in the preparation of this report is provided in appendix C.

Box 5.1 Snapshot of the Income and Asset Disclosure System in Indonesia

Indonesia's IAD system is managed by its Corruption Eradication Commission (KPK), a specialized and independent anticorruption agency with investigatory and prosecutorial powers and a broad mandate for prevention and enforcement. Since the system's inception in 2001, the KPK has focused on establishing mechanisms and capacity for managing its "wealth-reporting system" and, in particular, on increasing submission compliance among obligated officials. It has achieved notable gains on this front (from 56 percent compliance in 2006 to 85 percent in 2009), and is now focusing on strengthening its verification capacity. Amendments to the anticorruption law have been under discussion to enable the definition and enforcement of sanctions for violations of the disclosure law. The absence of sanctions for failure to disclose or for false disclosure has undermined the system's credibility as a viable corruption deterrent.

Key elements of the system include:

- **Detecting and preventing illicit enrichment.** The IAD system is managed by the KPK's Department for the Wealth Reports of State Officers (Wealth-Reporting Department, or LHKPN), a branch of its Prevention Division. KPK officials examine declarations for changes in wealth over time and for signs of illicit enrichment. The KPK does not examine wealth reports for potential conflicts of interest. By law, sanctions apply for the failure to submit a declaration, but the nature of sanctions is not specified, and to date no prosecutions have been brought for failure to submit a declaration or for false filing.
- **Advanced data management tools and targeted verification.** The KPK monitors and reports on submission compliance rates and is empowered to verify the content of declarations, which are submitted in hard copy. A sample of declarations is verified, targeting the declarations of officials in high-risk agencies. The KPK has introduced enhanced analysis and reporting using data warehouse and business intelligence tools; these tools provide for enhanced verification options and the publication of statistics and trends.
- **Public access.** Summaries of wealth disclosure reports are published in the *Official Gazette* and online on the Anticorruption Clearing House Portal website (http://acch.kpk.go.id/web/guest/statistik-kepatuhan). The portal also provides public access to compliance statistics and other reports on the system's performance.
- **Enhancing compliance through administrative channels and media pressures.** The KPK has achieved an increase in compliance, in part, by relying on the exertion of administrative and bureaucratic pressures *within* government agencies to create a culture of compliance through internal administrative processes. The KPK's collaborative efforts with line agencies and the credible threat of investigating agencies that are reluctant to engage proactively in corruption prevention, have been instrumental in its success.

are part of its Corruption Prevention Division. Since the system's inception in 2001, the KPK has focused its efforts on establishing the mechanisms and the capacity for managing its wealth-reporting system and on building compliance among obligated officials who are required to submit a declaration. The KPK views this effort as part of its integrated approach to fighting corruption, in which prevention and enforcement are two sides of the same coin and part of a long-term strategy. As noted by one of the KPK's deputy chairmen, "The KPK has been learning from counterparts in other nations, especially from Hong Kong SAR, China, that any serious anti-corruption program will need a minimum of two decades to produce real results. The KPK is dedicated to uprooting corruption in the long term, and indeed its strategies are long-term approaches."[3]

Background

Anticorruption efforts in Indonesia date back to the country's independence in 1950. An anticorruption agency, the State Apparatus Reform Committee (Paran), was established along with the requirement that all public officials submit income and asset declarations (*wealth reports*), although resistance from public officials contributed to the agency's failure to enforce this requirement. Anticorruption efforts fared little better under President Suharto, who took power in 1966 under the banner of a New Order Regime and a program of authoritarian rule. Despite the extensive anticorruption rhetoric of the new order, lawmaking and policy did little to tackle the problem. Successive anticorruption agencies met the same fate because of resistance from public officials, an inadequate mandate, and political acceptance of the status quo. Spurred by student protests in the 1970s, a program to tackle petty corruption did achieve some success.[4]

An economic and political crisis in 1998 brought an end to the Suharto regime, which had become inseparably tied in the public imagination to corruption. Popular unrest eventually forced Suharto's resignation. The so-called Reformasi era—as the post-Suharto period has been dubbed—brought a return to democratic elections with a multiplication of political party factions, a separation of powers, the decentralization of governance, and the deregulation and flourishing of politically vested media outlets. Anticorruption programs became banner features of all political programs, and open public dialogue—and outrage—about corruption became the norm.

The predecessor of the KPK, the Anti-Corruption Joint Team, was established in 1999. Its tenure was short lived because its mandate and structure were ruled irregular by the Supreme Court. The KPK's legal foundation was mandated in the 2002 Law on the Corruption Crime Eradication Commission, by which it was vested with investigatory and prosecutorial powers and established as independent from the branches of government. This law also has a comprehensive mandate for the prevention, supervision, and coordination of anticorruption efforts, as well as for public participation and outreach.

The IAD Legal Framework in Indonesia

The IAD legal framework in Indonesia was established by the following laws:

- Law No. 28 of 1999 on State Organizers Who are Clean and Free from Corruption, Collusion and Nepotism provides the primary legal framework for asset disclosure (Article 5 establishes the requirement, and Article 2 defines the State Organizers who are subject to the requirement).

Income and Asset Disclosure • http://dx.doi.org/10.1596/978-0-8213-9796-1

- Law No. 43 of 1999 amending Law No. 8/1974 on the Ordinance on Civil Service provides the extent of the coverage of the asset disclosure requirement.
- Law No. 20 of 2001, Amendment to Law No. 31/1999 on Corruption Eradication, provides greater clarity to the law by including text from the relevant articles of the criminal code to which the law refers.
- Law No. 30 of 2002 on the Corruption Crime Eradication Commission sets out the mandate and functions of the Corruption Eradication Commission, including its responsibility for implementing the IAD requirement.

IAD implementation procedures are set out in the Decree of KPK Commissioners No. 7 of 2005 on Assets Declaration and Examination Procedures. This decree covers:

- The definition of what is meant by assets
- Filing frequency and deadlines
- Submission procedures
- Examination procedures
- Channels of declaration
- The declaration forms (models A and B for first-time filing and subsequent filing, respectively)
- Cooperation between the KPK and other institutions

Coverage of Officials
The coverage of the reporting requirement is specified in Article 2 of Law No. 28 of 1999. Coverage was subsequently expanded following a presidential instruction in 2004 and a circular from the Ministry for Administrative Reform (MenPAN), as shown in table 5.1. In 2005, the requirement was further expanded by a MenPAN circular instructing all heads of agencies to issue a decree identifying and requiring that all positions prone to corruption, collusion, or nepotism submit a wealth report.

Content of Income and Asset Declarations
The content of the income and asset declaration form is shown in table 5.2. Staff in the data management unit of the KPK's Wealth-Reporting Department enter the contents of the wealth reports, which are submitted in hard copy, to their database, and publish summaries of the contents in the *Official Gazette*.

Filing Frequency
Officials are required to submit a wealth report within two months after taking and leaving office, after a promotion or transfer, on an ad-hoc basis upon a change in assets, or at any other time at the request of the commissioners. A *change in assets* is defined as a change in a previously reported item or items; the addition of an item or items not previously reported; and the elimination of a previously

Table 5.1 State Operators and Other Positions Required to Submit Income and Asset Declarations, Indonesia

State operators (covered by Law No. 28 of 1999, Article 2)	Other officials obligated to declare assets following Presidential Instruction No. 5 of 2004 on the Acceleration of Corruption Eradication (the requirement is made binding by the internal regulations of state institutions)

• State officials at the highest institution of the state
• State officials at the state supreme agencies
• Ministers
• Governors
• Judges
• Other state officials, in accordance with the provisions of legislation and regulations
• Other officials who have a strategic function in relation to the operation of the state in accordance with provisions of applicable legislation, including:
  • Directors, commissioners, and other appropriate officials of state-owned enterprises and the regional state corporations
  • Heads of the central bank of Indonesia
  • State higher education leaders
  • Echelon I officials within the civil service, military, and the Indonesian National Police
  • State prosecutor
  • Investigators
  • Clerks of court
	• Echelon II and other officials identified in the government or state institutions
	• All heads of office within the Ministry of Finance
	• Examiners of customs and excise
	• Tax examiners
	• Auditors
	• Officials who issue permits
	• Officer/head of community services unit
	• Regulatory officials
	• Other officeholders required to submit based on the decree of head of agency in their respective entity
	• Presidential and vice presidential candidates and potential candidates for regional head and deputy head of region

Source: Unofficial translation of Article 2, Law No. 28 of 1999.

reported item or items (sold, lost, legal issues, and so forth). Categories of items reported in changes include land, buildings, and securities; gifts (gratuities of a value of more than Rp 500,000 (about US$50) also have to be reported to the KPK.

Sanctions

By law, sanctions apply for the failure to submit a declaration, but the nature of these sanctions is not specified. To date, no prosecutions have been brought for failure to submit a declaration or for false filing. A draft Law on Corruption Eradication, if approved by the Indonesian Parliament, would introduce criminal sanctions for false filing. In the absence of sanctions, the KPK's strategy for enforcing compliance with the requirement to submit a wealth report is to work with ministries to encourage compliance through internal bureaucratic channels. This approach is in line with the KPK's strategy of integrating its prevention and enforcement efforts by working collaboratively with agencies to improve their internal oversight and corruption prevention mechanisms. The KPK applies pressure selectively by launching sting operations on agencies that appear reluctant to put weight behind their prevention measures.[5] Unsurprisingly, this approach is not as feasible with legislators, the Attorney

Table 5.2 Contents of the Income and Asset Declaration, Indonesia

	Disclosure requirement	Publicly available
Personal data		
Name	✓	✓
Place and date of birth	✓	✓
Official title	✓	✓
Gender	✓	
Work address	✓	✓
Spouse's name	✓	✓
Position		
Information about the employment position	✓	✓
Information about official duties	✓	
Information about outside employment	✓	
Assets		
Fixed assets: land and buildings	✓	✓
Movable assets: transportation equipment and other machines	✓	✓
Other movable assets and business interests: livestock, fisheries, plantation, agricultural, forestry, mining, and other business	✓	✓
Securities and cash equivalents	✓	✓
Income		
Annual taxable income	✓	✓
Loans		
Debts	✓	✓
Administrative data		
Date of wealth report	✓	✓
Report number	✓	✓

Source: Unofficial translation of the declaration form.
Note: Data are made public in a summary of the declaration. Asset values are given in the aggregate and not itemized beyond broad categories.

General's Office, or the national police. In the case of parliamentarians, compliance has instead been pushed by the party political machinery, largely thanks to the pressure exerted by media exposure of noncompliant party members.[6]

Monitoring, Oversight, and Verification

The KPK monitors and reports on submission compliance rates and is empowered to verify the contents of declarations, which it does on a sample basis, targeting the declarations of officials in high-risk agencies. Although the law provides no sanctions for failure to declare or for false filing, the detection of irregularities in an asset declaration can lead to a corruption investigation and potentially to prosecution for criminal corruption offenses, for which the KPK has substantial resources and powers. In addition, media interest in the wealth reports of politicians and senior civil servants can prompt an investigation.[7] However, no instances of a direct correlation between a wealth report and a corruption investigation were reported by officials interviewed for this study.

Public Access to Income and Asset Information

Public access to IAD information is mandated by law. The KPK publishes summaries of wealth reports (these summaries include all new reports and changes to submissions, listing total value of assets; see table 5.2). These are made public through the *Official Gazette*, which is usually printed quarterly. All government offices are required to keep copies of the *Official Gazette* in their library and to make them accessible to the public.

The public does not have the right to view the nonpublic information in wealth reports; however, law enforcement agencies and sometimes quasi law enforcement agencies can view this information by means of a written request to the KPK. A KPK investigator is assigned to each request and it is carefully examined before the request is fulfilled.

Mandate and Structure of the IAD Agency

The KPK is a special law enforcement body, independent from the executive, legislature, and judiciary. It has the authority to coordinate with and supervise the Attorney General's Office and the national police in handling corruption cases. The presiding authority of the KPK is the Board of Commissioners. The KPK is headed by five commissioners—one chairman and four deputy chairmen. Each deputy chairman is head of one of four divisions: Prevention; Repression; Information & Data; and Internal Monitoring and Public Complaints. A fifth division, which handles the internal administration of the agency, is headed by a secretary general.

The KPK has five categories of duties, authorities, and obligations (Article 6, Law No. 30 of 2002). They are to:

- Coordinate with institutions authorized to combat acts of corruption
- Supervise institutions authorized to combat acts of corruption
- Conduct preliminary investigations, investigations, and prosecutions of acts of corruption
- Conduct corruption prevention activities
- Conduct monitoring of state governance

The KPK is authorized to conduct pre-investigations, investigations, and prosecutions of corruption cases that:

- Involve law enforcers, state officials, and other individuals connected to corrupt acts perpetrated by law enforcers or state officials
- Have generated significant public concern
- Have lost the state at least Rp 1 billion (US$100,000)

The KPK is not charged with investigating corruption in the private or financial sectors (unless a case involves state funds).

The department responsible for income and asset declarations (the Directorate of Recording & Examining the Wealth Reports of State Officials) is part of the KPK's Prevention Division (see figure 5.1). This division is responsible for the receipt, review, and analysis of wealth reports for false filing or irregularities that may suggest illicit enrichment. Another directorate in that division is responsible for receiving and monitoring gratuity (gift) reports. The KPK's monitoring of gifts is seen as integral to its prevention efforts. Gifts valued over Rp 500,000 (about US$50) must be reported. Gratuity reports include:

- The name and complete address of both the giver and the recipient of the gratuity
- The civil service position of the state official
- The place and time the gratuity was received
- The value of the gratuity or gratuities

Within 30 days of receiving the report, the KPK must determine the status or probity of the gift. In so doing, the commission can call the recipient of the gratuity to testify. In 2005, there were 50 "gratification reports"; in 2006 there were 326; in 2007 there were 249; in 2008 there were 224; and in 2009, through December 15, there were 287.

Resources and Procedures of the IAD System

Facilities and Use of Technology

The KPK is housed in a modern headquarters in Jakarta, the capital of Indonesia. The Wealth-Reporting Department is housed in separate facilities. The KPK is awaiting approval from the Parliament for funds for a third building, since the current premises are inadequate. All the premises are government owned. All submissions (mailed and delivered in person) are filed in a secure building accessible only by authorized personnel.

Indonesia's asset declaration submission system is paper-based, but KPK's administrative and operational data management procedures are information technology (IT)-based. A majority of the staff in the Wealth-Reporting Department are data-processing agents. They enter all the information from declarations into a custom-built IT system. For each team of 8 to 10 data operators, there are line managers who troubleshoot problems and scan the supporting documentation (land titles and so on). The IT staff formally review the declarations (to validate the data rather than verify its accuracy; that is, to check the completeness and consistency of dates, personal information, values and totals, and so forth). The department has a database and data warehouse system that enables KPK analysts to examine the data for verification purposes.

The Wealth-Reporting Department has also implemented a sophisticated analysis and reporting system to allow the KPK to analyze wealth-reporting data and obtain institutional performance reports, such as the submission compliance rates (overall, by government office, by province, by sector, by age, and so forth). Other kinds of reports, such as Total Harta (Total Assets) reports, collate all declared assets and their values, which can then be viewed across a number of dimensions. The Wealth-Reporting Department has a network that supports secure data processing by hundreds of personnel simultaneously with a number of server computers that run the ICT application. The data are also backed up periodically to tape backups, which are then placed in a secure off-site location.

The Wealth-Reporting Department archives all hard copies of declarations. This involves large volumes of paper, since the declaration form can run to 17 pages and may possibly include dozens or even hundreds of scanned pages of land and vehicle deeds and other information. These are kept in safe file cabinets for up to seven years after submission (although none of the reports have been destroyed since the establishment of the KPK).

Human Resources

Five commissioners and two advisers lead the commission's 639 staff, of whom 80 are employed by the Wealth-Reporting Department. Although a large institution by the standards of many anticorruption agencies, the KPK staff could be considered small given the agency's broad mandate, Indonesia's geographically dispersed territory, and its population of 220 million.

The KPK uses competitive recruiting to hire new staff, requires staff to have relevant work experience qualifications, conducts annual employee reviews to monitor performance, and provides individualized training and professional development to staff. The KPK also has job profiles that clearly delineate staff responsibilities for every position, and conducts thorough background checks as part of its hiring processes. The KPK has a code of conduct and an internal whistle-blowing system. Salaries are higher than they are in other government agencies, and increases in salary are based on satisfactory performance. The KPK is not authorized to appoint investigators or prosecutors. Currently, these are seconded from the Attorney General's Office and the national police.

Budget

The KPK has an independent budget that undergoes annual parliamentary review and approval. Historically, it has suffered from a shortfall between approved budgets and actual amounts disbursed by Parliament. It is subject to audit by the Indonesian Supreme Audit Board. Despite significant resistance from members of Parliament to the KPK's broad authority, the KPK gained approval for a budget increase in 2010 to expand its facilities and hire new staff (see table 5.3).

Figure 5.1 Organizational Chart of the Corruption Eradication Commission (KPK), Indonesia

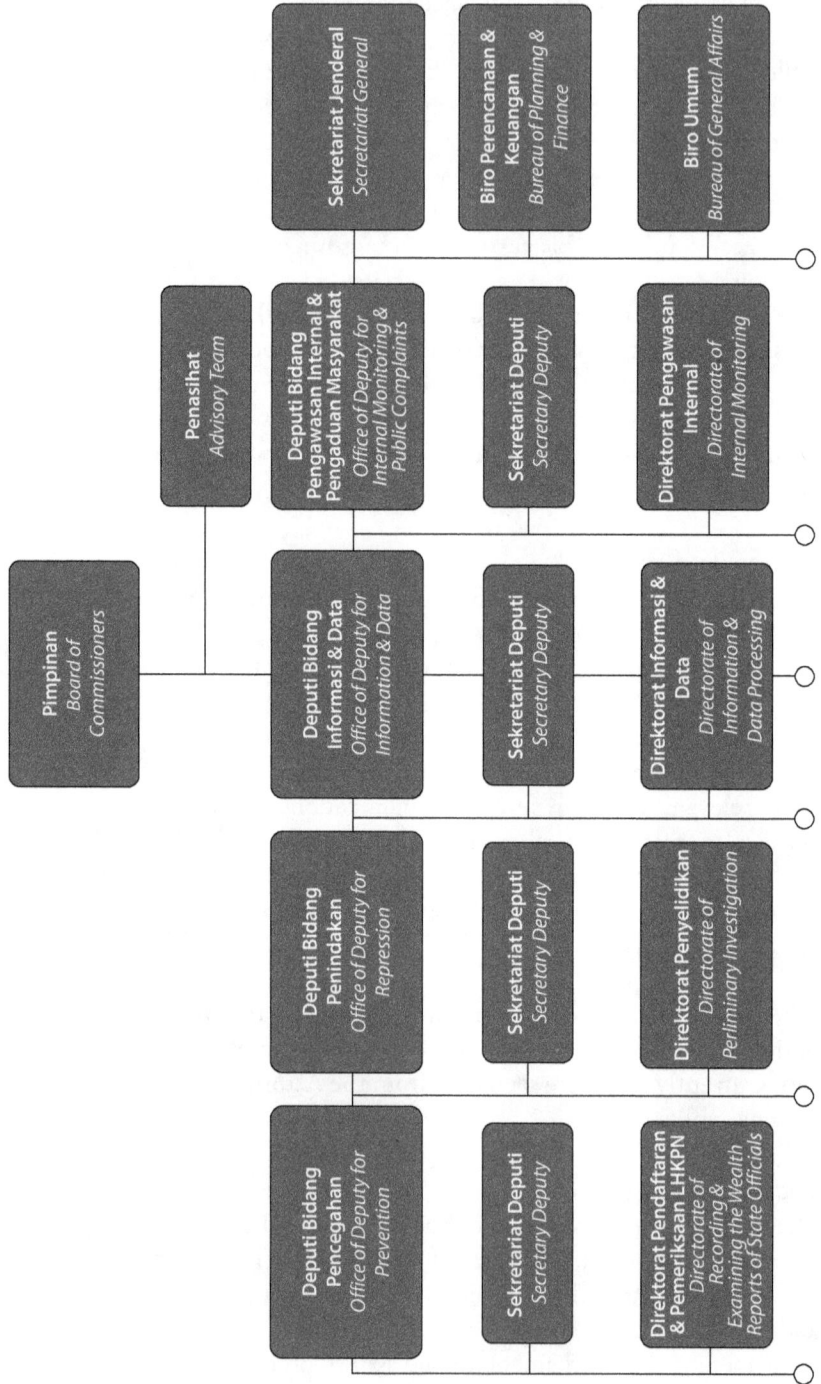

Pimpinan
Board of Commissioners

Penasihat
Advisory Team

Sekretariat Jenderal
Secretariat General

Biro Perencanaan & Keuangan
Bureau of Planning & Finance

Biro Umum
Bureau of General Affairs

Deputi Bidang Pengawasan Internal & Pengaduan Masyarakat
Office of Deputy for Internal Monitoring & Public Complaints

Sekretariat Deputi
Secretary Deputy

Direktorat Pengawasan Internal
Directorate of Internal Monitoring

Deputi Bidang Informasi & Data
Office of Deputy for Information & Data

Sekretariat Deputi
Secretary Deputy

Direktorat Informasi & Data
Directorate of Information & Data Processing

Deputi Bidang Penindakan
Office of Deputy for Repression

Sekretariat Deputi
Secretary Deputy

Direktorat Penyelidikan
Directorate of Perliminary Investigation

Deputi Bidang Pencegahan
Office of Deputy for Prevention

Sekretariat Deputi
Secretary Deputy

Direktorat Pendaftaran & Pemeriksaan LHKPN
Directorate of Recording & Examining the Wealth Reports of State Officials

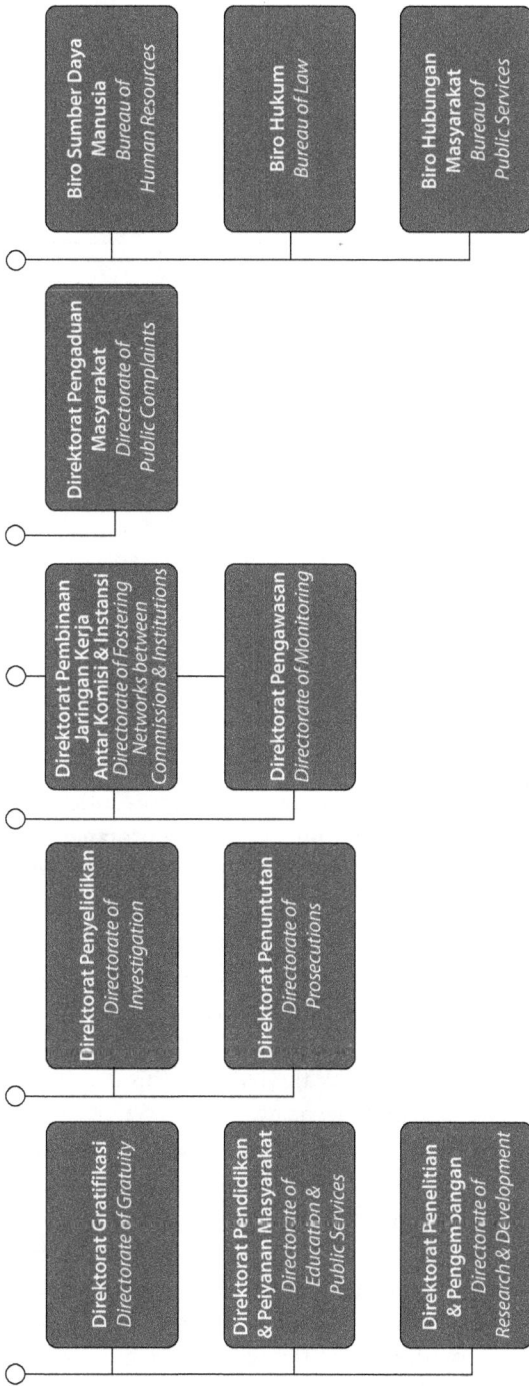

Biro Sumber Daya Manusia
Bureau of Human Resources

Biro Hukum
Bureau of Law

Biro Hubungan Masyarakat
Bureau of Public Services

Direktorat Pengaduan Masyarakat
Directorate of Public Complaints

Direktorat Pembinaan Jaringan Kerja Antar Komisi & Instansi
Directorate of Fostering Networks between Commission & Institutions

Direktorat Pengawasan
Directorate of Monitoring

Direktorat Penyelidikan
Directorate of Investigation

Direktorat Penuntutan
Directorate of Prosecutions

Direktorat Gratifikasi
Directorate of Gratuity

Direktorat Pendidikan & Pelyanan Masyarakat
Directorate of Education & Public Services

Direktorat Penelitian & Pengembangan
Directorate of Research & Development

Source: KPK.

Table 5.3 KPK Budget, Indonesia, 2009–10

2009 Budget

Rp 315 billion (approximately US$34.6 million) from the state budget (actual disbursement was 70 percent of the approved budget)

Rp 9.07 billion (approximately US$1 million) from donors (the European Union and the Canadian International Development Agency)

2010 Budget

Rp 398 billion (approximately US$43.8 million) from the state budget

Rp 27 billion (approximately US$3 million) from donors (the European Union and the Canadian International Development Agency)

Source: Interviews with KPK staff.

Regulatory Function

The KPK issues its own internal implementation regulations and operations manual. These are not publicly available.

Submission Compliance

Despite the absence of prosecutions for nonfiling and of clearly specified sanctions for violations of the wealth-reporting requirement, the compliance rate has steadily risen over the last few years. It is now nearing about 90 percent out of a total of over 116,000 required filers (see figure 5.2), although that percentage is lower for the national police and the Attorney General's Office. The KPK has achieved this result in part by relying on the exertion of administrative and bureaucratic pressures *within* agencies to create a culture of compliance through internal administrative processes. One example of such actions is illustrated by the Ministry of State Enterprises, a sector believed to be rife with corruption. The sanctions applied by the ministry for failure to submit a wealth report range from cancellations of promotions to reduced bonuses, and failure to submit is reflected in individual performance ratings. The Minister of State Enterprises is reported as saying, "even though the KPK does not sanction state officials who are late submitting their reports, the ministry feels discipline is necessary to promote good corporate governance."[8] Compliance is at about 90 percent, but the ministry did not expect 100 percent compliance, considering this to be difficult, if not impossible, to achieve. One of the reasons cited by the KPK for this difficulty is the inaccuracy of employment registries within agencies.

As noted, compliance rates are lower than average for the Attorney General's Office and the national police. In July 2010, of the 8,000 prosecutors and 7,000 police officers required to submit a wealth report, the commission had received 4,500 from the prosecutor's office and 5,100 from the police. In contrast, 92.5 percent of 7,000 state officials from the Finance Ministry had submitted their wealth reports and nearly 90 percent of Supreme Court judges had reported their wealth to the commission.[9] As noted, some of the compliance gap could be attributed to the transfer, resignation, or death of officials not reflected in official registers. Despite impressive gains in submission compliance, in the absence of sanctions for false filing, the process of submitting a wealth report can be viewed

Figure 5.2 Compliance Rates for Wealth Reporting, Indonesia

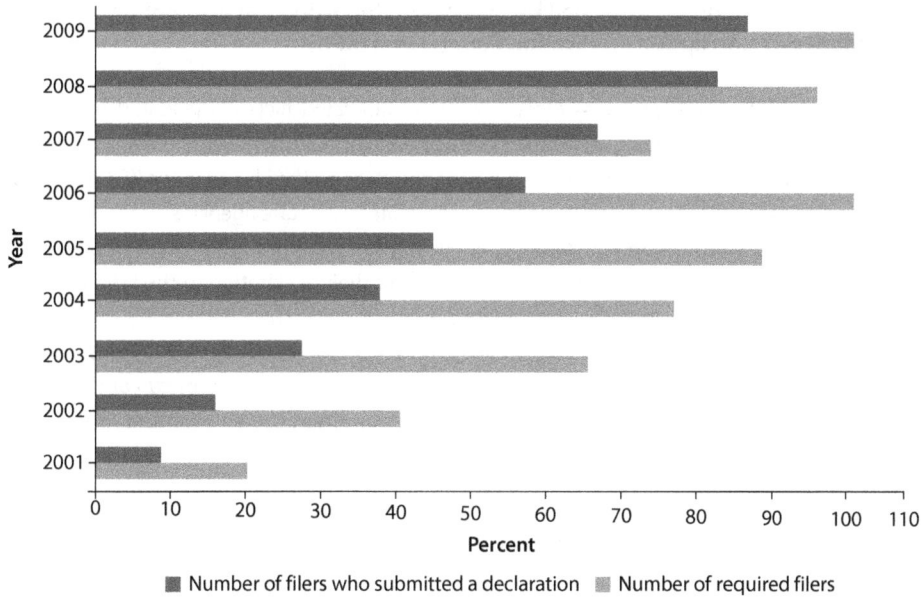

■ Number of filers who submitted a declaration   ▨ Number of required filers

Source: Jasin 2010, p. 27.
Note: Number of declarations and total number of filers shown for each year. Compliance rates rose from 56 percent in 2006 to 85 percent in 2009.

by public officials as an administrative formality rather than an ethical obligation that would carry consequences if not met.

Verification Function

The KPK's Wealth-Reporting Department reviews asset declarations for completeness and validates the consistency of the information listed in the declaration against supporting documentation (land titles, property deeds, and so forth). The KPK is also empowered to verify the accuracy of declarations by cross-checking these against other sources of data on income and assets (bank information, tax declarations, property registries, and so forth) and by reviewing declarations for changes over time. For verification purposes, 1 percent to 5 percent of declarations are selected. This is done manually by cross-checking other databases within the KPK and sometimes with the bureaus that register property and motor vehicles in Indonesia. The Financial Intelligence Unit is also consulted for some submissions.

Box 5.2 describes the procedures performed by the Wealth-Reporting Department.

Investigations and Prosecutions

The KPK has a mandate to prevent, investigate, and prosecute corruption (in cases involving at least Rp 1 billion [approximately US$100,000]). For enforcement purposes, the KPK has in-house investigators, a staff of prosecutors

---

Box 5.2   Procedures Performed by the Wealth-Reporting Department (LHKPN) of Indonesia's Corruption Eradication Commission (KPK)

- **Maintaining the register of filers.** The list of obligated filers is mandated by law and supplemented by binding decrees in state agencies (the law identifies filers by post; internal decrees identify additional filers on the basis of function). The LHKPN in the KPK manages a central list of obligated filers, for which it coordinates with state agencies.
- **Managing submission compliance.** Public officials (referred to as "State Operators" by the KPK) subject to the filing requirement submit their declaration to the LHKPN in hard copy either in person or by mail. Filers can also submit their declaration to a wealth-reporting coordinator in each state (where one has been appointed), who must forward the declaration to the KPK within one week. Filers can obtain a form by contacting the LHKPN to request one, or by downloading the form from the KPK website (http://www .kpk.go.id).

LHKPN staff provide the filer with a receipt either upon delivery or by mail (or by fax upon request). If the declaration is incomplete or incorrectly filled out, the KPK contacts the filer to request a completed or corrected form (as above, the corrected form can be submitted in person or by mail).

Completed declarations are processed (the entire declaration is scanned, the contents are entered into the database, and the declaration is given a number that filers must cite on subsequent declarations). The KPK archives the original hard copy of declarations in filing cabinets located on several floors of a secure building. The declaration form is 17 pages long, and when completed with supporting documentation (copies of land and property titles and other information), can run to hundreds of pages.

Summaries of declarations are published in the *Official Gazette* and must also be posted on a notice board in the agency where the official is employed. A copy of this notice is sent by the agency to the KPK.

(seconded from the Attorney General's Office), and—perhaps most significantly—a special Anticorruption Court presided over by ad-hoc judges (selected and screened rather than just drawn from the ranks). KPK investigators have the authority to gather evidence (from wiretaps, bank accounts, and tax statements) and to make arrests and seize assets. Investigators and commissioners work closely together, and the Board of Commissioners reviews all cases to ensure that only those with sufficient evidence to secure a conviction are taken to court (hence the 100 percent conviction rate).[10] The KPK is also strategic in choosing which cases to pursue; cases are selected if it is believed they will send a signal that the KPK is aggressively pursuing corruption at high levels of government and across sectors. As noted, however, no instances of corruption investigations or prosecutions directly related to an income and asset declaration have been reported by officials interviewed for this study.

Interagency Collaboration

The KPK is mandated to coordinate its corruption investigations with the national police and the Attorney General's Office, but also to supervise the work of these agencies in handling corruption cases. This has contributed to the frequently difficult relations between these institutions, not least when corruption charges were brought by the Attorney General's Office against two of the commissioners.

Public Access to Income and Asset Declaration Information

Law mandates that summaries of wealth reports and compliance information be publicly available. This is accomplished through the *Official Gazette* and by individual line agencies. The KPK is also working on making information on compliance and other statistical reports available on its Anticorruption Clearing House portal website, currently under development. A beta version of the Anticorruption Clearing House was released in December 2010 with statistical reports on compliance. A user can search and analyze the data according to a number of factors and print reports. This resource is publicly available at http://acch.kpk.go.id/web/guest/statistik-kepatuhan (authorized users have access to advanced features, but most of the site does not require registered user login) (see table 5.4).

Table 5.4 Wealth-Reporting Data Available to the Public, Indonesia

Summaries of the declarations are published in the Official Gazette. *Asset totals are given in aggregate.*

I. Personal data

  1. Name
  2. Position
  3. Place and date of birth
  4. Gender
  5. Spouse's name
  6. Work address
  7. Reporting date

II. Property data

  A. Fixed assets: land and buildings
  B. Movable assets:
      a. Transportation equipment and other machines..............Rp
      b. Livestock, fisheries, plantation, agricultural, forestry, mining, and other business..............Rp
      c. Other mobile property..............Rp
          1. Other movable assets originating from own products, acquired from 2002 until 2008 with a minimum sale price of Rp 500,000
  C. Securities
  D. Currency and cash equivalents
  E. Receivables

Total property (II) ....Rp

III. Loans..............Rp

IV. Total property (II – III) ....Rp

Source: Unofficial translation of categories of disclosed information available to the public from the KPK website.

Income and Asset Disclosure • http://dx.doi.org/10.1596/978-0-8213-9796-1

Education and Outreach

The KPK provides guidance to filers on completing a declaration both through its website (http://www.kpk.go.id) and in person at the KPK. Officials can make an appointment at the KPK for that purpose (the KPK website specifies that this assistance is free of charge and officials can charge their travel expenses to the KPK). Requests can also be made for KPK staff to conduct training workshops in government agencies. The KPK has been very effective at rallying public support and raising awareness about corruption through communication campaigns and publications aimed at changing public understanding of what constitutes corrupt practices. The wealth-reporting requirement is not an integral element of public awareness campaigns, although the KPK works proactively with government agencies to raise awareness of, and compliance with, the requirement. Public support for the KPK was manifested through a show of widespread public outrage expressed on social networking sites when unfounded corruption charges were brought against two of the commissioners in a perceived attempt to weaken the KPK. Those charges were subsequently shown to have been manufactured.

Summary of Key Findings

Indonesia's income and asset declaration system is managed by its national Corruption Eradication Commission, a specialized and independent anti-corruption agency with a broad mandate to prevent, investigate, and prosecute corruption. Fierce opposition to the KPK has caused it to suffer setbacks that, although serious, have to date hindered but not derailed the institution. The KPK's wealth-reporting function is managed by a department within its Prevention Division. Since the system's inception in 2001, the KPK has focused on establishing the mechanisms and the capacity for managing its wealth-reporting system and on building compliance among officials required to submit a declaration.

By law, sanctions apply for failure to submit a declaration, but the nature of sanctions is not specified and to date no prosecutions have been brought for failure to submit a declaration or for false filing. The administration of the wealth-reporting requirement has thus not become an integral tool in either investigating or prosecuting corruption in Indonesia. Wealth reports serve more as an obligation and a reminder to officials of their duty to integrity while in public office rather than as a tool for enforcing ethical standards. Proposals under discussion to amend the legal framework to provide sanctions for noncompliance could change this, however.

A key finding from this study is that, despite the absence of prosecutions or clearly specified sanctions for violations of the wealth-reporting requirement, compliance rates have steadily risen over the last decade (from 56 percent in 2006 to 85 percent in 2009). The KPK has achieved this result, in part, by relying on the exertion of administrative and bureaucratic pressures *within* agencies to create a culture of compliance through internal administrative processes.

The KPK has been able to do this through collaborative efforts with line agencies, and because its broad mandate—and its credibility in exercising it— poses a plausible threat of investigations and other inconveniences to agencies that are reluctant to engage proactively in corruption prevention. The extent to which the wealth-reporting requirement is viewed as a bureaucratic formality by individual filers remains a question, however, which tougher sanctions or other explicit consequences—such as the possibility of a corruption investigation for violations—could help to address.

Notes

1. Among these results are conviction rates in corruption prosecutions of 100 percent, with all convictions upheld on appeal by the country's Supreme Court, as well as substantial recovery of stolen state assets.

2. These charges were intended to cripple the KPK, since any commissioner under criminal investigation is suspended from duty, and a quorum of its board of commissioners is required for it to operate. The KPK was operating with only one or two active commissioners for much of 2010.

3. Jasin 2010, p. 27.

4. Jasin 2010, p. 27.

5. Sting operations could involve an undercover KPK investigator or police officer offering a bribe to an official, or surprise site visits when it is suspected that evidence of corruption will be discovered.

6. A number of nongovernmental organizations (which are highly politicized in Indonesia) have taken great interest in wealth-reporting compliance by members of Parliament. A member of a nongovernmental organization interviewed for this report noted that a large number of parliamentarians have been shown not to have a tax number, indicating that they had not declared their taxes.

7. The wealth report of the head of Indonesia's State Audit Agency was the object of intense media scrutiny in June 2010, with media reports alleging his failure to disclose all of his assets (see Handayani et al. 2010, p. 40).

8. Baskoro 2010.

9. Rachman and Rayda 2010.

10. Between 2003 and 2009, the KPK successfully prosecuted over 150 senior officials, including some very high-profile figures. Of these, 68 percent received sentences of two to five years, 10 percent received sentences of five to ten years, and less than 5 percent received sentences of more than ten years. When appealed, these decisions were upheld by the Supreme Court. In contrast to the KPK's success, the Courts of General Jurisdiction in Indonesia have an almost 50 percent acquittal rate on (more minor) corruption cases brought by the Attorney General's Office.

References

Baskoro, F. M. 2010. "Indonesian State-Owned Enterprise Ministry Plans Sanctions over Tardy Wealth Reports." *The Jarkarta Globe*, August 18. http://www.thejakartaglobe .com/business/indonesian-state-owned-enterprise-ministry-plans-sanctions-over-tardy -wealth-reports/391677.

Handayani, A. L., B. Riza, M. Nafi, and Yuliawati. 2010. "A Gift by Any Other Name." *Tempo* (June 23–29): 40.

Jasin, M. 2010. "Article 2 of the International Covenant on Civil and Political Rights." *The Indonesian Corruption Eradication Commission* 9 (01) (March 1), p. 27. A consultation on corruption and counter-corruption across Asia. Indonesia. http://www.article2.org/mainfile.php/0901/367.

Rachman, A., and N. Rayda. 2010. "19 Indonesian Lawmakers Still Have No Wealth Reports." *The Jarkarta Globe*, August 21. http://www.thejakartaglobe.com/news/19-indonesian-lawmakers-still-have-no-wealth-reports/392073.

CHAPTER 6

Jordan

Yousef Nasrallah

Overview

Jordan's income and asset disclosure (IAD) system (see box 6.1) is based on its Income and Asset Disclosure Law of 2006.[1] The law created an Income and Asset Disclosure Department within the Ministry of Justice to receive, maintain, and administer the asset declaration program of all three branches of government. As of November 2011, the department was in its third year and its second round of asset declarations.

Although Jordan's IAD regime is in its early stages, as in many countries, the establishment of a disclosure requirement reflects a government commitment to fight corruption. Jordan's Income and Asset Disclosure Law aims to combat illicit enrichment and, to that end, the law establishes "illicit enrichment" as a criminal offense. The Income and Asset Disclosure Department is not mandated to look into potential conflicts of interest of public officials; there is a separate conflict-of-interest law for civil servants and another for the judiciary. The IAD system is, thus, not complementary to the conflicts-of-interest regime, suggesting a possible missed opportunity that could be had by combining or establishing economies of scope in anticorruption efforts.

Asset declarations are sealed and confidential. They are not examined unless a complaint is filed and the head of the Cassation Court authorizes the commission to unseal the declaration and verify its contents. All procedures taken in relation to submission compliance, review, investigation, and prosecution are also deemed confidential and not available to the public.

Background

Jordan played a principal role in the drafting process of the United Nations Convention against Corruption (UNCAC). It was among the first countries to sign and ratify the UNCAC, endorsing it on December 9, 2003, and ratifying it

This report is based on desk research and the findings of a visit to Jordan in July 2010 undertaken on behalf of the Stolen Asset Recovery (StAR) Initiative and the Governance & Public Sector Management Unit of the World Bank to examine the country's IAD system.

Box 6.1 Snapshot of the Income and Asset Disclosure System in Jordan

Jordan's IAD system is based on its Income and Asset Disclosure Law of 2006. The law created an Income and Asset Disclosure Department in the Ministry of Justice to receive, maintain, and administer the asset disclosure program of all three branches of government. The IAD system in Jordan aims to detect and prevent the illicit enrichment of public officials through the abuse of public office or title. Although Jordan's IAD regime is in its early stages, as in many countries, it reflects the government's overall commitment to fighting corruption. According to Jordan's Income and Asset Disclosure Department, in 2008–09, 3,953 of the 4,117 individuals subject to the law submitted their asset declarations. Although there have yet to be any investigations into the content of income and asset declarations—which are sealed and not subject to scrutiny—there have been several convictions for failure to submit an IAD form. For the district of Amman, five cases were referred to the First Instance Court in 2008. All individuals prosecuted in these cases were convicted and fined. In June 2010, another five cases were referred by the prosecutor's office and are pending.

    Key elements of the IAD system in Jordan include:

- **A focus on the detection of illicit enrichment.** Jordan's Income and Asset Disclosure Law aims to detect and combat illicit enrichment; to that end, the law establishes "illicit enrichment" as a criminal offense. Although the Income and Asset Disclosure Department is not mandated to look into potential conflicts of interest of public officials, there is a separate conflict-of-interest law for civil servants and another for the judiciary.
- **Verification only upon complaint.** Opening IAD envelopes is prohibited unless a complaint is filed against one of the filers. The head of the Income and Asset Disclosure Department must refer the matter with the sealed envelope that contains the asset declaration to the head of the Cassation Court, who alone has the mandate to look into the complaint and the income and asset declaration.
- **Strong sanctions.** The law provides for strong sanctions for noncompliance or other violations of asset disclosure obligations. Any covered official who does not submit his or her asset disclosure on the dates specified without legitimate excuse can be penalized by imprisonment, fine, or both. A filer who intentionally submits false information will be sentenced to prison for a term of six months to three years, although the law does not provide mechanisms for verifying the accuracy of declarations unless a complaint is filed.
- **Filing is centralized and in hard copy only.** A covered official must bring his or her declaration to the Income and Asset Disclosure Department, where it is sealed and placed in lockers in a storage room. General information about the filers, however, is entered into an electronic database.
- **Income and asset declarations are confidential.** Declarations, statements, notes, and any other documents are deemed confidential. The Income and Asset Disclosure Department must maintain asset declarations in sealed envelopes as received, and department staff are prohibited from opening the envelope, reading its contents, or releasing it to the public.

on February 24, 2005.[2] Jordan hosted both the first Conference of State Parties of the UNCAC in December 2006 at the Dead Sea,[3] and then a follow-up conference to coordinate efforts in combating corruption, in which the Arab Anti-Corruption and Integrity Network was established.[4] Currently, Jordan heads this network, which includes 14 Arab countries and approximately 40 agencies specializing in combating corruption.[5]

According to the UNCAC, State Parties are obliged to apply specific measures—particularly at the level of general administration—to support the development of preventive and disciplinary schemes for the elimination of corruption and to provide organizational tools for applying such measures. In this regard, several laws were introduced to complement existing laws and regulations in Jordan. For example, in addition to the law that Parliament passed ratifying the UNCAC,[6] the Anti-Corruption Commission Law was enacted in December 2006,[7] the Income and Asset Disclosure Law was published in the *Official Gazette* in November 2006,[8] and the Anti-Money-Laundering Law and Access to Information Law were passed by Parliament in 2007.[9] New agencies and departments were also established to implement the laws.

As a result of these anticorruption laws, an Anti-Corruption Commission was established and began work on January 1, 2008, in accordance with Law No. 62 of 2006.[10] The commission laid out a strategy for combating corruption during 2008–12. The commission has a broad mandate, which includes the right to:

- Investigate acts deemed to be corruption offenses as stipulated in the law
- Take preventive measures, such as raising public awareness regarding the risks of corruption and enhancing cooperation with civil society organizations
- Enforce the law on offenders of corruption crimes
- Publish periodic reports
- Coordinate and cooperate with local, regional, and international institutions to enhance measures on combating corruption

Between January and June 2010, the Information and Investigation Department at the Anti-Corruption Commission investigated 711 cases of corruption; 122 of these cases were referred to the public prosecution department.[11] The prosecution then referred 101 cases out of the 122 that were referred to the courts. Some of the remaining cases were dismissed; others are still under investigation.[12] However, none of the cases were actually the result of IAD filings, since the declarations are sealed and not verified unless there is a formal complaint, which has never happened.

The law calls for the establishment of the Income and Asset Disclosure Department at the Ministry of Justice. The department started its work after September 2007, when the Council of Ministers issued instructions on organizing the Income and Asset Disclosure Department on April 10, 2007. The Ministry of

Justice provided the department with offices and furnished it with the required logistics and employees to carry out its mission.

The Income and Asset Disclosure Law aims to detect and prevent the illicit enrichment of public officials through the abuse of public office or title.[13] For that purpose, the law established the *offense of illicit enrichment*, which is defined as a significant increase in assets of a public official, or of his or her spouse or minor children, that cannot reasonably be explained as being the result of his or her lawful income. It is common in the region to include an illicit enrichment offense within IAD laws. In this regard, the department is considered complementary to the already-existing departments that are mandated to enhance integrity in the public sector, protect public funds, and curb corruption.[14]

The IAD Legal Framework in Jordan

Income and Asset Disclosure Law No. 54 of 2006 provides the legal framework for asset disclosure in Jordan. The law establishes the Income and Asset Disclosure Department at the Ministry of Justice, which shall be affiliated with the Minster of Justice,[15] headed by a Cassation Court judge, nominated by the High Judicial Council,[16] and mandated to receive and maintain all asset declarations of specified officials subject to this law within due dates specified by the law. The law, in conjunction with the amended instructions for organizing the Income and Asset Disclosure Department and the income and asset declaration form, provides extensive management of the IAD system.[17]

Despite the fact that the Income and Asset Disclosure Department is not mandated to verify asset disclosures, which by law are required to remain in sealed envelopes, the law specifies the competent body and sets out the means and procedures for verifying asset disclosures if a complaint is filed against an official. Although the law outlines a mechanism for verification, the fact that the declarations are sealed and that all procedures associated with declarations are confidential poses the potential risk—or creates a perceived risk—of arbitrariness or the possibility of the misuse of the system through the selective use of investigations or prosecutions.

While the Income and Asset Disclosure Law covers all three branches of government, the main focus of the discussion in this study is on the executive branch.

Coverage of Officials

Article 2 of the Income and Asset Disclosure Law specifies the individuals who are subject to an income and asset declaration (table 6.1).

Since its inception, the Income and Asset Disclosure Department has completed one round of income and asset declaration submission, which for 2008–09 included 4,117 individuals.[18] For the second round, which started in January 2010, the asset disclosures of 1,655 public officials were received through

Table 6.1 Positions Subject to IAD Filing Obligations, Jordan

Functionaries	Senior civil servants	Managers
Prime minister	Senior public officials	Public agencies
Ministers	Heads of ministerial departments	Public institutes and municipalities
Judges	Heads of government offices	Companies where the government holds over 50%
Speakers and members of the national assembly	Ambassadors	Heads and members of the Central Committees of bids, civil and military special bids committees, bids and procurement committees in government departments, official institutions and municipalities

Table 6.2 Contents of the Income and Asset Declaration, Jordan

Assets

Real estate (commercial and private)

Land

Movable assets (money and deposits in banks, stocks, bonds, and vehicles)

Liabilities

Debts owed by filer to any individual or commercial entity

Foreign assets, cash, investments, and liabilities

All assets, cash, investments, and liabilities held or owed abroad

June 2010.[19] Spouses and minor children of covered officials are included in the primary filer's declaration form, as stipulated in Article 5(a) of the Income and Asset Disclosure Law and Article 7 of the Amended Instructions of Organizing the Income and Asset Disclosure Department.

Content of Declarations

The Income and Asset Disclosure Law and the Amended Instructions, which includes the IAD form issued by the Council of Ministers, require specific classes of income and assets to be declared. What constitutes asset disclosure was initially ambiguous. The amendments on the instructions issued by the cabinet on March 24, 2009, clarify the concept of IAD and do not limit disclosure to the sum of movable or immovable assets and financial interests owned by the public official; rather, disclosure also includes the sum of monetary loans and obligations the public official owes (table 6.2).[20]

The filer must sign a statement affirming the accuracy of the information included in the declaration. The standardized filing form, which was issued by the cabinet, reflects the statutory requirements of the Income and Asset Disclosure Law of 2006. The 10-page form includes excerpts of the relevant articles of the Income and Asset Disclosure Law; definitions of the terms used in the form; and charts to describe moveable and immoveable property owned by the official, sources of increases in property, and rights to and obligations of the public official, his or her spouse, and minor children. The declaration form is available in hard copy.

Filing Frequency

The law and the Amended Instructions specify the exact deadlines for filing asset declarations. All covered individuals, spouses, and minor children must declare their assets on the approved declaration form within the first three months of receiving the form upon taking office.[21] While in office, covered individuals are required to file in January upon the expiration of two years from the previous declaration, thus potentially allowing for almost three years between filings. For example, if an official took office in February 2008, he or she would be required to submit a declaration in January 2011. Officials must also submit a new declaration for the covered period upon leaving office.[22]

As an exception to the general rule regarding the time frame for submitting entry declarations, employees who work at the Anti-Corruption Commission and the Anti-Money-Laundering and Financing Terrorism Unit, which is affiliated with the governor of the central bank, are required to submit their asset disclosures before assuming office.[23]

Submission Compliance and Content Verification

In the case of failure to submit asset declarations prior to the legally mandated deadlines, the department notifies those officials who failed to declare their assets and requests submission within a month after receiving the notice of this requirement, in accordance with the civil procedures law.[24]

The IAD system in Jordan does not provide for an automatic verification of asset declarations. All completed asset declarations of covered public officials are submitted to the Income and Asset Disclosure Department at the Ministry of Justice.[25] According to Article 5(e) of Law No. 54 of 2006 and Article 7(c) of the Amended Instructions, all asset disclosure forms must be deposited in a sealed envelope provided by the Income and Asset Disclosure Department. Article 2 of Law No. 54 requires the employing agencies to provide the Income and Asset Disclosure Department with the names of the holders of covered positions within two months of being subject to the law.[26] The Income and Asset Disclosure Department must prepare a database that contains the names, positions, and addresses of covered officials and the due dates of each official required to submit an asset disclosure.[27] The department also notifies those who fail to disclose their assets on the specified dates in accordance with the civil procedures law. Such individuals must then submit their asset declarations to the same department that should have received it earlier within one month from receiving notification.[28]

The opening of income and asset declaration envelopes is prohibited unless a complaint is filed against a filer. If a complaint is filed, the head of the Income and Asset Disclosure Department must refer the matter with the sealed envelope that contains the asset declaration to the head of the Cassation Court, who is the only person with the mandate to look into the complaint and at the IAD form. If allegations are substantiated, the head of the Cassation Court refers the matter to at least one commission, which is formed by the High Judicial Council annually and composed of a Cassation Court judge and two other judges at the appellate level,[29] to verify the contents of the income and asset declaration and take appropriate action.[30]

Sanctions

The law provides for strong sanctions for noncompliance or other violations of asset disclosure obligations. According to Article 12 of Law No. 54 of 2006, any covered official who does not submit his or her asset declaration on the dates specified without legitimate excuse and despite being notified as stipulated in Article 5(d) of the same law, shall be penalized by imprisonment, a fine, or both.[31] Fines range from JD 5 (approximately US$7) to JD 200 (approximately US$282), as stipulated in Article 22, and the penalty of imprisonment ranges from one week to three years, as stipulated in Article 21 of the Amended Penal Code No. 16 of 1960. A filer who intentionally submits false information will be sentenced to prison from six months to three years,[32] although the law does not provide mechanisms for verifying the accuracy of declarations unless a complaint is filed.

Public Access to Declarations

Asset declaration forms, statements, notes, or any other documents secured under Article 8 are deemed confidential, as stipulated in Article 9 of the Income and Asset Disclosure Law. The Income and Asset Disclosure Department must maintain asset declarations in sealed envelopes as received, and it is prohibited, under legal liability, for any department staff to open the envelope or read its contents.[33] Therefore, the asset declarations of covered officials are not publicly available.

Mandate and Structure of the IAD Agency

As mentioned, asset disclosure is handled by the Income and Asset Disclosure Department of the Ministry of Justice. The department's mandate is to receive and maintain all asset disclosures of public officials subject to the Income and Asset Disclosure Law.

The mandate of the Income and Asset Disclosure Department includes the obligation to:

- Prepare and propose any necessary amendments to the instructions that regulate the tasks of the department that were issued according to Article 3 of the law
- Provide the competent authorities with the required IAD forms, follow up with them until they receive the forms, and deal with any data clarifications or notifications concerning the forms
- Build a specific database to include the data required of covered officials, such as names, positions, addresses, the date of the submission of the form or clarifications, or any information concerning the declaration forms in cooperation with the information technology department

- Follow up with the competent authorities to make sure that covered officials submit their forms on time
- Take all necessary precautions to maintain the confidentiality of the information, data, clarifications, and documents presented to the department, and to secure all asset disclosure forms in their sealed envelopes and provide them to the head of the Cassation Court upon request and as stipulated in the law
- Receive notifications of failure to provide the required data within the specified period according to the law, notify those public officials who did not submit their asset declaration forms that they should provide the information within one month of receiving the notification, and maintain all sealed notification envelopes
- Provide assistance and required information regarding covered officials to the commissions formed by the High Judicial Council to verify asset disclosures
- Receive complaints and reports regarding any of the covered officials and, if necessary, refer the matter to the head of the Cassation Court
- Contribute to enhancing the integrity and transparency principles in Jordanian society by coordinating with competent authorities
- Participate in activities and conferences that are related to illicit wealth
- Maintain all documents or decisions referred to the department by the chief prosecutor
- Conduct the necessary administrative and logistical work of the department in coordination with other departments at the Ministry of Justice

The department currently has five employees, all of whom were previously employed in various departments within the Ministry of Justice (a ratio of five staff to 4,100 filers). Figure 6.1 provides the structure of the Income and Asset Disclosure Department at the Ministry of Justice.

Resources and Procedures of the IAD System

To assess the functioning and the unique characteristics of the asset disclosure process in Jordan, a set of processes and correlating indicators have been developed. These focus on the practical aspects of implementing the asset disclosure process and consider the availability of physical facilities, technology, human resources, administrative capacity, and other factors. By mapping Jordan's structure and capabilities against this framework, it is possible to gain a better understanding of the strengths and weaknesses of the implementation of Jordan's asset disclosure system.

Facilities and Use of Technology

The Income and Asset Disclosure Department is housed in the Ministry of Justice. The total space allocated for the five employees working in the department is 70 square meters, excluding the office of the head of the department and the storage room. According to those working at the Income and Asset

Figure 6.1 Organizational Chart of the Income and Asset Disclosure Department at the Ministry of Justice, Jordan

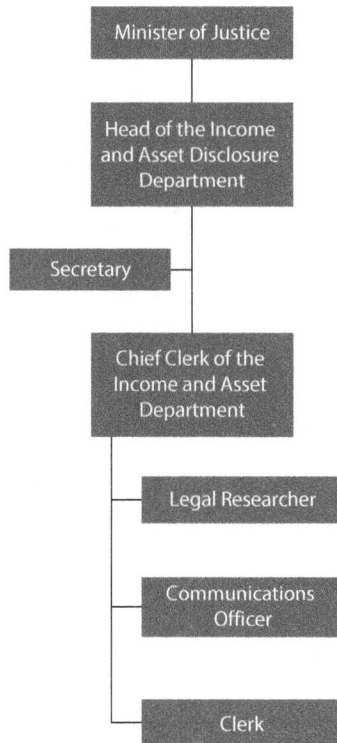

Source: Income and Asset Disclosure Department, Ministry of Justice, Jordan.

Disclosure Department, the offices are adequately heated and maintain uninterrupted electricity. The building also has storage capacity for holding the physical asset declarations of all public officials subject to the law. These declarations are held in metal lockers. There are eight lockers, each containing four shelves that hold 400 declarations each. Of the eight lockers, almost three lockers have been used to secure the declarations. The storage room is secured by a locked door and there are only two copies of the key. One copy is held by the head of the department and the other by the communications officer, who is in charge of receiving asset declarations from public officials. The law is silent on how long the department should maintain these declarations, so it is unclear how long these facilities will be adequate. The statute of limitations for an illicit enrichment offense is five years from the date the public official is no longer subject to the Income and Asset Disclosure Law, assuming that no investigation was started prior to this date.[34]

The Income and Asset Disclosure Department uses the information technology professionals employed by the Ministry of Justice, who facilitate the use of computers, software, and networking. Each employee at the Income and Asset Disclosure Department has a computer. Asset declarations are submitted only in hard copy. Information technology equipment is used to transfer general information regarding filers to an electronic database for submission compliance management.

Human Resources

The Income and Asset Disclosure Department is part of the Ministry of Justice. All five employees previously worked at the ministry before being reassigned to the Income and Asset Disclosure Department. The department provides in-depth orientation and training in all administrative processes, laws, and regulations. Currently, the staff use only Microsoft Word and Excel, so there is no need for extensive computer training. In conformity with Jordanian civil service standards, the department conducts performance evaluations semiannually. The department provides explicit job descriptions to its staff, which clearly delineate their responsibilities, and has produced an operations manual designed to familiarize department staff with the declaration process.

Budget

The department is financed under the budget of the Ministry of Justice. The head of the department and staff indicated that they are provided with everything they need to operate effectively. Staff salaries are similar to the salaries of equivalent positions in other government offices.

Regulatory Function

The Income and Asset Disclosure Department is authorized to prepare and propose to the cabinet, through the Minister of Justice, any necessary amendments to the instructions that regulate the tasks of the department as outlined in Article 3 of the Income and Asset Disclosure Law of 2006. The first instructions for organizing the Income and Asset Disclosure Department were issued by the cabinet on April 10, 2007; the amendments to the first instructions were issued on March 24, 2009. Currently, new amendments are considered by the department for submission to the Cabinet.

Managing Submission Compliance

All covered individuals, their spouses, and their minor children must declare their assets on the approved declaration form within the first three months of receiving the form, as stipulated in Article 3(c) of the Income and Asset Disclosure Law.[35] Then, within the month of January following the expiration of two years from the previous declaration, officials must submit a new declaration covering the period, and then again upon leaving office.[36] As an exception to the general rule regarding the time frame for submitting asset disclosures, employees who work at the Anti-Corruption Commission[37] and those who work at the Anti-Money-Laundering and Financing Terrorism Unit (which is affiliated with the governor of the central bank) submit their IAD forms before assuming office.[38]

However, in practice, the department grants second-time filers three months, starting from the month of January, to submit his or her asset disclosure, similar to the deadlines required the first time. The department also gives those who leave public office, and those who are no longer subject to the provisions of this law, three months to submit their final asset disclosure. In the case of failure to submit the asset declaration by the deadline specified by the law, the department notifies the covered official of this error and requests, in accordance with the civil procedures law, that the declaration be submitted within a month after receiving the notice.[39]

Because of the timing of the legal submission requirement, there is potential for a discrepancy in filing frequency. More specifically, if a public official submits his or her asset disclosure on December 31, he or she must submit a second time during the month of January after the expiration of 24 months if he or she is still subject to the law, as stipulated in Article 5(b) of the law. However, if the public official submits his or her asset disclosure on January 1, he or she must submit the following asset disclosure during the month of January after the expiration of 24 months from the previous declaration while being subject to the provisions of this law. Therefore, in the second case, the public official gains another year and must submit his or her asset disclosure in the third year.

According to statistics provided by the Income and Asset Disclosure Department, in 2008–09, 3,953 of the 4,117 individuals subject to the law submitted their asset declarations. Another 753 public officials were judicially notified to submit their asset declarations within one month of receiving the notification, and 164 cases were referred to the public prosecutor for noncompliance even after having been notified. As of June 2010, 1,655 public officials submitted their asset declarations. Another 331 public officials were judicially notified to submit their asset declaration within one month of receiving the notification, and 11 cases were referred to the public prosecutor for noncompliance even after having been notified.

As required by the Criminal Procedures Law, the public prosecutor must open an investigation and request an official reason for failure to submit an asset declaration. Some public officials provided proof of a legitimate excuse for non-compliance with the specified deadlines, which included a letter from their respective agency with his or her passport showing that he or she was abroad on an official trip during that period, or his or her name was mistakenly given to the Income and Asset Disclosure Department and he or she is no longer subject to the law. The latter circumstance was particularly relevant for the ministerial procurement committees, which change membership every six months. In such cases, the prosecutor has the discretion to drop the case. However, if no legitimate excuse is provided, the public prosecutor orders the official to submit the asset declaration form and provide a receipt as proof of submission. The public prosecutor then refers the case to the First Instance Court, which is presided over by one judge. For the district of Amman, and according to the public prosecutor, five cases were referred to the court in 2008. All were convicted and fined.

Fines range from JD 5 to JD 200, as stipulated in Article 22 of the Amended Penal Code No. 16 of 1960. As of June 2010, five cases had been referred to the public prosecutor's office. All were referred to the court, and in summer 2010, final judgments were pending.[40]

Content Verification

The IAD system, as established by the Income and Asset Disclosure Law, does not provide for automatic verification, and the articles regarding verification have not been activated or exercised. A verification procedure is triggered only if a complaint is filed at the Income and Asset Disclosure Department against one of the filers. The head of the department must refer the complaint with the sealed IAD envelope to the head of the Cassation Court. The head of the Cassation Court is the only one with the authority to look into the complaint and open the sealed envelope. If allegations are substantiated, the matter is referred to the commission established to verify asset declarations. The commission is composed of a Cassation Court judge and two other judges at the appellate level, formed by the High Judicial Council annually to verify asset disclosures.[41]

During the verification process, the commission has the power to request data, explanations, and documents from the public official or any other authority, regardless of any conflicting law. If the commission discovers a significant increase in the assets of the public official, or of his or her spouse or minor children, and this increase is not commensurate with his or her legitimate financial resources, the commission requests an explanation of the discrepancy and any supporting data. If the official cannot reasonably explain to the commission that the increase is the result of his or her lawful income, the commission refers the documents to the competent investigation and prosecution authorities. If the commission, while auditing the financial disclosure form, discovers that there is sufficient evidence of illicit enrichment, the commission is empowered to issue an order preventing the official, his or her spouse, and his or her minor children from disposing of their property and to take any other precautionary measures necessary to implement the order. Conversely, if the commission finds the evidence insufficient to prove illicit enrichment, the commission can decide not to proceed with the case.[42]

Investigatory Function

Investigations into an official's asset disclosure can be triggered as a result of the formal verification process performed by the commission established according to Article 7 of the Income and Asset Disclosure Law. If the commission discovers a significant increase in the assets of the public official, or of his or her spouse or minor children, and this increase is not commensurate with his or her legitimate financial resources, the commission requests an explanation of the discrepancy and any supporting data. If the official cannot reasonably explain to the commission that the increase is the result of his or her lawful income, the commission refers the documents to the competent investigation and prosecution authorities, as stipulated in Article 8(a/2) of the law. The law does not specify the competent authority for investigation and prosecution, but it implies that it should be either the Public Prosecution Office or the Anti-Corruption Commission.[43] However, as of 2010, no cases have been referred to the commission, nor has there been any subsequent investigation or prosecution. Therefore, this article has not been exercised.

Interagency Collaboration

Despite the fact that no IAD form has yet to be verified, the Income and Asset Disclosure Law provides the commission entrusted with verifying declarations with significant powers to exercise its mandate. Article 7(b) gives the commission the authority to request any data, explanations, or documents from the filer or any other agency, regardless of any conflicting law.

Public Access to Declarations

Asset declaration forms, statements, notes, or any related documents secured under Article 8 of the law are deemed confidential, as stipulated in Article 9 of the law. The Income and Asset Disclosure Department must maintain asset declarations in sealed envelopes as received, and under Article 5(e/1) of the law, department staff are prohibited, under legal liability, from opening the envelope or reading its contents. Therefore, the asset declarations of covered officials are not publicly available.

Box 6.2 presents the sequence of procedures performed by Jordan's Income and Asset Disclosure Department.

Summary of Key Findings

Income and asset disclosure in Jordan is a recent development. The IAD system represents a positive, albeit somewhat limited, step toward enhancing integrity and transparency in the public sector and introduces a preventive measure to protect public funds and curb corruption. The IAD system in Jordan represents, to some degree, what is politically feasible and institutionally practicable in Jordan, taking into account legal and other more practical challenges that limit its effectiveness. Although UNCAC was initially a driving force behind the creation of the Income and Asset Disclosure Department in Jordan, there is now both impetus and consensus within the government to advance the anticorruption agenda, and progress in deepening the implementation of the UNCAC provisions.

The primary functions of the Income and Asset Disclosure Department during its first three years have been to serve as a depository for declarations and to provide guidance to filers to assist them in the proper completion of the forms. Over the course of the first three years, marked improvements have been made in the implementation of the IAD system. For example, although the Income and Asset Disclosure Department initially faced some challenges from officials covered by the law, the current (second) round of disclosures shows

Box 6.2 Sequence of Procedures Performed by Jordan's Income and Asset Disclosure Department

Developing and maintaining a register of filers
- The chief clerk of the department prepares official letters to be sent to the different government agencies, ministries, and concerned bodies every two years.[a] The concerned bodies are required to provide the names of officials to whom the law applies.

Notifying filers of the obligation to submit a declaration
- Upon receiving the names, the communications officer at the department prepares the asset declaration forms and the specified envelope with an official letter to be sent to the bodies concerned.
- The secretary enters the names provided to the department into the computer database.
- The communications officer packages the forms and their specified envelopes and sends them through a mailing company to the concerned bodies.

Managing the receipt of declarations
- When a covered official brings his or her asset declaration form to the Income and Asset Disclosure Department, the communications officer receives the envelope and provides the filer a serially numbered receipt and keeps a copy of the receipt for the file. The officer checks the official's identification, makes a copy of it, and then asks the official to fill out a general information form. The communications officer stamps the envelope "confidential" to guarantee that no one opens it and asks the filer to sign the envelope after it is sealed. The officer then stores the form in lockers in the storage room.[b]

Monitoring submission compliance
- The secretary enters all the information contained in the general information form into the database on the computer and records the filer's personal information in a designated registry.
- If a covered official does not submit his or her declaration within three months of receiving the IAD form, the department notifies the official of this failure and requests submission within a month after receiving the notification, in accordance with the civil procedures law.
- The communication officer documents, in a registry, all data regarding the notifications sent to those who have not submitted their declarations by the due dates.
- If a covered official does not submit his or her declaration after the specified period without a legitimate excuse, a letter is sent to the public prosecutor to investigate and refer the defendant to the competent court.

Responding to allegations and complaints
- If the chief clerk receives any complaints or reports regarding one of the filers, the information about the complainant must be collected and then documented in a special registry. The secretary enters all the data regarding the complaint into a computer database.
- The head of the department refers the complaint, along with the defendant's IAD envelope, to the head of the Cassation Court for assessment.

box continues next page

Box 6.2 Sequence of Procedures Performed by Jordan's Income and Asset Disclosure Department
(continued)

- After reviewing the complaint, and if allegations are substantiated, the head of the Cassation Court refers the matter to at least one commission composed of a Cassation Court judge and two other judges at the appellate level, formed by the High Judicial Council annually, to verify the asset declaration form and undertake the proper procedures.[c]
- If the commission finds that there is sufficient evidence of illicit enrichment, the commission refers the matter to the competent authorities for investigation and prosecution.

a. Article 2 of the Income and Asset Disclosure Law.
b. The Amended Instructions added a paragraph to Article 7 of the instructions to give filers a chance to correct any mistake mentioned in the declaration by submitting a written request within one week from the date he or she submits his or her asset declaration. The new form must be attached to the old one.
c. Article 5(e) of the Income and Asset Disclosure Law.

---

increased familiarity with the law and more dedicated offices in agencies providing assistance and advice to covered officials. As a result, by 2010, all high-level public officials had submitted their asset declarations by the deadline specified by the law.

Since establishing the Income and Asset Disclosure Department and implementing its legal provisions, several gaps and ambiguities remain in the law, resulting in some constraints on its implementation and enforcement. These ambiguities include questions about specifically to whom the law applies, the optimal filing frequency, and the required period of time for maintaining declarations. Another significant problem is the extreme confidentiality of the forms, coupled with the provision that declarations shall be opened and investigated only if someone accuses the filer of a crime, thus creating a risk of real or perceived bias in the selection of declarations for review and potential prosecution.

One lesson that may be drawn from Jordan's current system is that there is a need to ensure that such laws do not allow for ambiguities and subjective interpretation. Another lesson is that a sustainable balance between maintaining confidentiality and providing for some form of scrutiny of the declarations is crucial. The Income and Asset Disclosure Department is studying the possibility of verifying asset declarations and the best approaches for doing so; however, no consideration is being given to allow public access to declarations. As of this writing, the department is working to address some of the other shortcomings within the system and will propose amendments to both the law and the Amended Instructions to the Council of Ministers.

Notes

1. The Income and Asset Disclosure Law No. 54 of 2006 was published in *Official Gazette* No. 4790 on November 1, 2006, p. 4257.

2. http://www.unodc.org/unodc/en/treaties/CAC/signatories.html.

3. Pursuant to Article 63 of the convention, the Conference of the State Parties to UNCAC was established to improve the capacity of and cooperation between states parties to achieve the objectives set forth in the convention and to promote and review its implementation.

4. The Arab Anti-Corruption and Integrity Network was established in Amman in July 2008 to provide regional knowledge networking, capacity development, and policy dialogue to fight corruption across the Arab region. In addition, Jordan is supporting the regional initiative to draft an Arab League convention on combating corruption.

5. Interview with H.E. Dr. Abed Shakhanbeh, chairman of the Anti-Corruption Commission, Amman, July 10, 2010.

6. Law No. 28 of 2004 on ratifying UNCAC was published in *Official Gazette* No. 4669 on August 1, 2004.

7. The Anti-Corruption Commission Law No. 62 of 2006 was published in *Official Gazette* No. 4794 on November 30, 2006, p. 4534.

8. The Income and Asset Disclosure Law No. 54 of 2006 was published in *Official Gazette* No. 4790 on November 1, 2006, p. 4257. With regard to IAD, a legal committee was established in April 2002 by decision of the prime minister. The committee was composed of nine members and includes judges, lawyers, and public administration members, and is authorized to review, prepare, and draft the Illicit Wealth Law. A debate immediately ensued over the proposed title due to the sensitivity of public perception of public officials. The initial proposal was the Illicit Wealth Law, but the committee ultimately agreed upon the Income and Asset Disclosure Law. A heated debate ensued in Parliament regarding the bill, specifically as to whom the law should apply. Some members of Parliament opposed being subject to the law, arguing that it is unconstitutional. Finally, the Income and Asset Disclosure Law passed on September 19, 2006. Interview with Judge Dr. Nazem Aref, head of the Financial Disclosure Department, Amman, July 11, 2010.

9. Anti-Money-Laundering Law No. 46 of 2007 and Access to Information Law No. 47 of 2007 were published in *Official Gazette* No. 4831 on June 17, 2008.

10. Anti-Corruption Commission Law No. 62 of 2006 was published in *Official Gazette* No. 4794 on November 30, 2006, p. 4534.

11. The term *corruption* is defined through offenses listed in Article 5 of the Anti-Corruption Commission Law No. 62 of 2006. The following offenses are deemed to be corruption: (1) crimes violating the duties of public office and public trust as stipulated in Amended Penal Code No. 16 of 1960, (2) economic crimes as defined in Economic Crimes Law No. 11 of 1993, (3) any act or abstinence from acting that leads to transgression and encroachment on public funds, (4) misuse of power in violation of the law, (5) acceptance of favoritism and nepotism (*wasta*) that would invalidate a right and validate a void, and (6) all Acts mentioned in international conventions on anticorruption that have been ratified or signed by Jordan.

12. Interview with H.E. Dr. Abed Shakhanbeh, chairman of the Anti-Corruption Commission, Amman, July 10, 2010. Information presented is as of June 2010.

13. *Oudeh* is the concept that asset disclosure includes all rights, debts, and obligations (Al-Rraqad 2009).

14. The criminal offense of illicit enrichment directly addresses one of the intrinsic difficulties of anticorruption law enforcement: the requirement that the prosecution provide evidence of the criminal activity from which the individual has

profited. The criminalization of illicit enrichment allows for a prima facie case of corruption to be established simply by determining that an individual's wealth is disproportionate to his or her legitimate income, thus arguably shifting the burden of proof from the prosecution to the official to legitimize the source(s) of wealth. The term *illicit enrichment* is also used to refer to the focus of IAD systems that monitor income and asset declarations for suspicious changes in the wealth of public officials, although, in many countries, an unjustified increase in wealth may not in itself constitute a criminal offense. For more information on illicit enrichment, see Muliza et al. 2012.

15. Article 3 (a) of Income and Asset Disclosure Law No. 54 of 2006 and a conference call with Dr. Salah Albashir, former Minister of Justice, on July 15, 2010.

16. Letter No. 2/1/1741 issued on December 20, 2006, by the head of the Cassation Court and the High Judicial Council, to the Minister of Justice naming Judge Dr. Nazem Aref as the head of the Income and Asset Disclosure Department at the Ministry of Justice according to Decision No. 137 of 2006 issued by the High Judicial Council on December 17, 2006.

17. The first instructions were issued by the Council of Ministers in April 2007. These instructions were amended in March 2009 in accordance with the provisions of the asset disclosure law. The most important amendments to the first instructions (1) redefined *asset disclosure* by adding debts and obligations that have a monetary value to be disclosed for himself or herself and his or her spouse and minor children; and (2) added a paragraph that allows the filer to review the IAD in person within a week from when he or she submits his or her assets disclosure, to correct any mistakes and to attach the new envelop to the old one.

18. Statistics provided to the author by the Income and Asset Disclosure Department.

19. Information presented in this chapter is as of June 2010.

20. Articles 2(a) and 7(b) of the Amended Instructions of Organizing the Income and Asset Declaration Department; and Al-Rraqad (2009).

21. Article 5(a) of the Income and Asset Disclosure Law and Article 7 (a/1) of the Amended Instructions of Organizing the Income and Asset Disclosure Department.

22. Article 5(b) of the Income and Asset Disclosure Law and Article 7 (a/2, 3) of the Amended Instructions of Organizing the Income and Asset Disclosure Department.

23. Article 8(f) of Law No. 62 of 2006 of the Anti-Corruption Commission.

24. Article 5(d) of the Income and Asset Disclosure Law No. 54 of 2006.

25. Article 3(b) of the Income and Asset Disclosure Law and Article 5(c) of the Amended Instructions of Organizing the Income and Asset Disclosure Department.

26. Article 4 of the Income and Asset Disclosure Law and Article 4 of the Amended Instructions of Organizing the Income and Asset Disclosure Department.

27. Article 5(a) of the Amended Instructions of Organizing the Income and Asset Disclosure Department.

28. Article 5(d) of the Income and Asset Disclosure Law.

29. According to an interview with Judge Krayyem Tarawneh, head of the Judicial Inspection Department, judges at the appellate level are at the grade in which they serve on the Court of Appeal. At the time of writing, Judge Krayyem Tarawneh was also head of the commission to verify asset disclosures.

30. Article 5(e) of the Income and Asset Disclosure Law.

31. Article 12 of the Income and Asset Disclosure Law No. 54 of 2006.

32. Article 13 of the Income and Asset Disclosure Law No. 54 of 2006.

33. Article 5(e/1) of the Income and Asset Disclosure Law.

34. Article 10 of the Income and Asset Disclosure Law.

35. Article 3(c) of the Income and Asset Disclosure Law and Article 7(a/1) of the Amended Instructions of Organizing the Income and Asset Disclosure Department.

36. Article 5(b) of the Income and Asset Disclosure Law and Article 7(a/2, 3) of the Amended Instructions of Organizing the Income and Asset Disclosure Department.

37. Article 8(f) of Law No. 62 of 2006 of the Anti-Corruption Commission.

38. The Anti-Money-Laundering and Financing Terrorism Unit was established according to Article 7 of Law No. 46 of 2007 on Combating Money Laundering, which was published in *Official Gazette* No. 4831 on June 17, 2007. As indicated by the Income and Asset Disclosure Department, submitting asset declarations regarding employees at the unit is required according to internal instructions.

39. Article 5(d) of the Income and Asset Disclosure Law No. 54 of 2006.

40. Interview with Judge Dr. Hasan Al-Abdallat, the first public prosecutor of Amman, July 14, 2010.

41. Articles 5(b) and 7 of the Income and Asset Disclosure Law. Interview with Judge Krayyem Tarawneh, head of the Judicial Inspection Department. At the time of writing, he was also head of the commission to verify asset disclosures.

42. Article 8 of the Income and Asset Disclosure Law of 2006. Interview with Judge Krayyem Tarawneh, head of the Judicial Inspection Department. At the time of writing, Judge Tarawneh was also head of the commission to verify asset disclosures.

43. Interview with H.E. Dr. Abed Shakhanbeh, chairman of the Anti-Corruption Commission, Amman, July 10, 2010.

References

Al-Rraqad, M. 2009. "Financial Disclosure: Rights, Debts, and Obligations." *Alghad Newspaper*, March 26, 2009. http://www.alghad.com/?news=405804.

Muliza, L., M. Morales, M. Mathias, and T. Berger. 2012. *On The Take: Criminalizing Illicit Enrichment to Fight Corruption*. Stolen Asset Recovery (StAR) Series. Washington, DC: World Bank. http://star.worldbank.org/star/publication/take-criminalizing-illicit-enrichment-fight-corruption.

CHAPTER 7

Kyrgyz Republic

Aisuluu Aitbaeva

Overview

The income and asset disclosure (IAD) system in the Kyrgyz Republic (see box 7.1) is governed chiefly by the 2004 Law on Asset Declaration, which requires all civil servants—including high-level public officials (the president, the prime minister, ministers, and members of Parliament)—to declare their income and assets. Since this report was researched in August 2009, the Kyrgyz Republic has experienced a period of conflict and political instability, resulting in changes to governance structures.[1] These changes include proposals to amend the IAD legislation, as well as renaming the Civil Service Agency formerly responsible for IAD administration, so that it is now called the State Personnel Service.[2] Based on available information, new developments are indicated where possible in the findings of this report.

The Kyrgyz IAD system has achieved a high level of compliance with the requirement to submit declarations, although the system lacks both serious sanctions for violations and mechanisms for formal verification and public scrutiny of declarations, suggesting that its powers of prevention and enforcement are limited.

The administration of income and asset declarations places emphasis on the *submission* of asset declarations by public officials, but little emphasis on ensuring that the contents of declarations are accurate. Although the IAD system lacks any verification mechanism because of this oversight in the law, as of the writing of this report the government was taking steps to redress this problem. In May 2009, the head of the presidential administration of the Kyrgyz Republic established a Working Group for the Development of an Asset Declaration

This report is based on desk research and the findings of a visit to the Kyrgyz Republic in August 2009 undertaken on behalf of the Stolen Asset Recovery (StAR) Initiative and the Governance & Public Sector Management Unit of the World Bank to examine the country's IAD system. Special thanks for assistance in the preparation of this report go to Bekbolot Bekiev (Millennium Challenge Account Threshold Program); Jackie Charlton (UK Department for International Development); Bakytbek Sagynbaev and Zulfiya Aitieva (State Personnel Service); and Stephanie Trapnell, Natalia Pisareva, Gregory Kisunko, and Maksat Kobonbaev (World Bank).

Box 7.1 Snapshot of the Income and Asset Disclosure System in the Kyrgyz Republic

The IAD system in the Kyrgyz Republic is governed chiefly by its 2004 Law on Asset Declaration and a number of subsequent regulations. The Law on Asset Declaration requires all civil servants, including high-level public officials (the president, the prime minister, ministers, and members of Parliament) to declare their income and assets. The agency responsible for the implementation of the IAD system was, until 2009, the Civil Service Agency of the Kyrgyz Republic, now named the State Personnel Service. The Kyrgyz IAD system has achieved a high level of compliance with the requirement to submit declarations, although the system lacks both serious sanctions for violations and mechanisms for either formal verification or effective public scrutiny of declarations. This suggests that its powers of prevention and enforcement are limited.

Key elements of the IAD system include:

- **A design intended to prevent illicit enrichment.** Asset disclosure is a component of the national fight against corruption and is mainly intended to prevent illicit enrichment.
- **Paper submission and centralized administration process.** Asset declarations are submitted in hard copy. High-level public officials submit declarations directly to the State Personnel Service; all other civil servants submit declarations to specialized officers appointed within each agency, who then transport all paper declarations to the Civil Service Agency (later renamed the State Personnel Service), where they are permanently stored.
- **No content verification mechanism.** The State Personnel Service may only collect and examine declarations. No mechanism exists for cases where discrepancies are found. The law does not authorize any agency to deal with content verification. This issue is currently being addressed by the government and reforms are under consideration.
- **No sanctions for high-level public officials.** The law does not provide for serious sanctions for noncompliance by high-level public officials. The only remedy provided in the law is the publication of the names of nonfilers in the media.
- **Public access is granted only to the declarations of high-level public officials.** Summaries of asset declarations of high-level officials are published in the official bulletins and on the Web. Declarations of all other civil servants are confidential.

Content Verification Mechanism. The working group includes representatives of the presidential administration, the Civil Service Agency, the Prosecutor General's Office, the Ministry of Interior, the Financial Police, Financial Intelligence, the Ministry of Justice, and the Millennium Challenge Account Threshold Program. The main purpose of the working group is to develop a verification mechanism of the contents of income and asset declarations and promote interagency cooperation and information sharing for investigative purposes.

The Kyrgyz government has acknowledged that existing law is deficient in terms of sanctions for violations of income and asset declaration requirements by public officials. Thus, as part of the reform, the government intends to introduce administrative and criminal liability for noncompliance with IAD requirements.

Background

After gaining independence in 1991, the Kyrgyz Republic set the objective of becoming a democratic state with a free market economy. The Kyrgyz government was determined to devote itself to international cooperation and development. Despite all its efforts, however, corruption at all levels continued to grow; this is still a serious challenge. IAD was formally introduced by the Law on Civil Service adopted in 1999, which required all civil servants to declare their income and assets. Because there was no specialized depository body, the declarations were to be submitted to tax authorities. According to the 1999 Law on Civil Service, the information contained in declarations was categorized as "official secrets," with disclosure resulting in liability. However, the law did not describe the procedure for submitting the declarations, it was not clear about what was to be declared, and there were no sanctions for noncompliance.

In the early 2000s, the attention of the international community focused on combating corruption, and in 2003, the Kyrgyz Republic became the first Commonwealth of Independent States country to sign the United Nations Convention against Corruption.[3] Despite the fact that the convention had yet to be ratified, the Kyrgyz government started taking steps toward better accountability and transparency standards. In 2003, the new Law on Combating Corruption also came into force, but it mentioned only vaguely the obligation of civil servants to declare income and assets.

The 1999 Law on Civil Service was subsequently replaced by a new Law on Civil Service, which came into force in 2004. The new law was more complex than its predecessor in terms of its IAD requirements. Unlike the 1999 law, where IAD requirements were compressed into a single three-paragraph article, the new Law on Civil Service devoted an entire chapter to the declaration of income and assets by civil servants. The improvement was obvious: the new law listed the types of income and assets to be declared, specified the procedure for submitting the declarations, and envisaged sanctions for noncompliance with declaration requirements. The law also introduced an additional requirement: civil servants must file income and asset declarations for their immediate family members as well as for themselves. According to the 2004 Law on Civil Service, information in the declarations of civil servants was to be made available upon request (see table 7.1).

Table 7.1 Comparison of IAD Provisions, the Kyrgyz Republic

	1999 Law on Civil Service[a]	2004 Law on Civil Service	2004 IAD Law[b]
Clear procedures	None	✓	✓
Types of income	None	✓	✓
Public access	None	✓	✓
Sanctions	None	✓	None

a. The 1999 Law on Civil Service was replaced by the 2004 Law on Civil Service.
b. The 2004 IAD Law covers only high-level public officials.

In 2004, another IAD law was adopted—the Law on Declaration and Publication of Information on Income and Assets, Liabilities and Property of Political and Other Special State Appointees and Their Immediate Family Members (the 2004 IAD Law). This law required high-level public officials— including the president, the prime minister, and members of Parliament—to declare their income and assets. As with the 2004 Law on Civil Service, the IAD Law laid out the procedure for submitting declarations, listed the types of income and assets to be declared, and required the submission of declarations also for immediate family members of the filers. Also, according to the IAD Law, the summaries of the declarations of high-level public officials were to be published, including on the Internet.

Simultaneously, the Civil Service Agency was created to administer both the Law on Civil Service and the IAD Law. The agency became a central organ to deal with civil service matters, including IAD. However, the agency lacked some important powers, which will be discussed further below.

In March 2005, only a year after the Civil Service Agency came into existence, the Kyrgyz Republic, following the examples of Georgia and Ukraine, was shaken by its own "Tulip Revolution." A few of the commonly cited reasons leading to the overthrow of the government were the difficult economic situation, deep-rooted corruption, nepotism, and tribalism. The parliamentary elections held in February–March 2005, which were declared short of international standards,[4] became the ultimate trigger for revolution. The first president, Askar Akayev, resigned, and the new president, Kurmanbek Bakiyev, was elected.

Although the new government took several steps to strengthen its position in the anticorruption battle (including creation of the Anti-Corruption Agency and the National Council for Corruption Prevention in 2005), the IAD system saw no drastic change since 2004. Only in 2009 did the president issue a decree approving the country's new anticorruption strategy,[5] as well as the action plan for its implementation, both of which listed IAD policy as an important part of anticorruption efforts. (See figure 7.1 for a historical time-line of IAD legislation.)

The Civil Service Agency, in 2009, had achieved a 99.7 percent compliance rate among high-level public officials (out of a total of 1,389 people occupying political or special state positions), and a 95.4 percent compliance rate among the rest of civil servants (out of a total of 15,877 civil servants), but the agency and the IAD system as a whole face problems that the government is trying to tackle.

The Kyrgyz IAD system lacks a content verification mechanism. According to Civil Service Agency officials, it does not have enough authority to deal with matters related to verification of the accuracy and content of asset declarations. The wording of the law concerning the agency's authority to verify the contents of declarations is vague. Establishing a content verification mechanism will require amending the relevant IAD laws through an act of Parliament. The government addressed this problem by establishing a working group

Figure 7.1 IAD Historical Timeline, the Kyrgyz Republic

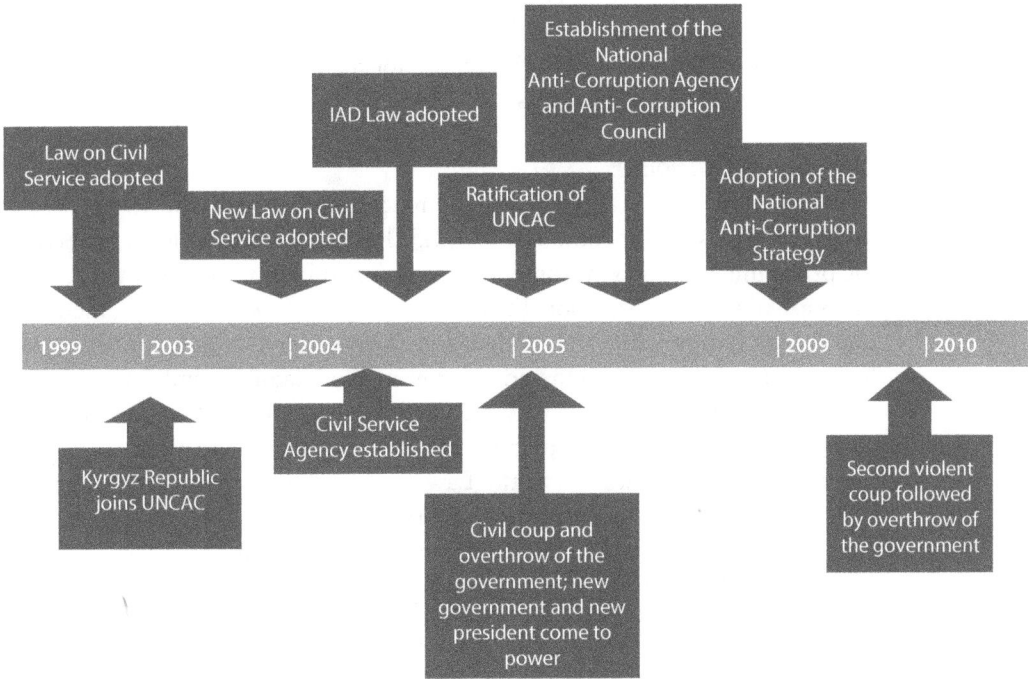

Establishment of the National Anti-Corruption Agency and Anti-Corruption Council

IAD Law adopted

Law on Civil Service adopted

New Law on Civil Service adopted

Ratification of UNCAC

Adoption of the National Anti-Corruption Strategy

1999 | 2003 | 2004 | 2005 | 2009 | 2010

Kyrgyz Republic joins UNCAC

Civil Service Agency established

Civil coup and overthrow of the government; new government and new president come to power

Second violent coup followed by overthrow of the government

Note: UNCAC = United Nations Convention against Corruption.

in May 2009, the main purpose of which is to propose a verification mechanism for submitted asset declarations.

Another issue of concern is the absence of sanctions for noncompliance with disclosure requirements by high-level public officials. According to one expert consulted for this study, members of Parliament have expressed their intention not to submit asset declarations, given the lack of any sanctions for nonfilers. For this reason, administrative and criminal sanctions for noncompliance with asset disclosure requirements by all public officials has been proposed, including sanctions for those occupying high public positions.

In addition to the above factors, some people think that the entire IAD system is nothing more than a tool used by the government to reassert itself in the eyes of the public. With no effective enforcement mechanism, the system is often characterized as a public relations effort rather than a genuine effort to prevent unethical conduct.

The IAD Legal Framework in the Kyrgyz Republic

IAD in the Kyrgyz Republic is mainly regulated by the 2004 Law on Asset Declaration, which covers political appointees, elected officials, and their immediate family members; and the 2004 Law on Civil Service, which imposes on other categories of public officers the obligation to declare their assets and liabilities. The procedure, terms, and time limits for asset disclosure by civil servants is laid out in the Regulation of Procedure, Terms and Time-Frames of Income and Asset Disclosure by Civil Servants adopted on April 5, 2005. Finally, the Anti-Corruption Law (2003) provides for mandatory disclosure of any bank accounts owned by civil servants.

Coverage of Officials

Article 1 of the Law on Asset Declaration identifies, by post, officials required to declare property and income (table 7.2). These officials include the president, the prime minister and government ministers, members of Parliament, justices of the Supreme and Constitutional Courts, and other officials occupying high positions in the government. These officials are also required to submit declarations for their spouses and children and other immediate family members.

Articles 3 and 33 of the Law on Civil Service impose the same duty on civil servants "holding administrative public positions" and their immediate family members. In addition to the Law on Asset Declaration and the Law on Civil Service, the Anti-Corruption Law requires persons intending to work as civil servants to declare their assets and income. Former high-level public officials are also required to file asset declarations for two years after leaving office.

Content of Declarations

The Law on Asset Declaration and the declaration form issued by the Civil Service Agency require specific types of income and assets to be declared (table 7.3). The covered persons are obliged to declare real estate, movable property, cash, securities, loans and liabilities, and all types of income. The assets and income of spouses and children and other immediate family members must also be declared. The law does not specify any thresholds for income and assets declared by officials in political and special state posts. However, a threshold

Table 7.2 Coverage of Officials, the Kyrgyz Republic

High public officials[a]	Civil servants
President	"Civil servant is a citizen of the Kyrgyz Republic
Prime minister	holding an official position within the public
Members of Parliament	body who carries out professional activity on
Chairman and judges of the Supreme Court	a full-time basis in exchange for monetary
Vice prime ministers	reward from the state budget, exercising
Prosecutor General	powers provided to him or her due to the
Chairman of the Chamber of Accounts	position held and being accountable for the
Chairman of the National Bank	execution thereof, . . ."[b]
Chairman of the Central Election Commission	
Heads of local and central Finance Police	
Heads of local administrations and mayors of Bishkek and Osh cities	

Source: Author's compilation, based on the 2004 Law on Asset Declaration.
a. List is not exhaustive.
b. Definition under Article 1b of the 2004 Law on Civil Service.

Table 7.3 Contents of the Income and Asset Declaration, the Kyrgyz Republic

	Disclosure requirement	Publicly available
High-level public officials		
Personal data		
Name	✓	✓
Contact details (address, phone, etc.)	✓	
Position		
Title	✓	✓
Date of appointment	✓	✓
Income		
Income (monetary and in form of property)	✓	✓
Source and location of income	✓	
Assets		
Movable property—title and location	✓	
Value of movable property	✓	✓
Immovable property—title and location	✓	
Value of immovable property	✓	✓
Assets in charter capitals of companies	✓	
Assets in property trust	✓	
Stocks—title and location	✓	
Value of stocks	✓	✓
Liabilities		
Amount of loan or other liability	✓	
Paid amount, unpaid amount, interest rate	✓	
IAD declarations of spouses and children		
Summaries of IAD declarations of spouses and children	✓	✓
Civil Servants		

Source: Author's compilation, based on the 2004 Law on Asset Declaration.

exists for income and assets declared by other civil servants. Income from gambling, gifts, prizes, donations, inheritance, and other income derived from contracts must meet a threshold equivalent to US$211. The income and asset declaration consists of three sections—income, assets, and liabilities. High-level public officials and civil servants file the same form. Declarations of immediate family members are annexed to the declaration of the principal filer. The form is available on the Civil Service Agency website.

Filing Frequency

The Law on Asset Declaration and the Law on Civil Service specify deadlines for submitting declarations. According to the Law on Asset Declaration, all public officials are required to submit declarations within 30 days of their election or appointment, and then annually (no later than March 1). Declarations must also be submitted within 30 days after leaving office and for the subsequent two years. Neither law contains provisions requiring public officials or civil servants to file new declarations upon changes in assets in between the filing periods.

Sanctions

One notable weakness of the Kyrgyz legislation, and particularly of the Law on Asset Declaration, is that it does not provide for any liability for high-level public officials for nonfiling, late filing, or the submission of false information. Publication of the list of nonfilers is the only censure provided by the IAD Law. The Law on Civil Service, however, does provide for administrative sanctions for civil servants, including removal from office. Whereas ordinary civil servants can be dismissed from office for nonsubmission of their declaration under the 2004 Law on Civil Service, high-level public officials do not face any sanctions for noncompliance with the IAD Law. Given the extent of corruption in the Kyrgyz Republic, the absence of sanctions for high-level public officials is of particular concern.

Monitoring, Oversight, and Verification

According to Articles 5 and 6 of the IAD Law, the depository body is the Civil Service Agency, which was created pursuant to the Law on Civil Service. High-level public officials submit their income and asset declarations directly to the Civil Service Agency, which publishes summaries of declarations on its website and in the official bulletin. Civil servants submit their declarations to their respective agencies, and the agencies are responsible for forwarding the declarations to the Civil Service Agency, where they are processed in the Income and Asset Disclosure Department. The decentralized collection of declarations is regulated by the Regulation of the Organizational Process of Asset Declaration. This regulation lays out the procedure of collecting the declarations, their safekeeping, and their proper delivery to the Civil Service Agency. Each agency is responsible for keeping a standardized registry of filers, and the hard copy of the completed declaration form must be strictly accounted for. The regulation provides for the liability of the head of the agencies for violation of the regulation's provisions; however, it neither specifies the form of liability nor refers to the application of a specific law.

Although the verification of the contents of declarations is within the competency of the Civil Service Agency, there are no explicit procedures established for verifying the contents. To address this gap, the Kyrgyz government adopted the Action Plan for Realization of the National Anti-Corruption Strategy for 2009–2011, which includes the objective of developing content verification mechanisms for asset declarations by public officials and their immediate family members, and established the working group mentioned above.

In February 2008, the Civil Service Agency adopted the Rules of Monitoring and Evaluation of the Compliance with Asset Disclosure Legislation of the Kyrgyz Republic. Pursuant to these rules, the Civil Service Agency annually monitors the performance of state agencies with regard to compliance with IAD legislation. The monitoring takes place after completion of the declaration campaign and must ensure, among other things, that the IAD-dedicated officer within the agency is appointed, that the registry of filers is properly kept, and that rules of registering and safekeeping the completed declaration forms are observed.

Public Access to Declarations

According to Article 7(1) of the Law on Asset Declaration, the Civil Service Agency is required to publish summaries of the information contained in income and asset declarations of high-level public officials and their immediate family members in the official bulletin of the Civil Service Agency and on the agency's website. Some information—such as address, telephone numbers, and location of property—are considered confidential and cannot be published.

Because of the high volume of declarations received each year (approximately 17,000) and the small number of staff processing the submissions (four in the IAD Unit), declarations of civil servants are not proactively published, but must be made available upon individual request. Similar to the publication requirements for the declarations of high-level public officials, the contact details, title, and location of the property of civil servants cannot be disclosed. Declarations of immediate family members of civil servants are confidential.

Mandate and Structure of the IAD Agency

Under the laws of the Kyrgyz Republic, the Civil Service Agency is a central state authority and is responsible for the development and realization of the state policy for the employment and obligations of the civil service. The Civil Service Agency was created with enactment of the new Law on Civil Service and the Law on Asset Declaration, and was vested with exclusive powers in matters related to civil service, including aspects of IAD. Thus, the Civil Service Agency is the principal body responsible for the implementation of the IAD system. However, as mentioned, the agency's content verification powers are vague.

The agency currently employs 95 people dedicated solely to IAD functions, and is headed by the director, who is appointed by the president. The agency is organized into 10 small departments and three large regional offices. Figure 7.2 presents an organizational chart of the Civil Service Agency.[6]

Housed within the Civil Service Agency, the Asset Disclosure Department is the primary unit responsible for the IAD process. Under Article 6 of the Law on Asset Declaration, the Asset Disclosure Department has the powers to:

- Maintain the register of filers and the declarations register, ensure their safe-keeping, and provide confidentiality and secrecy of information that cannot be disclosed
- Provide declaration forms, clarifications, and guidance to the filers
- Inform the filers about the need to provide timely declarations and undertake measures to ensure the completeness and truthfulness of submitted declarations and information indicated in the declarations
- Review declarations; when necessary, send a letter of inquiry to the tax inspection office to confirm fullness and authenticity of information provided in the declaration; review information received from state bodies, local self-governments, commercial and noncommercial organizations, and citizens

Figure 7.2 Organizational Chart of the Civil Service Agency, the Kyrgyz Republic

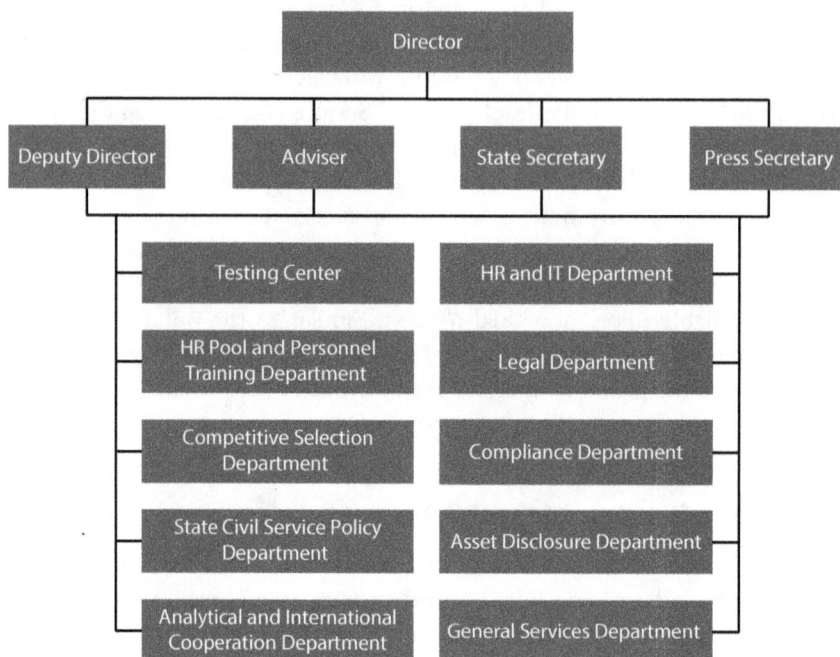

Source: Civil Service Agency, the Kyrgyz Republic.
Note: HR = human resources; IT = information technology.

with regard to the income, liabilities, and assets of the persons covered by this law; if necessary, confirm the information provided in the declaration together with the filer

• Publish summarized data on income and assets of high-level and other state officials and their immediate family members

The Asset Disclosure Department is responsible for setting the format and procedure for completing, submitting, registering, and storing the asset declarations of civil servants. It also accepts and reviews declarations of high-level public officials and civil servants, keeps the record of filers and submitted declarations, stores them safely, and ensures the safety of confidential information. It publishes consolidated information on the income and assets of high-level public officials and of their close relatives, in accordance with laws of the Kyrgyz Republic.

The Civil Service Agency's role has essentially consisted of the storing and record keeping of declarations. The Asset Disclosure Department annually receives the asset declarations of slightly more than 15,000 civil servants and approximately 1,400 political appointees (high-level public officials). After the declarations are submitted and the agency processes them, they are simply bundled and stored, since there is no prescribed mechanism for the agency or any other authority to handle the declarations.

The Asset Disclosure Department has four employees and is led by a department head who is responsible for department operations and who reports directly to the director of the Civil Service Agency.

Three other employees of the Asset Disclosure Department (one senior specialist and two lead specialists) report directly to the department head and the director of the Civil Service Agency, and are responsible for all routine work associated with the asset declaration process (figures 7.3 and 7.4).

Figure 7.3 The IAD Process for High-Level Public Officials, the Kyrgyz Republic

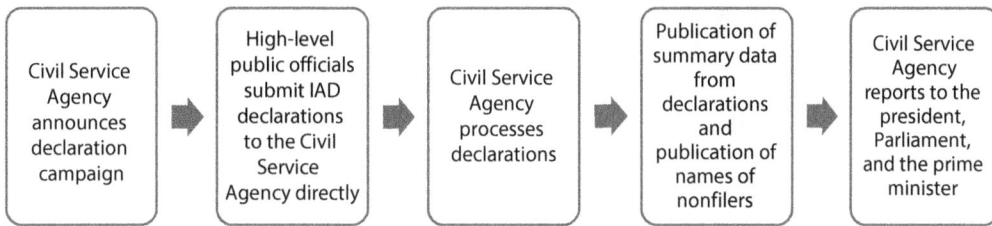

Figure 7.4 The IAD Process for Civil Servants, the Kyrgyz Republic

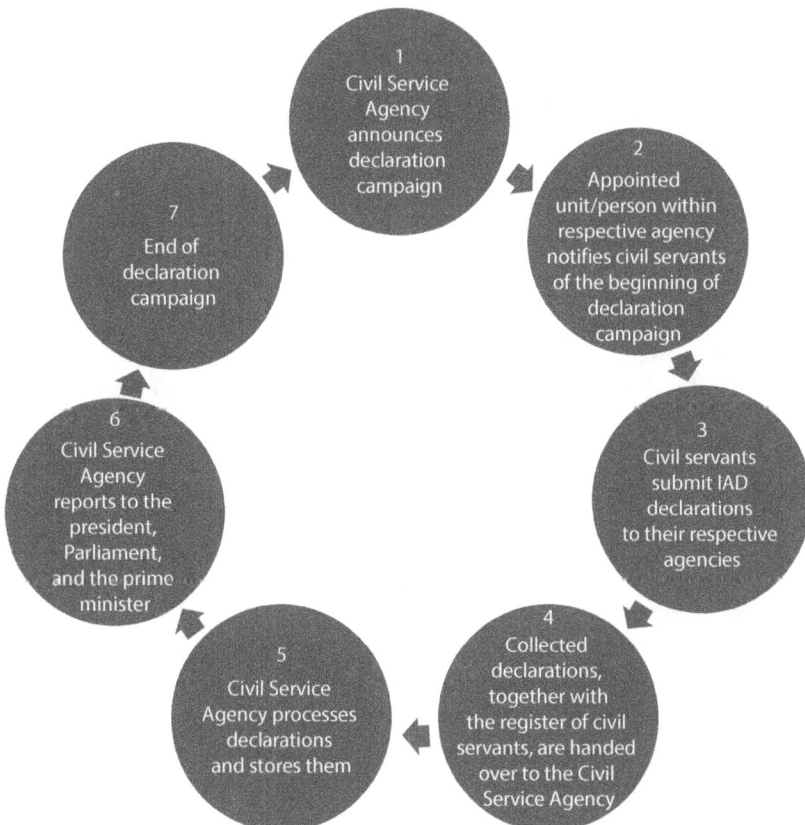

Resources and Procedures of the IAD System

Facilities and Use of Technology

The Civil Service Agency shares a building with the Central Electoral Commission of the Kyrgyz Republic. According to the Asset Disclosure Department, the building is adequately heated and maintains uninterrupted electricity.[7] All asset declarations are stored in locked metal safes in one of the rooms of the Asset Disclosure Department and in the adjacent isolated hallway. The declarations are stored for seven years, after which they are destroyed. Because of a lack of physical space for storing declarations, a proposal has been made to reduce the storage time for declarations of civil servants to only two years, and to three years for the declarations of persons occupying political and special positions.

Three of the four members of the Asset Disclosure Department share one room. Some of the declarations are also stored in the same room inside lockable shelves. All staff members have their own work computer equipped with database management software to process the submitted asset declarations.

Declarations are submitted in hard copy, and staff manually input the information contained in the declarations into the computer. After the declarations have been processed, the summary data are published on the Civil Service Agency website and in the official bulletin.

The working group has put forth several proposals regarding the transition of the Civil Service Agency IAD system to an automated regime for electronic submission of declarations. They are:[8]

- IAD declarations would be submitted to the Tax Inspectorate, which already has a fully automated system. The Tax Inspectorate will also be empowered to verify and investigate information provided in the declarations. However, this scenario would undermine the status of the Civil Service Agency, since it was initially created to deal with all matters related to public service. Delegation of part of its functions to the Tax Inspectorate would deprive the agency of its exclusive jurisdiction over public service matters.
- Declarations would be submitted to the Tax Inspectorate for verification, but suspicious declarations would be forwarded to the Civil Service Agency for further investigation.
- The Civil Service Agency would transition to a fully automated IAD system and would collect, verify, and investigate declarations, thus keeping all its functions and status as a body dealing with all matters of public service.

Human Resources

There are four staff members in the Asset Disclosure Department: department head, senior specialist, and two lead specialists. Given the large number of declarations received annually (roughly 17,000), each staff member must deal with 4,250 declarations. This is a symptom of broader budgetary constraints.[9]

As with all other state institutions, the Civil Service Agency hires personnel on the basis of competitive selection under the Law on Civil Service. The Civil

Service Agency announces the competition and coordinates the hiring process. All personnel must hold a degree from an institution of higher education and must know how to use computers and computer software. All of the members of the Asset Disclosure Department are career civil servants.

Under the 2004 Law on Civil Service, training is conducted at the initiative of the civil servants, manager, or state secretary of a public body. Staff also may participate in seminars and workshops dedicated to IAD. The law requires that performance evaluations be conducted once every three years.

Budget

The Civil Service Agency is financed from the state budget. The salaries of the agency officers, like those of all civil servants, are surprisingly low and do not correspond to the cost of living.

In 2008, the Kyrgyz Republic and the United States signed a Millennium Challenge Account Threshold Program Assistance Agreement, under which the Kyrgyz Republic would receive a grant of about US$15 million. Part of these funds would be allocated to finance improvements to the IAD system and to further develop the system's implementation mechanisms.[10] The overall Civil Service Agency's budget has been growing since 2008; in 2010, the budget nearly tripled (see figure 7.5 for a comparison of allocation and expenditures). It is not known, however, what proportion of the budget is allocated specifically to IAD administration.[11]

The Civil Service Agency also issued a standardized asset declaration form, which was approved by the director of the agency and reflects all statutory requirements. It is available both in hard copy and on the Civil Service Agency website.

Regulatory Function

The Civil Service Agency can issue rules regulating specific areas of its operation. It can also issue orders, instructions, and other regulations concerning civil service

Figure 7.5 Annual Budgets of the Civil Service Agency, the Kyrgyz Republic, 2008–10

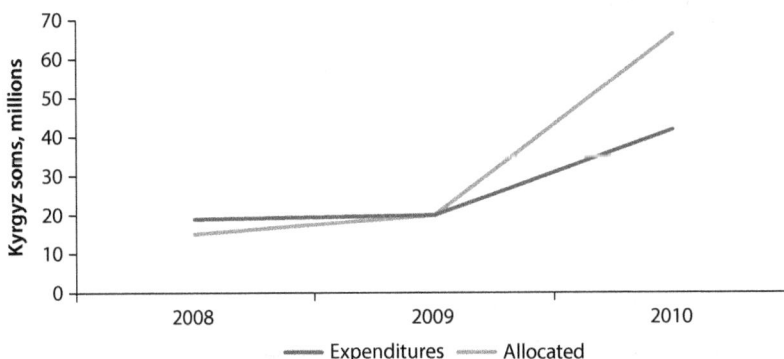

Source: Civil Service Agency, the Kyrgyz Republic.

matters that are mandatory for all other agencies. For example, the agency has produced the Regulation of Procedure, Terms and Time-Frames of Income and Asset Disclosure by Civil Servants, which contains procedural provisions and guidelines for submitting income and asset declarations by high-level public officials and all civil servants. The agency has also issued the Regulation of the Organizational Process of Asset Declaration, which contains guidelines for state agencies with regard to collecting and safekeeping declarations, keeping the register of filers, and delivering the declaration forms to the Civil Service Agency; and rules of monitoring, instructions for filing the asset declaration form outlining the procedure, and rules of monitoring state agencies by the Civil Service Agency in matters related to IAD.

Managing Submission Compliance

Under the Kyrgyz law, the Civil Service Agency has the authority to collect and review the asset declarations submitted by covered officials. The Asset Disclosure Department annually receives about 17,000 declarations of both civil servants and high-level public officials. Processing is done manually by only four people in the Asset Disclosure Department, including the department head, who is not involved in the technical work. Processing entails typing the information contained in the declarations and uploading it to the computer, and organizing the declarations alphabetically and chronologically; the hard copies are collected and stacked in the lockers after the information has been entered into the computers.

The Asset Disclosure Department has been able to closely monitor the submission compliance of asset declarations and produce accurate statistics. As of 2008, the Civil Service Agency had completed four rounds of asset declarations and, as of this writing, was in its fifth round. As of March 20, 2009, the agency had received 1,385 asset declarations from high-level public officials, which is 99.7 percent of the total number of 1,389 high-level public officials (table 7.4).

Table 7.4 Compliance Rate, the Kyrgyz Republic

Year	Political and other special positions (high-level officials)			Administrative positions (all civil servants)		
	Total number of filers	Actual number of submissions	Filed/ nonfiled	Total number of available civil service positions/ number of positions filled	Actual number of submissions	Filed (%)
2005	—	—	—	—	12,253	—
2006	1,003	911	91/9	15,718/14,774	12,739	86.2
2007	991	972	98/2	15,400/14,476	14,018	96.8
2008	1,407	1,395	99/1	15,877/14,969	15,141	95.4
2009	1,389	1,385	99.7/0.3	—	15,829	—

Source: Civil Service Agency, the Kyrgyz Republic.
Note: — = not available.

The data in table 7.4 illustrate that the compliance rate has increased each year. However, the statistics show only the overall compliance of *all* political officials and of *all* civil servants; they fail to reflect a detailed breakdown of the compliance rate by location, level, or affiliation, which is especially important to demonstrate transparency.

High-level public officials who fail to submit their income and asset declarations do not face serious sanctions; the names of the offenders are published in mass media outlets, and their violation is communicated to the president of the Kyrgyz Republic, the prime minister, and the speaker of Parliament. Civil servants who fail to file declarations face stricter sanctions, including reprimand, demotion, or dismissal.

According to the Civil Service Agency, it has been especially difficult to collect declarations from former public officials, who are required to file declarations for two years after termination of their office, pursuant to the IAD Law. The complications arise because of the change of address of former public officials, their relocation abroad, retirement, illness, and low awareness about the law's requirements.

Content Verification

Under the Law on Asset Declaration, the Civil Service Agency of the Kyrgyz Republic is authorized to review the asset declaration and, if necessary, request clarification from the tax authorities if the information in the declaration is found to be incomplete or false. There are few methods of content verification, and they include checking for incompatibilities between public function and private interests, checking for internal consistency within the form, comparing two or more forms from the same filer over time, cross-checking declarations with external records (registries, banks, tax agencies, and so forth), and lifestyle checks. Given the popular opinion that the Civil Service Agency does not have sufficient powers of content verification, even though the law leaves room for interpretation, it seems that the agency uses a strict interpretation of the provision and narrows content verification to only cross-checking with external records. The problem lies in the absence of provisions requiring external record holders to release their records to the Civil Service Agency for content verification purposes.

There has been some discussion about granting verification and investigation powers to the Tax Inspectorate, since it has the necessary infrastructure to perform content audit. However, the Civil Service Agency would then no longer serve the purpose for which it was created—to deal with all matters associated with the civil service. To avoid this, it was suggested that the Tax Inspectorate only collect and verify declarations and the Civil Service Agency investigate suspicious cases. The other option is to keep all powers within the Civil Service Agency. The agency would collect, verify, and investigate.

Box 7.2 presents details of IAD procedures performed by the Civil Service Agency of the Kyrgyz Republic.

Box 7.2 IAD Procedures Performed by the Kyrgyz Republic's Civil Service Agency

The Civil Service Agency is responsible for collecting income and asset declarations of all civil servants (15,877) and persons occupying political and other special state positions (1,389) in 2009 (the time of writing this report). This means that the Civil Service Agency must collect and store slightly more than 17,000 declarations. Because of the insufficient physical capacity of the Civil Service Agency, declarations are sometimes kept within a civil servant's own agency.

Managing the receipt of declarations

To facilitate the work of the Civil Service Agency, the law provides for the collection of declarations of civil servants by respective agencies. The head of that agency appoints a special person, usually within the human resources department, to be responsible for collecting declarations.[a] It is the responsibility of the person within the agency to transfer declarations to the Civil Service Agency. Other responsibilities of this person include notifying civil servants about new rounds of submission of asset declarations; ensuring the safekeeping of asset declarations, and their storage, where applicable; and keeping the registry of civil servants within their agency who have an obligation to declare.

The Asset Disclosure Department of the Civil Service Agency is then responsible for processing submitted income and asset declarations in accordance with the IAD legislation. According to the law, the Asset Disclosure Department has the authority to examine the contents of the declarations. However, should it find that the contents are not accurate or there are discrepancies between declarations, there is no legal framework for further action. Therefore, in practice, the Civil Service Agency can do little with submitted declarations other than to publish and store them.

Data management and publication of compliance results

After receiving the asset declarations, the staff of the Asset Disclosure Department manually input the information contained in the declarations into computers. If a public official fails to submit the declaration, the agency will publish his or her name in the mass media and will send the notice to the president of the Kyrgyz Republic, the prime minister, and the speaker of Parliament (see figures 7.3 and 7.4).

a. Regulation of the Organizational Process of Asset Declaration of the Kyrgyz Republic, January 9, 2007.

Investigatory Function

The Civil Service Agency does not have an investigatory function with relation to asset declarations. As part of its verification mandate, the agency is authorized to review information contained in the asset declaration and, if necessary, to request information from the tax authorities for clarification. It may also examine information submitted by the state bodies, local governments, commercial and noncommercial organizations, and individuals related to the income, liabilities, and property of persons covered by law and, if necessary, ask the filers to clarify information contained in declarations.

Interagency Collaboration

The Civil Service Agency does not have the authority to directly access the databases and information of other state bodies. However, this can be done through formal requests of the agency. Interagency collaboration is characterized as satisfactory by officials; however, since the agency does not perform verifications, this cooperation has not been tested. The Civil Service Agency can request information from the land registry and the motor vehicle registry. However, none of these entities is required to release information to the Civil Service Agency.

The IAD Law contains provisions on cooperation between the Civil Service Agency and the Tax Inspectorate. Upon request of the Civil Service Agency, the Tax Inspectorate is obliged to clarify any incomplete or false information submitted by the filers in the asset declarations. Again, this has not been tested in practice.

Public Access to Declarations

According to IAD Law, the Civil Service Agency is responsible for publishing the summaries of 1,389 declarations of high-level public officials on the agency's website and in the agency's official bulletin. However, there has been criticism in the press that the Civil Service Agency had removed the information on asset declarations of high-level public officials from its website. The time between the collection of declarations and their publication is not clearly specified in law, but practice shows that the time period is not more than five months.

The summaries of income and asset declarations of all other civil servants are made publicly available in accordance with the procedures specified by the Civil Service Agency. Access to declarations is provided upon individual request to the Civil Service Agency. The agency must respond to the request within one month from the date of receipt of the request, unless the response time has been extended by the director of the agency or his or her deputy. If the Civil Service Agency denies access to the declarations of civil servants, its refusal may be appealed administratively or in court.

The summary of the declaration includes the list of immovable property of the filer, total value of immovable property, transportation vehicles and stocks, and annual income. The high-level public officials' summary data also include information on income and assets of their immediate family members.

Education and Outreach

The Civil Service Agency publishes asset declaration manuals and guidelines on its website. The agency has also compiled all relevant laws and regulations, including various blank forms used in the asset declaration process by both civil servants and Civil Service Agency staff. The compilation is in the form of a brochure and can be used by filers, Civil Service Agency officers, and the general public.

Summary of Key Findings

This study found that, despite the lack of an effective content verification mechanism and the absence of serious sanctions for noncompliance, the IAD compliance rate by high-level public officials and other civil servants in the Kyrgyz Republic is high, and reached 99.0 percent and 95.4 percent, respectively, in 2009.[12] However, paradoxically, such a high compliance rate might indicate that something is wrong with the income and asset disclosure system, especially given the fact that no sanctions apply to high-level public officials and no effective verification mechanism is in place. In the absence of verification mechanisms or sanctions for filing violations, the requirement to submit a declaration becomes a formality with limited effectiveness as either a prevention or an enforcement mechanism. The Civil Service Agency was created as a central organ to deal with all issues related to civil service, including asset disclosure by civil servants. However, the law is not clear on the core functions of the IAD process, most notably verification and investigation, and sanctions for noncompliance. Although the IAD Law contains vague language on the content verification function of the Civil Service Agency, there is no established content verification mechanism.

To fill this gap, the government established a working group responsible for developing a mechanism of effective asset declaration verification. There have also been proposals to introduce criminal and administrative liability for noncompliance with asset disclosure legislation. There are currently no serious liability provisions in the asset disclosure laws for failure to file asset declarations.

The working group submitted its proposal on the new verification mechanism. In mid-2010, the Kyrgyz government underwent major reforms, which included folding the functions of the National Anti-Corruption Agency into the Civil Service Agency and renaming the Civil Service Agency the State Personnel Service, along with other internal reforms.

Notes

1. While this study was being prepared in early 2010, the Kyrgyz government underwent a period of political instability and a change of government structure. In April 2010, the Kyrgyz Republic experienced a second revolution followed by tragic ethnic clashes in the south of the country. A new government came to power and new parliamentary elections were held in October 2010.

2. For clarity, we refer to the "Civil Service Agency" throughout the chapter when referring to this body.

3. The Anti-Corruption Strategy of the Kyrgyz Republic national strategy is available at http://www.adc.kg/index.php?option=com_content&view=article&id=15&Itemid=&lang=en.

4. OSCE 2005.

5. This is the National Strategy of Fight Against Corruption in the Kyrgyz Republic; http://spf.gov.kg/index.php?option=com_content&task=view&id=415&Itemid=#.

6. The structure may have changed as a result of events in the Kyrgyz Republic that occurred after this report was drafted.

7. The end of 2008 and 2009 were marked by an energy crisis in the Kyrgyz Republic. All buildings were subject to rotating blackouts because there were insufficient power resources.

8. This list of proposals is based on an informal conversation with one of the asset disclosure experts in the Kyrgyz Republic.

9. Burdescu et al. 2010.

10. Millennium Challenge Account Threshold Program Assistance Agreement, Annex 1. See http://www.mcc.gov/documents/agreements/tpaa-english-kyrgyzrepublic.pdf.

11. www.budget.kg.

12. That is, 99 percent of high-level officials occupying political or special state positions.

References

Burdescu, R., G. J. Reid, S. E. Trapnell, and D. W. Barnes. 2010. "Income and Asset Disclosure Systems: Establishing Good Governance through Accountability." *Economic Premise* 17 (June), Poverty Reduction and Economic Reduction Network, World Bank, Washington, DC.

OSCE (Organization for Security and Co-operation in Europe). 2005. Press release in Russian, February 28. http://www.osce.org/item/8941.html.

CHAPTER 8

Mongolia

Daniel W. Barnes

Overview

On November 1, 2006, Mongolia enacted the Anti-Corruption Law of 2006, which created a comprehensive income and asset disclosure (IAD) system (see box 8.1). It also created a new, independent agency to fight corruption and administer the IAD program. In 2011, the Independent Agency against Corruption (IAAC) was in its third year and had completed the third round of asset declarations in Mongolia.

In many respects, the IAAC has achieved remarkable success in a very short time. The submission rate of income and asset declarations has reached 99.9 percent, and declarations have been used in the prosecution of at least one high-ranking government official for underlying corrupt acts that were substantiated, in part, through the use of his declaration. However, the legal framework surrounding broader issues of corruption remains vague. For instance, the law neither provides a definition of a conflict of interest nor prohibits such a conflict. Nor is there an explicit law against illicit enrichment by public officials (though there are antibribery laws and other criminal laws that cover most elements of illicit enrichment).

The Mongolian IAD system places an emphasis on submission verification and public availability of all declarations. However, because of budgetary and staffing constraints, the IAAC physically stores the asset declarations of only the top 256 government officials. The remaining 50,000+ declarations continue to be stored within the individual agencies where the filers work. This presents a significant obstacle to making the declarations easily accessible to the public.

This report is based on desk research and the findings of a visit to Mongolia in March 2009 undertaken on behalf of the Stolen Asset Recovery (StAR) Initiative and the Governance & Public Sector Management Unit of the World Bank to examine the country's IAD system. Please note that all data reflect conditions as of March 2009 and do not include developments subsequent to that date. Special thanks are extended to Zahid Hasnain (Senior Public Sector Specialist, East Asia Economic Policy and Public Sector Department) for his assistance throughout the preparation of this report. Further thanks are extended to Verena Fritz (Senior Governance Specialist, Governance & Public Sector Management Unit, Poverty Reduction and Economic Management Sector) for her review of the case study early in the project.

Box 8.1 Snapshot of the Income and Asset Disclosure System in Mongolia

Created by the Anti-Corruption Law of 2006, the IAD system in Mongolia is scaling up its capacity. The law created the Independent Agency against Corruption (IAAC), which is responsible for the management of the IAD program. Entering its third year, the IAAC has achieved significant progress in a relatively short time, and currently reports a 99.9 percent submission compliance rate. Despite its success on that front, the IAAC has faced some challenges with regard to resources and obtaining cooperation from outside agencies and banks. However, these challenges are slowly being overcome with increased coordination. Mongolia's experience is a useful example of the gradual implementation of an IAD system at the early stages.

Key elements of the system include:

- **A design intended to detect and prosecute illicit enrichment.** The Anti-Corruption Law and the IAAC were designed with the purpose of combating illicit enrichment. However, the IAAC has repeatedly expressed a desire to expand the system to include conflicts of interest, which will require the adoption of a law by Parliament defining conflicts of interest and giving the IAAC the power to monitor them.
- **Decentralized submission system, with centralized monitoring.** Currently, only the top 256 government officials declare their income and assets directly to the IAAC. The remaining 50,000+ officials submit declarations to designated ethics officers in their individual agencies, enabling the IAAC to monitor submission compliance with a staff of nine. Given the resource constraints faced by the IAAC and government, this appears to have been an effective approach to ensuring compliance in the absence of electronic filing or submission systems.
- **Verification procedures and trained staff who investigate.** The IAAC has the power to verify the content of declarations, but currently verifies content only if an allegation of wrongdoing is made against an official. This is due, in part, to resource constraints, to the decentralized paper submission process, and, presumably, to the very large size of the disclosing population. The IAAC has plans to create an electronic submission and verification system to better streamline the process.
- **Administrative sanctions for noncompliance that are enforced.** Administrative sanctions are the only sanctions available for failure to file or for disclosing false information, but they are enforced swiftly: 50 civil servants were dismissed in 2008 for failing to submit asset declarations. Criminal sanctions are available for underlying corrupt acts, and income and asset declarations have already been used in such prosecutions.
- **Public access to income and asset declarations.** Access to modified versions of all income and asset declarations is granted to the public. These versions contain summaries of classes of assets and their total values, which enable limited lifestyle checks should members of the public wish to perform such checks. However, despite access being free, the majority of the public seem to be unaware of the existence of these declarations and their content.

Further, the press is relatively weak in Mongolia, and includes little investigative journalism, thus raising questions about the ability of the press to adequately monitor the IAD system.

Moreover, the Mongolian system places relatively little emphasis on verifying the accuracy of asset declarations. This appears to have been a conscious decision, in recognition of the difficulty of verifying the declarations against other government databases—such as the land registry and traffic registry—which may or may not be accurate themselves. In the presence of an active press and lifestyle checks by community groups or the IAAC itself, the database verification system could indeed be unnecessary, but such is not the case in Mongolia.

In the end, this study found that Mongolia and the IAAC have implemented the IAD system quite quickly and have achieved what appears to be an extremely high submission rate. The agency has expressed a desire to increase its budget and staffing levels while also recognizing the challenges posed by the verification process and engaging the media.

Background

Mongolia has been the focus of significant research in the last few years into perceptions and patterns of corruption. For instance, Transparency International has conducted surveys in Mongolia since 2004 and scored perceptions of corruption inside the country at 2.7 (on a 10-point scale, with 1 corresponding to high perceptions of corruption and 10 corresponding to no perception of corruption) for four of the last five years.[1] Furthermore, a joint U.S. Agency for International Development and Asia Foundation corruption assessment, performed in June 2005, found that the distinction between the private and public sector in terms of corruption has been eroding steadily, with conflicts of interest becoming more common throughout the government.[2]

Indeed, with the fall of communism and the transition to capitalism in Mongolia, new opportunities for corruption by public officials were created. Throughout the 1990s, public perceptions of corruption rose. Then, during the 2001 presidential campaign, the candidates for that office voluntarily declared their assets as a mechanism to demonstrate their commitment to combating corruption and to demonstrate their own fidelity to the rule of law.

However, during 2000–04, the State Great Khural (Parliament) was controlled by a single party with an absolute majority. This control, according to individuals interviewed during the mission to Ulaanbaatar, dampened incentives for changing the existing framework for nonpublic disclosure of assets.

The parliamentary elections of 2004 seem to have changed this dynamic. Corruption was highlighted by both of the main parties during the campaign, and transparency with respect to assets held by public officials became an increasingly important element of the discourse surrounding corruption issues.

The election produced near parity in the State Great Khural between the two largest political parties. This balance is believed to have opened political space to allow serious debate about the adoption of a new anticorruption law and, therefore, a new asset declaration regime. Adding to the dialogue surrounding IAD issues in Mongolia was the push, since 2000, by the United Nations Development Programme for public disclosure of assets. The result was the creation of a parliamentary working group on anticorruption that included members from different parties.

Simultaneously, civil society groups, alternative political parties, and nongovernmental organizations all became actively engaged in applying pressure on the working group. In combination with perceived public support for the public disclosure of assets, the working group ultimately endorsed the concept, and the State Great Khural adopted the Anti-Corruption Law in 2006.

The new law created the IAAC, which is responsible for the administration of the new IAD system. The structure of both the law and the IAAC will be discussed in detail below.

The IAAC was, in 2011, in its third year and had completed its third annual round of the collection of income and asset declarations of public officials. As will be discussed below, the compliance rate with the requirement to submit an asset declaration has steadily risen and was currently 99.9 percent in 2011. Despite the success of the IAAC in ensuring the timely submission of the declarations, however, there are lingering concerns about the IAD process.

For instance, members of Parliament have expressed concern that the IAD system can be used as a weapon against political enemies. Because the IAAC is required to investigate the validity of an asset declaration by a public official if an allegation of lying is made against that official, there is a worry that baseless charges may be made by politicians or those aligned with a certain politician against political rivals. Even if the official is found to have accurately declared his or her assets, the fear is that the allegation alone could prove politically devastating, particularly since there is now an official apparatus for investigating these charges, which may lend credibility to charges in the eyes of the public.

Whether or not these concerns have a basis in fact, their very existence has the potential to weaken political support for the IAD system in the short to medium term. If, however, the IAAC demonstrates its independence and decisively acts to either clear allegations or prosecute instances of corruption, this perception could be weakened.

Connected to this concern that the system could be used as a political weapon is the perception that the civil service remains highly political. Although, by law, the IAAC is an independent body and its employees must remain nonpartisan, the public perception of the overall government is one of politicization. Recent efforts may be changing the reality of politicization, even if perceptions are slow to change. For instance, the Law on Civil Service requires that most civil servants be nonpartisan by prohibiting political party membership and encouraging increasingly meritocratic forms of hiring and promotion.

Despite these legal changes, it has been asserted that the public continues to believe that the rule of law is weak in Mongolia. In addition to perceptions that the rich can bribe judges to rule in their favor, there is also a belief that the inability to strictly enforce contracts has provided incentives for corruption in the first place. Individuals enforce their own contracts with bribes and are then able to hide their illicit dealings, making it very difficult for the IAAC to reveal corrupt acts or the existence of illegally obtained assets.

This difficulty is reinforced by perceptions that official records—such as the land registry and the tax registry—do not reflect the true holdings of individuals. For instance, if an individual has not registered his or her house, and then fails to declare that house on his or her asset declaration, the IAAC will fail to discover this omission on the asset declaration when it checks the land registry.

Because of these concerns, there is a lingering belief that the IAAC only *collects* income and asset declarations but does not actually do anything with them. In part, this is probably the product of high expectations when the Anti-Corruption Law was adopted in 2006. As noted, the law was enacted as the culmination of years of both grassroots and high-level political activism on corruption.

With the 2008 presidential and parliamentary elections, the Mongolian People's Revolutionary Party seized control of the majority of parliamentary seats. In the wake of this, and as a result of a nearly decade-long campaign against corruption, nongovernmental organizations and parliamentarians themselves have begun voicing the belief that fatigue is developing in the public with respect to anticorruption efforts. Because of this, the political will to maintain a focus on the IAAC appears to be waning, particularly with the onset of the financial crisis in the fall of 2008.

The IAD Legal Framework in Mongolia

The 2006 Anti-Corruption Law provides the legal framework for IAD in Mongolia. The law provides extensive coverage and, in conjunction with the IAD form issued by the IAAC, requires all public officials to declare specific categories of assets.

Coverage of Officials

Article 4 of the Anti-Corruption Law of 2006 specifies the persons subject to an income and asset declaration. Specifically, Article 4.1.1 covers the following individuals: "Officials holding political, administrative or special office of the state, whether appointed or elected, whether permanently or temporarily." This language covers the head of government, ministers, members of Parliament, and civil servants of the national government, as well as governors of the local *aimags* (provinces). However, Article 4 also covers candidates for election and certain nongovernmental organization officials.

In short, the breadth of the law's coverage is extensive. Indeed, in the third and most recent round of declarations, 52,800 individuals submitted asset declarations to the relevant authorities. Furthermore, the asset declaration form approved by Parliament requires covered individuals to declare the assets and income of family members, as well as their own.

Table 8.1 Contents of the Income and Asset Declaration, Mongolia

Personal data

Name

Date of birth

Marital status

Assets

Real estate

Movable assets

Cash and investments

Cash

Investments

Liabilities

Loans

Liabilities

Income

All income and sources

Content of Declarations

The law and the asset declaration form issued by the IAAC, with approval by Parliament, requires specific classes of assets and income to be declared. Mongolia requires all covered individuals to declare their real estate, movable assets, cash, investments, loans and liabilities, and all income (table 8.1). The declaration form itself requires that the income and assets of family members of covered individuals also be included.

Filing Frequency

The Anti-Corruption Law of 2006 also specifies the exact deadlines for filing asset declarations. All covered individuals must declare their assets, using the approved declaration form, within 30 days of their election or appointment to office. Then, by February 15 of every year, officials must submit a new declaration. If a "substantial" change in income or assets occurs after the yearly declaration, the official is required to notify the IAAC of the change. Mongolia does not require asset declarations upon leaving office or at any time after the public official has left office.

Submission Compliance and Content Verification

According to Article 11 of the Anti-Corruption Law of 2006, the depository body for asset declarations depends upon where the public official works. For top officials, the depository body is the IAAC, which was also created by the 2006 law. These officials include the president, prime minister, ministers, members of Parliament, and governors of *aimags*. The remainder of covered officials are required to submit their asset declarations to the designated ethics official of the agency that employs them. The IAAC is also required by law to monitor the submission process to ensure that all covered public officials comply with the requirement to declare their assets.

Furthermore, the IAAC is responsible for verifying the accuracy of submitted income and asset declarations in certain instances, as prescribed by Article 13 of the Anti-Corruption Law. The agency has been provided the authority to verify declarations at its discretion, but is specifically required to analyze those declarations that contain clerical errors and to analyze the declarations of officials who have complaints alleging inaccuracies on their declarations lodged against them.

Sanctions

The Anti-Corruption Law creates administrative sanctions for public officials who fail to abide by the asset declaration requirement. Specifically, an official who fails to file, files late, provides false information on a declaration, or provides an incomplete declaration may be suspended from duties or dismissed from office. The law does not provide for fines or criminal sanctions.

These sanctions are distinct from those that already exist in the criminal code regarding corrupt acts. Should the income and asset declaration of a public official reveal underlying criminal behavior, that revelation may be used during the investigation into that wrongdoing. The sanctions outlined above would have no bearing on the imposition of further sanctions—be they fines, criminal sanctions, or further administrative sanctions—for a finding of guilt for other behavior outside the specific requirement to declare assets.

Public Access to Declarations

Finally, Article 14 of the Anti-Corruption Law of 2006 mandates that the asset declarations of all officials be made available to the public. This requirement takes different forms, depending on the seniority of the official. In effect, the asset declarations of the top 256 public officials in Mongolia are published annually in the country's *Government News Magazine* (*Turiin medeelel*).

Although the income and asset declarations of civil servants are not published in the media, they must be made available, upon request, to the public. Again, the IAAC is the responsible agency for facilitating the availability of these asset declarations, although the individual agencies within which any given official works physically maintain the asset declarations.

Mandate and Structure of the IAD Agency

As noted, the IAAC was created as an independent body by the Anti-Corruption Law of 2006. Its mandate is to prevent corruption, investigate instances of corruption, and raise public awareness regarding the fight against corruption in Mongolia. Although its mandate extends beyond the IAD regime, it is the principal agency responsible for the implementation and execution of that system.

The agency has 90 employees and is headed by a commissioner general who is nominated by the president and appointed by Parliament. The IAAC is organized into four departments and four services: the Investigation Department, the Prevention and Public Awareness Department, the Supervision and Analysis Department, and the Administrative Department. The services are the Research

Figure 8.1 Organizational Chart of the IAAC, Mongolia

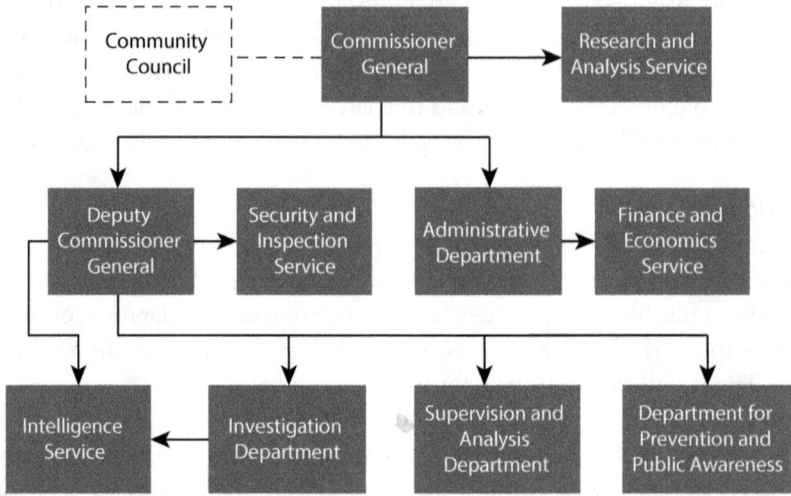

Source: IAAC, Mongolia.

and Analysis Service, the Intelligence Service, the Security and Inspection Service, and the Finance and Economics Service (figure 8.1).

The primary unit responsible for implementing and overseeing the IAD system is the Supervision and Analysis Department, which has the explicit authority to:

- Oversee the IAD system, including administration, submission, and storage of declarations
- Collect and store declarations from high-level officials, as defined in Article 14 of the Anti-Corruption Law of 2006
- Collect summaries of the declarations of all other officials
- Verify that all declarations are submitted and initiate sanctions against those who fail to comply
- Prepare reports for the public regarding compliance with the requirement of officials to declare their assets; respond to requests from the public for information within three days
- Provide training for declarers and answer, within three days, requests for guidance by declarers

Functions and Tasks of the Supervision and Analysis Department of the IAAC

There are three main functions carried out by the Supervision and Analysis Department.

Submission and Storage of Asset Declarations

- Maintain the IAD submission system: organize IAD submissions, oversee storage in state and local administrative organizations, incorporate IAD reports, and ensure public dissemination of enforcement procedures for the reporting and disclosure of income and asset declarations

- Receive and store declarations from high-level officials
- Publish the declarations of high-level officials in the *Government News Magazine*
- Conduct training for filers on how to properly prepare their income and asset declarations, and training for officials responsible for receiving and storing the declarations of officials within their agencies
- Create a toolkit and manuals to facilitate this training
- Upon the request of a declarer, orally or in writing, provide preliminary advice on how to file the income and asset declaration form, how to provide additional information on the form, and how to register the form, while maintaining strict confidentiality of all communication with the filer

Review of Asset Declarations
- Verify the submission of declaration by officials
- Review the list of officials who are required to declare their assets
- Perform inspection of declarations in accordance with legal review procedure: Inspections are performed randomly, in response to a complaint, upon late submission, when there is a lack of explanation as to the source of an asset, or other missing information on the declaration
- Supervise activities of all officials within government agencies in charge of receiving asset declarations

Research and Analysis
- Analyze income and asset declaration submission statistics and prepare reports on the administration of the IAD process
- Assess the implementation and execution of IAD registration, storage, and reporting, and prepare proposals to improve the process and resolve any problems
- Conduct surveys among declarers and the public for the purpose of analyzing the functioning of the IAD system; create a database for IADs and statistics related to the system

In addition, the Supervision and Analysis Department is required to issue regular reports to the commissioner general that verify that (1) all operational procedures were strictly adhered to, (2) stakeholders within and outside the public administration were consulted, (3) all deadlines were met, (4) the integrity of the report has been maintained at all times, and (5) the report contains reasonable proposals and the data included have been verified.

Structure and Organization of the Supervision and Analysis Department of the IAAC
The Supervision and Analysis Department is led by a department head who is responsible for the day-to-day operations of the department and who reports directly to the commissioner general of the IAAC. The department head is responsible for managing the department by ensuring organizational coherence,

assigning functions to individual employees, monitoring job performance and task completion, and reviewing the products of the employees' work. The department head is also responsible for coordinating the work of his or her department with the other IAAC departments through direct communication with the heads of those departments and in conjunction with the commissioner general.

Under the department head are two senior officers and seven other officers. The senior officers are responsible for monitoring and directing the activities of the seven officers and for facilitating the review of income and asset declarations. The seven officers are assigned a subset of the top 256 income and asset declarations to process, and are also responsible for the review and verification of the summaries of the income and asset declarations submitted to the IAAC by the other government agencies.

Fundamentals of the Income and Asset Declaration Process in Mongolia

Although the IAAC is the principal agency responsible for administering the IAD system in Mongolia, in reality, the agency has direct control over the declarations of only the top 256 public officials. The system, as outlined in the Anti-Corruption Law of 2006, relies on a decentralized submission and collection process. All public officials, aside from the top 256, are required to submit their income and asset declarations to their direct employing agency. In practice, this means that each agency designates at least one official to be responsible for physically receiving the declarations of all covered officials within that agency.

This official is responsible for entering the subtotals for each type of asset (real estate, bank accounts, and so forth) held by each filer into a Microsoft Excel spreadsheet. This spreadsheet is then sent to the IAAC for review. Any declaration that is not filled out completely or that contains any errors is flagged for review by the IAAC. Anyone may report suspected infractions of the income and asset declaration requirement or suspected corruption to the IAAC. The income and asset declaration of an official against whom an allegation has been made must also be verified for accuracy.

The verification process is regulated by internal rules of the Supervision and Analysis Department and follows a set procedure. Broadly speaking, an officer will be assigned the task of verifying any given declaration and will contact the appropriate government or private entity to verify the assets declared. This may entail contacting the land registry, traffic registry, and private banks. If discrepancies are discovered, the case is referred to the Investigation Department, which is responsible for investigating whether the public official in question has committed a corrupt act.

If no underlying crime is uncovered, the official will face only dismissal or a reduction in pay for presenting false information on his or her asset declaration. If, however, the Investigation Department uncovers evidence of corruption or another crime, the case is referred to the Ministry of Justice for prosecution. Decisions regarding whether to actually prosecute are made solely by the Ministry of Justice.

Resources and Procedures of the IAD System

To assess the functioning and the unique characteristics of the IAD process in Mongolia, a set of processes and correlating indicators have been developed. These focus on the practical aspects of implementing an IAD process and take into account the available physical facilities, technology, human resources, administrative capacity, and so forth. By mapping Mongolia's structure and capabilities against this framework, we hope to gain a better understanding of possible strengths and weaknesses of the implementation of the country's IAD system.

Facilities and Use of Technology

The IAAC is housed in a building originally built in 1960. It contains 22 rooms with an average size of 9 meters by 16 meters, within each of which three to four officials work. This results in an average space per employee of 36 to 48 square meters. According to the IAAC, the building is adequately heated and has uninterrupted electricity. The building maintains storage capacity for holding the physical income and asset declarations of the top 256 filers. These declarations are held in metal lockers that are sealed with wax seals. The declarations are stored in this building for two years; they are then sent to an archive for the remaining three years they are required to be maintained.

The IAAC maintains a dedicated staff of information technology professionals who facilitate the use of computers, software, and networking by all public officials responsible for executing the IAD system. Every officer within the Supervision and Analysis Department has his or her own computer to use at the office. All asset declarations are transferred from hard copy to spreadsheets for easier use and analysis.

Currently, asset declarations are submitted only in hard copy. The IAAC has developed a proposal to create an online portal through which all filers would be able to submit their income and asset declarations in electronic form. However, by the end of 2011, this proposal was still in its early stages.

Human Resources

As an independent agency, the IAAC uses competitive recruitment to hire new staff. Potential hires must have relevant work experience and a minimum of four years of postsecondary education, although many have the equivalent of a Master's degree and all personnel are required to know how to use computer software. Because the agency was only beginning its third year at the time this report was compiled, it was not possible to determine the three-year turnover rates for staff.

The agency provides explicit job descriptions to its staff, which clearly delineate their responsibilities. It has also produced operating manuals designed to familiarize both the agency staff and income and asset declaration filers with the declaration process.

The IAAC provides in-depth orientation at the time of hiring all personnel, who receive training in all administrative processes and in all laws and regulations

Income and Asset Disclosure • http://dx.doi.org/10.1596/978-0-8213-9796-1

governing the IAD system. In conformity with Mongolian civil service standards, the IAAC conducts yearly reviews of employee performance.

Budget

The IAAC is guaranteed a certain level of budget continuity by the Anti-Corruption Law of 2006. In 2008, the IAAC received 3.8 billion Mongolian togrogs (approximately US$2.9 million). The salaries of the officers in the Supervision and Analysis Department are, anecdotally, higher than those of civil servants of equivalent seniority throughout the Mongolian government. Specific salary figures were not, however, supplied. Despite the relatively solid funding for the provision of salaries, the IAAC budget allowed for only six officers, two senior officers, and one department head to handle the 52,800 declarations submitted in February 2009. The IAAC is directly responsible for receiving declarations from only the top 256 officials in the country. The remaining declarations are received by approximately 1,190 officials within 120 public organizations. However, the IAAC also receives summaries of all declarations from those 120 public organizations, and it is expected to provide oversight of all these organizations for their role in the IAD system. The IAAC maintains an accounting system in accordance with that used by other government agencies, and the details are published on both the IAAC and Ministry of Finance websites.

Regulatory Function

The IAAC Supervision and Analysis Department indicated that it produces a yearly report containing recommendations for alterations to the IAD system that can be adopted by the IAAC commissioner general in the form of legally binding requirements.

The standardized filing form, which was produced by the IAAC and approved by Parliament, reflects the statutory requirements provided for by the Anti-Corruption Law of 2006—as well as additional reporting requirements such as those for spouses and children—for all assets that are declared on the form, rather than only the specific classes of assets provided for in the law.

The filing form, including an example of a filled-out form, is available both in hard copy upon request and on the IAAC website. In 2009, the department prepared a new asset declaration form, with additional guidance contained on the form. The IAAC has stated that it plans to submit the form to Parliament for approval for use as the declaration form for all filers in subsequent years.

Further, as discussed below in the section on interagency collaboration, the IAAC has forged agreements with banks to verify data provided on the asset declaration forms against records maintained by the banks, including the balances of accounts. Mongolian law was unclear on whether banks were required to provide this information, so the IAAC opted to negotiate with each individual bank to obtain access to their records. These agreements, however, were negotiated and were not the result of a legally binding regulation issued by the IAAC. Because of this, the ability of the IAAC to issue regulations that clarify legal issues remains unclear.

Managing Submission Compliance

The Anti-Corruption Law of 2006, which created the IAAC, gives the IAAC the explicit authority to receive and review income and asset declarations by covered public officials.

However, as mentioned, the IAAC is directly responsible for receiving the declarations of only the top 256 public officials (the president, members of Parliament, *aimag* governors, and a few other positions provided by statute). The remainder of the declarations (52,800 of them in 2009) are received by the agencies within which these other public officials work. According to the IAAC, approximately 1,190 officials are responsible for collecting declarations within 120 public organizations. These officials collect the income and asset declarations of all covered officials by February 15 of every year, then enter the data into spreadsheets and send these spreadsheets and reports to the IAAC by March 1 of every year.

Within the IAAC, there are six officers who are ultimately responsible for handling all 52,800 declarations. On average, each of these staff members is responsible for the declarations of 35 high-level officials and 10,000 public servants from 18 public organizations. Despite the large numbers, the officers within the Supervision and Analysis Department of the IAAC have been able to closely monitor and verify the submission of declarations by all covered officials. In large measure, this is because of the decentralized nature of the IAD system in Mongolia, where designated IAD officials within individual agencies of the government are responsible for the initial submission of a declarant's IAD form.

Covered officials who fail to declare their income and assets face immediate dismissal from office, and the Supervision and Analysis Department has been able to implement this sanction in the first three years it received declarations. In 2009, 64 individuals submitted their income and asset declarations late, and 37 failed to submit them at all (out of 52,800 filers). All 37 who failed to file were fired from their jobs, and the IAAC was, at the time of writing, investigating the 64 individuals who submitted their declarations late. If a valid reason is presented for the tardiness of submission, an individual may only face suspension of pay for a few months. However, most late filers will be dismissed from public service for their failure to abide by the deadline.

In order to execute this submission verification function, the IAAC keeps a regularly updated list of all parties obligated to declare their income and assets. Further, the IAAC communicates directly with those obligated through correspondence, through the 1,190 officials in the 120 public organizations responsible for receiving declarations, through its website, and through the media.

Content Verification

Mongolia's IAD system has been focused primarily on ensuring compliance with the requirement to submit an income and asset declaration. Although verification audits do occur, they are distinctly limited, in part because of the number of officers available to perform the task. The Anti-Corruption Law does provide the legal authority to the IAAC to conduct verification audits at its discretion, but the law also requires audits for any income and asset declaration that contains any readily observable errors (such as failing to provide explanations for the sources of assets or failing to disclose certain types of assets).

Further, the law requires the IAAC to investigate the income and asset declaration if an allegation of corruption or of lying on the declaration is made against a particular public official. These allegations can be made by any member of the public, anonymously or not. In 2008, five of the income and asset declarations of the top 256 officials were audited because of allegations of corruption, suggesting that this avenue of political persecution is not being heavily used, as had been feared. The audits found no inaccuracies in the declarations; however, one of the accused was prosecuted for corruption and electoral code violations, and was found guilty in 2008.

The IAAC does not use random audits to verify the accuracy of declarations. The agency has a policy designed to shield it from charges of politically motivated investigations, whereby it does not audit any asset declaration unless a specific allegation has been made, or if the public official has failed to properly complete the declaration form. During research for this report, different officers within the IAAC, on two different occasions, stressed the agency's efforts to maintain its independence and ensure the public's continued perception that it does not have political motivations. However, despite these policies, relying on accusations as the primary trigger for an audit still allows for politicization of the IAD system, albeit on the part of the accusers rather than the IAAC. As mentioned, Mongolia has a highly partisan society, which poses significant risks for an anticorruption agency attempting to remain independent and nonpartisan.

Importantly, because Mongolia does not have a conflict-of-interest law, verification audits are designed solely to determine whether an income and asset declaration is accurate. However, despite the emphasis on determining accuracy, there is no criminal law against lying on a declaration. The sole sanction for lying on a declaration is dismissal from public service. In terms of criminal liability, the sole use of the declaration form is as an additional resource during an investigation or prosecution of an underlying corrupt act.

Box 8.2 provides an overview of the procedures performed by Mongolia's IAAC.

Investigatory Function

The IAAC has two investigatory functions. One resides primarily within the Supervision and Analysis Department and is focused on determining the accuracy of income and asset declarations. The other investigatory function is housed within the Investigation Department, which is the principal organ for performing detailed investigations into corrupt acts by public officials. The officers within this department perform undercover operations and investigate all aspects of possible instances of corruption. They can access income and asset declaration forms during these investigations.

To verify the accuracy of declarations, officers in the Supervision and Analysis Department check the declaration against official records, such as the land

---

Box 8.2 IAD Procedures Performed by Mongolia's IAAC

Receipt of hardcopy declarations

Although the IAAC is the principal agency responsible for administering the IAD system in Mongolia, in reality the agency directly handles the declarations of only the top 256 public officials. The system, as outlined in the Anti-Corruption Law of 2006, relies on a partially delegated submission and collection process. All public officials, aside from the top 256, are required to submit their asset declarations to their direct employing agency. In practice, this means that each agency designates at least one official to be responsible for physically receiving the declarations of all covered officials within that agency.

Data entry for administrative and submission compliance purposes

The official designated by each agency is responsible for entering into a spreadsheet the subtotals for each type of asset (real estate, bank accounts, and so forth) held by each filer. This spreadsheet is then sent to the IAAC for review. Any declaration that is not filled out completely or that contains errors is flagged for review by the IAAC.

Verification of declarations

The verification process is regulated by internal rules of the IAAC Supervision and Analysis Department and follows a set procedure. Broadly speaking, an officer will be assigned the task of verifying any given declaration and will contact the appropriate government or private entity to verify the assets declared. This may entail contacting the land registry, traffic registry, and private banks. If discrepancies are discovered, the case is referred to the Investigation Department, which is responsible for investigating whether the public official in question has committed a corrupt act.

Receipt and response to corruption allegations

Anyone may report suspected infractions of the income and asset declaration requirement or suspected corruption to the IAAC. The declaration of an official against whom an allegation has been made must also be verified for accuracy.

Application of administrative sanctions and referral of cases for investigation or prosecution

If no underlying crime is uncovered, then the official will face only dismissal or a reduction in pay for presenting false information on his or her declaration. If, however, the Investigation Department uncovers evidence of corruption or another crime, the case is referred to the Ministry of Justice for prosecution. Decisions regarding whether to prosecute are made solely by the Ministry of Justice.

---

registry, traffic registry, and bank records. These officers do not, however, perform lifestyle checks. The Investigation Department may perform such checks, but the officers within this department are not responsible for verifying the accuracy of declarations. Rather, their investigations are concerned with discovering evidence of a corrupt act. Because of this, a detailed description of their work is not included in this report.

Income and Asset Disclosure • http://dx.doi.org/10.1596/978-0-8213-9796-1

Interagency Collaboration

The Supervision and Analysis Department reports that it has received excellent cooperation from all government agencies with which it communicates in the process of verifying asset declarations. Because the Anti-Corruption Law of 2006 provides significant authority to the IAAC, these other government agencies have been responsive during the verification process. The head of the Supervision and Analysis Department was not aware of any instances of a government agency failing to provide requested information.

However, a source of concern is the accuracy of the records maintained by the land registry and the tax service. According to various nongovernmental organizations, many Mongolians fail to register their land in an effort to avoid paying the registration fee. This problem is compounded by unclear property rights for sections of Ulaanbaatar and by communal property rights in rural areas. It is alleged that buildings are constructed on public parks in Ulaanbaatar or other vacant lots, regardless of whether the builder has a legal right to erect a building on that location, and that these buildings are not registered with the land registry.

A similar concern was raised regarding the tax administration. Nongovernmental organizations, local business leaders, and members of the government all asserted that many businesses and individuals maintain two sets of records, one for the tax authorities and one that reflects reality. In 2008, a law was enacted that provided a six-month amnesty for all businesses and individuals during which they could report their true income and assets to the tax administration without fear of penalties or prosecution.

Some 2,908 companies declared their true assets, representing 5 percent of registered companies in Mongolia. However, only 769 individuals declared their true income and assets to the tax administration. The amnesty revealed US$3.923 billion in assets that had previously been hidden. The tax revenue generated by this newly declared wealth is approximately US$370 million out of a yearly government of Mongolia budget of approximately US$2 billion.

Public Access to Declarations

According to the Anti-Corruption Law of 2006, the IAAC is responsible for facilitating the public availability of summaries of the income and asset declarations of public officials. The agency publishes summaries of the declarations of the top 256 public officials annually in *Government News Magazine*, the official government news magazine, and on the IAAC website (www.iaac.mn/).

Although they are not published in the media, the income and asset declarations of civil servants are required to be available, upon request, to the public. Again, the IAAC is the agency responsible for facilitating the availability of these declarations, although the individual agencies within which any given official works physically maintains the declaration. According to the head of the Supervision and Analysis Department, no one has requested a copy of the asset declaration of an official who is not in the top 256 group.

Box 8.3 IAD Compliance Rates at Mongolia's IAAC

The IAAC completed the third round of asset declarations in February 2009. Since 2006, the number of officials who failed to file income and asset declarations has decreased and the percentage of officials who file their declarations by the deadline has steadily increased. The overall compliance rate was 99.9 percent by February 2009, which reflects a strong emphasis on monitoring submission by all covered officials. Since 2006, nearly all high-level public officials, as defined by the Anti-Corruption Law, have submitted their income and asset declarations by the February 15 deadline (see table B8.3.1).

Table B8.3.1 Compliance and On-Time Rates, Mongolia

Compliance rates			
Year	Nonfiled (#)	Filed (#)	Compliance rate (%)
2007	1,237	41,884	97.0
2008	333	47,285	99.3
2009	37	52,800	99.9
Late submission rates			
Year	Filed late (#)	Filed on time (#)	On-time submission rate (%)
2007	574	40,647	98.6
2008	184	46,952	99.6
2009	64	52,763	99.9

Source: IAAC, Mongolia.

Education and Outreach

The IAAC places an emphasis on helping filers understand their obligation to declare their income and assets. Accordingly, the IAAC issues clarifying memos to filers regarding the proper completion of the forms. It also conducts training for filers on how to prepare their income and asset declarations, and training for officials responsible for receiving and storing the declarations of officials within their agencies. To accomplish these tasks, the agency has created a toolkit and manuals to facilitate training.

Furthermore, upon the request of a declarer, the IAAC will provide preliminary advice on how to file the income and asset declaration, how to provide additional information on the declaration, and how to register the declaration. Finally, the IAAC buys ads in local newspapers and magazines and on billboards announcing the requirement to submit income and asset declarations in a further effort to communicate the importance of complying with this requirement. Box 8.3 provides further information on compliance rates.

Summary of Key Findings

The Independent Agency against Corruption has demonstrated a clear ability to enforce compliance with the obligation for public officials to declare income and assets. The agency carefully monitors the list of officials required to submit declarations and swiftly implements sanctions against those who fail to comply. They have achieved this success in a decentralized system where declarations are received by over 120 public organizations, demonstrating an ability to monitor a widely dispersed system. The real measure of success for the income and asset disclosure system in Mongolia, though, will be in a heightened ability to prevent corruption, uncover instances of corruption, and prosecute offenders.

The continuing challenges to the IAD system in Mongolia include the following:

The IAAC was created as an independent agency with the authority to perform numerous functions, including registering income and asset declarations and investigating alleged corrupt acts. However, the exact role the IAD system is meant to play in the fight against corruption remains somewhat unclear.

Covered officials may be dismissed from their position for failing to declare their income and assets or for lying on their declaration, but there are no criminal penalties for false statements on the forms. The criminal code remains vague on the subject of illicit enrichment, the underlying crime that is most often the basis upon which an IAD regime is built. Furthermore, there is no law against having a conflict of interest while serving in public office.

As a result, the IAD system in Mongolia appears to be primarily concerned with establishing a baseline of the income and assets of all public officials. The Anti-Corruption Law of 2006 emphasizes the public availability of the declarations, thereby signaling a focus on the transparency function of an IAD regime, rather than on law enforcement.

However, the relative weakness of the press in Mongolia raises questions about the efficacy of relying on the public availability of these declarations to improve governance outcomes. The stories in the media are generally paid for by private interests, and most media outlets are explicitly aligned with a political party. As a result, according to the experts consulted for the preparation of this report, it can be challenging to disseminate facts and figures about the IAD system that are believed by the public.

Mongolia's experience in setting up its IAD system offers a valuable example of experience in the gradual implementation of a system. The IAAC focused almost exclusively on attaining a 100 percent compliance rate with the requirement to submit declarations before expanding its efforts to verify the accuracy of declarations. Furthermore, because of resource constraints, the IAAC relied on the individual line agencies to receive declarations, rather than attempting to be the submission body for all declarations. However, the agency is now trying to implement an electronic submission system so that it can centralize its administration and oversight of the IAD system and reduce its reliance on the line agencies.

Notes

1. See the Transparency International Corruption Perceptions Index at http://www .transparency.org/policy_research/surveys_indices/cpi.
2. C&A with TAF 2005.

Reference

C&A (Casals & Associates, Inc.), in collaboration with TAF (the Asia Foundation). 2005. "Assessment of Corruption in Mongolia: Final Report." Submitted to USAID (U.S. Agency for International Development), August 31. http://pdf.usaid.gov/pdf_docs/PNADE136.pdf.

CHAPTER 9

Rwanda

Daniel W. Barnes

Overview

Rwanda created a powerful Office of Ombudsman in 2003, which was empowered with a broad anticorruption mandate, including an income and asset disclosure (IAD) system. The Rwandan IAD system (see box 9.1) is a targeted and robust system that emphasizes the detection and prevention of illicit enrichment. Although conflict-of-interest rules exist and are enforced, the IAD system is not used as a tool for monitoring conflicts of interest among government personnel. The system is run entirely by the Office of the Ombudsman of Rwanda, which is responsible for the collection of nearly 5,000 declarations every year.

Currently, Rwanda prohibits income and asset declarations from being made publicly available, and instead focuses on monitoring submission compliance and verifying the accuracy of a small sample of the declarations it receives each year. Although the Office of the Ombudsman could use more resources and personnel to enhance its monitoring of the IAD system, the office has achieved success to date by employing a phased implementation of its system. Rather than mete out sanctions for filing failures in the first year of operation, the Office of the Ombudsman instead chose to issue warnings to individuals who failed to submit their declarations or who were found to have incorrectly filled out their declarations. By the third year, however, the office began pursuing administrative sanctions for noncompliance and by its seventh year, the office referred cases to the Office of the Prosecutor General.

Compliance, though robust, has room for improvement. As of 2008 (the latest year for which figures are available), 91 percent of covered individuals submitted their declarations on time. Although compliance rates could be higher, Rwanda has managed to use the IAD system as an effective anticorruption tool by prosecuting high-ranking officials for corruption based on investigations stemming

This report is based on desk research and the findings of a visit to Rwanda in June 2010 undertaken on behalf of the Stolen Asset Recovery (StAR) Initiative and the Governance & Public Sector Management Unit of the World Bank to examine the country's IAD system. Special thanks are extended to Lewis Murara of the World Bank Rwanda Country Office for his assistance and review of this case study.

Box 9.1 Snapshot of the Income and Asset Disclosure System in Rwanda

The IAD system in Rwanda is administered by the Office of the Ombudsman of Rwanda, which operates as both a traditional ombudsman and an independent anticorruption authority. The ombudsman's office has phased in the system since its creation, and has rapidly increased compliance and facilitated prosecutions for corruption using IAD data. As of 2011, there were approximately 5,000 individuals who must declare their assets every year directly to the ombudsman's office, which maintains a staff of nine to oversee the submission and analysis of these declarations.

Key elements of the system include:

- **A design intended to detect and prosecute illicit enrichment.** The IAD system in Rwanda is designed solely to prevent, detect, and prosecute illicit enrichment. Rwanda adopted the Leadership Code of Conduct in 2008, which clearly limits the types of outside activities in which public employees may engage. However, the income and asset declarations of filers are not used to monitor conflicts of interest.
- **A modest increase in submission compliance rates.** In 2004, 84 percent of filers submitted their declarations on time. By 2008, on-time submission had risen to 91 percent.
- **An increasing use of technology.** The Office of the Ombudsman originally required IAD forms to be submitted in hard copy only. However, beginning in 2011, declarations can be submitted electronically.
- **Detailed verification procedures.** The Office of the Ombudsman verifies approximately 6 percent of the declarations it receives each year. It chooses which declarations to audit by targeting a portion of filers based on their position, and randomly chooses a sample of declarations to audit. These audits entail not only verifying that the assets and values declared match government and banking records, but also lifestyle checks and house visits.
- **Decentralized enforcement structure.** According to law, the Office of the Ombudsman has the power to recommend administrative sanctions (typically suspension of pay) against those who fail to file their declarations on time and without explanation. However, the ombudsman does not have the authority to enforce sanctions directly, but instead must rely on individual government agencies to administer the sanctions. This gap between recommendation and enforcement has already resulted in conflicts between individual agencies and the Office of the Ombudsman, necessitating the intervention of the prime minister to force the individual agencies to implement the sanctions.
- **Systematic use of income and asset declarations in corruption investigations.** Income and asset declarations are routinely and systematically used as an additional investigatory tool during corruption investigations of individuals who are required to declare their income and assets. In fact, numerous individuals have faced charges that included the crime of lying on their declaration, a crime punishable with prison time.
- **Asset declarations are confidential. No public access is granted.** Law No. 25 of 2003 specifically prohibits making income and asset declaration data publicly available to protect the privacy of filers.

from the verification process of their income and asset declarations. With Rwanda's rapid development and gradual increase in governmental capacity, the IAD system will likely provide an increasingly valuable tool for combating the illegal accumulation of assets by government officials and employees.

Background

The IAD system in Rwanda was created by the country's 2003 constitution, which also created the Office of the Ombudsman. This office, however, is a relatively unique institution and marries the responsibilities of a traditional ombudsman with those of an independent anticorruption agency. Its explicit mandate is to reinforce good governance in both public and private institutions by acting as a link between the public and these institutions, preventing injustice and corruption, receiving complaints from citizens, and administering the government IAD system. It is notable that injustice and corruption are linked by the terminology used by the ombudsman and by the structure and operations of the office. As a result, the office seeks resolution of specific problems that citizens experience when interacting with their government, but it also recommends structural policy reform measures to individual government agencies. The office then adds an additional layer of responsibility with its role as an investigator and monitor of corruption in agencies. From its founding, the IAD system has been integral to the ombudsman's mission.

The IAD Legal Framework in Rwanda

Article 182 of the 2003 Constitution created the Office of the Ombudsman and the requirement that certain public sector employees and officials declare their income and assets. Following the ratification of the Constitution, Law No. 25 of 2003 Establishing the Organization and Functioning of the Office of the Ombudsman was adopted, which clarified and expanded the IAD system in Rwanda. This law was, in turn, amended by Law No. 17 of 2005, which expanded and refined the operation of the system.

Coverage of Officials

Law No. 25 of 2003 specifies the persons subject to income and asset declarations. Specifically, Article 7 of that law requires the president, members of Parliament, ministers, certain high-ranking civil servants, and the spouses and children under 18 years of age of each of those individuals to declare their income and assets. In 2008, the law applied to 4,929 individuals across the government.

Content of Declarations

The law and the income and asset declaration form issued by the Office of the Ombudsman, with the approval of Parliament, requires specific classes of income and assets to be declared (table 9.1). Rwanda requires all covered individuals to declare their real estate, movable assets, cash, investments, loans and liabilities,

Table 9.1 Contents of the IAD Form, Rwanda

Personal data
Name
Date of birth
Marital status and name of spouse, if applicable

Assets
Real estate (commercial and private)
Land
Movable assets (livestock, cars, and any movable asset worth twice the yearly salary of the filer)

Cash and investments
Cash (both foreign and domestic)
Shares in companies or cooperatives

Liabilities
Debts owed by the filer to any individual or commercial entity
Debts owed to the filer by any individual or commercial entity

Foreign assets, cash, investments, and liabilities
All assets, cash, investments, and liabilities held or owed abroad

---

Source: Office of the Ombudsman, Rwanda.

and all income. The declaration form itself requires that the income and assets of family members of covered individuals also be included.

Filing Frequency

Law No. 25 of 2003 also specifies the exact deadlines for filing income and asset declarations. All covered individuals must declare their assets, using the approved declaration form, within one month of beginning their official duties. Subsequent to the initial declaration, all declarants must submit a new declaration every year by June 30. All covered individuals must also submit a final declaration of their income and assets (and those of their spouses and children under age 18) within 15 days of leaving office.

Submission Compliance and Content Verification

According to Article 7 of Law No. 25 of 2003, the depository body for income and asset declarations is the Office of the Ombudsman. The text of the law simply specifies that the Office of the Ombudsman shall receive the declarations of all persons whose positions are named in the law. There is, however, no specific legal requirement that the Office of the Ombudsman monitor the submission process, and there is no requirement in the law that the Office of the Ombudsman verify the content of declarations. In practice, however, Rwanda's IAD system performs both functions, as will be discussed below.

Sanctions

Law No. 25 of 2003 empowers the Office of the Ombudsman to request individual agencies to apply administrative sanctions against individuals who fail to declare their income and assets. However, the law does not provide clear guidance regarding the exact form or magnitude of sanctions that can or should be applied for certain filing failures (such as late filing, incomplete filing, or nonfiling).

Although the Penal Code does not specifically mention the IAD system, certain provisions of the code can be applied to key filing failures. Specifically, under the crime of perjury, anyone who lies on their income and asset declaration can be prosecuted.

Public Access to Declarations

All income and asset declarations are private and cannot be made publicly available, according to Law No. 17 of 2005, which amended Law No. 25 of 2003. Prior to the enactment of the amendments contained in Law No. 17, the law was silent on the issue of whether declarations should be made publicly available. With the passage of Law No. 17, Rwanda firmly embraced confidentiality for public officials and employees. However, as will be seen below, the Office of the Ombudsman now verifies the content of a subset of declarations every year in an effort to ensure full compliance with the law.

Mandate and Structure of the IAD Agency

As noted, the Office of the Ombudsman was created as an independent body in 2003. Its mandate is to reinforce good governance in both public and private institutions by acting as a link between the public and these institutions, preventing injustice and corruption, receiving complaints from citizens, and administering the IAD system. Although its mandate is broad, it is the principal agency responsible for the implementation and execution of the IAD system.

The Office of the Ombudsman has 47 employees and is headed by a chief ombudsman, who is nominated by the president and approved by the Senate of Rwanda. He or she is appointed to a four-year term that can be renewed only once. By law, the chief ombudsman can be removed only by Parliament, though the specific mechanism by which Parliament could remove him or her is not clearly delineated. Under the chief ombudsman are two deputies who serve three-year terms that can be renewed only once.

The Office of the Ombudsman is organized into five units:

- The Declaration of Assets Unit
- The Fighting Injustice and Corruption Unit
- The Preventing Injustice and Corruption Unit
- The Monitoring of Incompatibilities of Officials Unit
- The Administration and Finance Unit

As the name implies, the primary unit responsible for the IAD system is the Declaration of Assets Unit. This department created the IAD form, updates the list of individuals required to declare their income and assets, receives and stores declarations from filers, and verifies the accuracy of a sample of the declarations.

Income and Asset Disclosure · http://dx.doi.org/10.1596/978-0-8213-9796-1

Figure 9.1 Organizational Chart of the Office of the Ombudsman, Rwanda

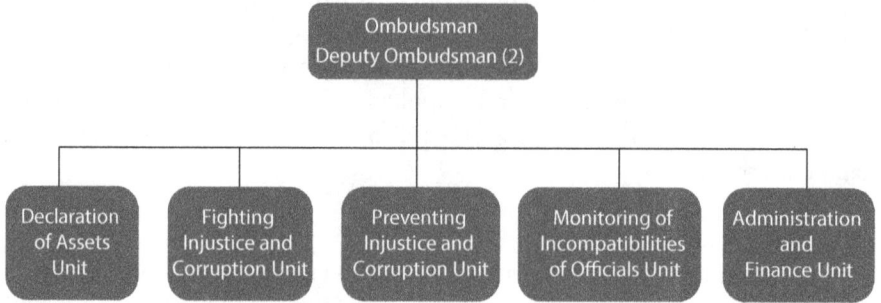

Source: Office of the Ombudsman, Rwanda.

The unit is also responsible for researching the effectiveness of the IAD system and for issuing requests to line agencies to impose administrative sanctions against individuals found not to be in compliance with the requirement to declare their income and assets. With a staff of nine, this unit handles almost every aspect of administering and enforcing the IAD system in Rwanda, with the exception of prosecuting criminal behavior, which is handled by the Office of the Prosecutor General.

See figure 9.1 for an organizational chart of the Office of the Ombudsman.

Resources and Procedures of the IAD System

The means by which Rwanda has implemented its IAD system is as important as the legal framework and organizational structure for understanding the overall functioning of the system. Using a set of in-practice indicators, a clear picture of the physical, budgetary, human resource, and enforcement capabilities of the Rwanda system was created, which is detailed below.

Facilities and Use of Technology

The Office of the Ombudsman is located in a converted private house in the administrative region of Kigali. The office comfortably accommodates a staff of 47, as well as storage facilities for administrative files; these include the original hard copies of the approximately 5,000 income and asset declarations received every year. These declarations are archived on the premises and are stored in locked metal cabinets.

The building has constant electricity service, but also maintains a backup generator to ensure an uninterrupted supply of electricity in case of service disruptions caused by inclement weather or other problems with the external electricity supply.

The Office of the Ombudsman uses a secure intranet system to manage files and workflow across all its departments. All personnel have dedicated computers for their use, along with dedicated sign-on credentials that provide access only to their individual unit's files in order to ensure security and the confidentiality of reports. This security is advanced and particularly important for investigations into discrepancies on IAD forms and other possible misconduct. In fact, the office uses a proprietary computer system, but one that is maintained by external information technology experts from the government's technology office.

Originally, income and asset declarations could be submitted only in hard copy, but the Office of the Ombudsman designed an online portal for the electronic submission of declarations. Although slated to be operational for the declarations required by June 30, 2010, the launch of the online submission system was delayed until 2011 to ensure that the system was functioning properly and filers were sufficiently acquainted with the new system.

Human Resources

The Office of the Ombudsman uses competitive recruitment to hire new staff for the agency. The process involves a civil service exam, a background check, and thorough vetting. All nonadministrative staff have a minimum of four years of postsecondary education equivalent to a Bachelor's degree and receive ongoing training. The Office of the Ombudsman has developed detailed job descriptions for its staff, along with operating manuals that provide guidance for administrative procedures. The agency also conducts yearly performance reviews for its entire staff to monitor and promote employee performance.

Budget

The budget of the Office of the Ombudsman is ultimately determined and allocated by the Parliament of Rwanda. However, the Ministry of Finance and Economic Planning plays an important role in determining the yearly allotment for the office. Every year, the Office of the Ombudsman submits a budget request to the ministry detailing its requirements and the functions to be supported by the requested budget. The ministry then determines the office's budget in the context of governmentwide spending priorities and prepares a budget allocation. The Parliament makes the final decision and appropriates funds. As such, the budget of the Office of the Ombudsman is subject to the same budgetary and political pressures as are the budgets of the majority of government agencies.

In 2009, the Office of the Ombudsman had a budget of RF 1.4 billion (US$2.7 million). This represents significant growth since the creation of the office in 2003, when it had an operating budget of RF 600 million (US$1.02 million). This reflects both robust presidential and parliamentary support for the office and strong donor community support. In fact, the donor community provides approximately 15 percent of the funding for the office. However, almost half of the government's entire budget comes from the international community, some of which is used in the government's budget allotment for the Office of the Ombudsman. Thus donor involvement is significant in the office, but is also consistent with overall donor support to the government. Unfortunately, the budget for the IAD system, (rather than the overall Office of the Ombudsman's office), was not available at the time of writing.

Importantly, while the salaries of the Office of the Ombudsman's staff were lower than those for other government agencies for a few years, the office has managed to equalize pay with that of peer elite institutions in the country, such as the Ministry of Finance, putting its salaries significantly higher than those of many other civil servants. This has greatly reduced loss of staff to other government agencies and has facilitated the retention of knowledgeable and capable staff. Unfortunately, the office did not have exact retention and turnover figures, but they were believed to be similar to those of other public sector institutions. A survey conducted in 2007 concluded that (1) the leaving rates captured by the survey are not sufficiently high to indicate a serious problem overall in the Rwandan public service, and (2) there may be problems with lower retention rates in particular organizations or in particular sectors (accounting, legal, information technology, finance) where the private sector is offering better pay, conditions, or management.

Further, the Declaration of Assets Unit within the Office of the Ombudsman has a staff of nine dedicated to distributing, collecting, and analyzing 4,929 declarations each year (table 9.2). This ratio of declarations to staff (548:1) has enabled the unit to closely monitor submission compliance rates and to issue warnings and demands for disciplinary measures against those who fail to file their income and asset declarations (the specifics of which will be covered below). However, because of resource constraints that limit both the number of staff and the resources available to them, only 6 percent of declarations are audited for accuracy each year. While this level of auditing still provides a deterrent effect, the Office of the Ombudsman has expressed its desire to audit a significantly greater proportion of declarations, if possible.

Regulatory Function

The Office of the Ombudsman has clear regulatory authority within its policy remit. The office plays an active role in the formulation of new policies regarding the IAD system and regarding corruption more broadly, with staff proposing draft legal language for possible new laws and amendments. Although the office issued numerous regulations at the time of its creation, few

Table 9.2 Number of Declarations Submitted and Analyzed by the Office of the Ombudsman and Number of Staff Responsible, Rwanda

Number of declarations received
4,929
Number of staff
9
Percent of declarations verified for accuracy
6%

Source: Office of the Ombudsman, Rwanda.

new regulations for the IAD system have been issued in recent years, since the system has not been significantly altered. The one exception, however, has been the revision of the declaration form itself over the last few years. Indeed, the filing form created by the Office of the Ombudsman reflects the statutory requirements of the law that created the system. However, the law was quite vague and left significant responsibility to the Office of the Ombudsman, so the office was able to determine the majority of the filing requirements pursuant to its regulatory authority. Because of this, the Office of the Ombudsman has revised the form each year as it learns from the successes and challenges of previous years.

Beyond its independent regulatory authority, the Office of the Ombudsman has played an active role in proposing new laws to Parliament, which would either clarify the office's responsibilities or expand the powers available to it. Many of these proposals concern policy areas other than the IAD system. However, a key area of concern has been the investigatory powers of the office, some of which are directly relevant to the auditing function within the IAD system.

Managing Submission Compliance

The Office of the Ombudsman closely monitors submission compliance every year. As noted in the legal framework section above, Law No. 25 of 2003 lists the positions that must file income and asset declarations. Some positions, however, are not explicitly named (such as "those in charge of receiving, managing and controlling the public finance and property"), so the Office of the Ombudsman continually works with line agencies to classify which positions must declare. Every year, beginning in February, the ombudsman contacts these agencies and collects a list of the individuals who currently fill all positions required to submit income and asset declarations. Using this list, the office distributes declaration forms and then monitors whether they are returned by June 30. In 2008 (the latest year with complete figures), 4,929 individuals were required to declare their assets.

These declarations are submitted, in hard copy, directly to the Office of the Ombudsman. Thus, the office is able to closely monitor who has submitted their declaration on time. The Asset Declaration Unit has a staff of nine who are responsible for receiving these 4,929 declarations, representing a staff-to-declaration ratio of 1 to 548. In 2008, 451 individuals failed to file their declarations by June 30, representing 9 percent of the filing population. The ombudsman contacted every individual to demand an explanation for their failure to submit their declaration. Although many responded to this warning by submitting their declaration, the Office of the Ombudsman ultimately requested that administrative sanctions be levied against 153 individuals.

The office responds to questions from individuals who are required to declare their income and assets. However, because of staffing and financial constraints, the office has produced only limited documentation that clearly explains the exact requirements for each section of the IAD form. There is a brief introduction to the IAD process contained in the front of the IAD form; however, it does not provide comprehensive information.

The Office of the Ombudsman can only request that the line agency impose the recommended sanction (typically, a suspension of up to two months' salary). This requires a high level of cooperation with every government agency. The Office of the Ombudsman reports that cooperation on the issue of imposing penalties has been mixed across the government. In fact, in one case, one ministry refused to impose the recommended penalty, which prompted the Office of the Ombudsman to appeal the decision to the prime minister of Rwanda, the only recourse for the Office of the Ombudsman with regard to administrative sanctions. In this instance, the prime minister ordered the ministry to comply with the ombudsman's request, but this example highlights the potential inability of the Office of the Ombudsman to effectively and consistently impose sanctions. As noted in *Public Office, Private Interests: Accountability through Income and Asset Disclosure*—the companion volume to these case studies—it is important that an IAD system impose fair and proportionate sanctions in a consistent and predictable manner to ensure that the system remains credible.

Content Verification

Rwanda's IAD system focuses on ensuring compliance with the requirement to submit a declaration, but it also audits a small portion of those submitted declarations to ensure that they are accurate *and* that the assets of the individual have been legally obtained. The auditing of declarations is not explicitly required by Law No. 25 of 2003 or its subsequent amendments, but the Office of the Ombudsman uses its broad investigatory powers granted by that law to audit selected declarations.

The office uses the following mixture of strategies to determine which declarations to audit:

- It randomly audits a small portion of all declarations.
- It chooses certain high-risk positions (such as procurement officers) to audit.
- It chooses certain agencies, or units within agencies, to target each year.
- It audits the declaration of any individual who has been accused of wrongdoing.

The Office of the Ombudsman audits approximately 300 of the 4,929 declarations submitted each year, or 6 percent of declarations.

The auditing process is rigorous and in depth. The audit compares the income and asset declarations of the individuals in question with their government and banking records. It also compares the declaration to previous declarations made by the individual, in a process known as *year-to-year reconciliation*. Any large changes in wealth or other discrepancies are investigated particularly thoroughly. Even in the absence of such discrepancies, Office of the Ombudsman staff will perform a full investigation, including visiting the individual's residence and interviewing friends and family members in an effort to determine whether the individual has assets not declared on their income and asset declaration form. This includes physical verification of assets to ascertain reasonableness of the declared value.

Although Rwanda has conflict-of-interest legislation, the income and asset declaration is *not* used to monitor possible conflicts of interest. Instead, the verification process is designed solely to determine whether an income and asset declaration is accurate.

Box 9.2 outlines the functions performed by Rwanda's Office of the Ombudsman.

Investigatory Function

The Office of the Ombudsman has the power of *police judiciaire*,[1] which is derived from the French justice system. This power has been extended to numerous government agencies in recent years and enables them to perform preliminary criminal investigations of suspected breaches of the law in their specific

---

Box 9.2 IAD Functions Performed by Rwanda's Office of the Ombudsman

Communicating with filers, receiving declarations, and monitoring submission compliance

The Office of the Ombudsman administers the IAD system and communicates with filers. Once a declaration has been completed and submitted to the office, the Declaration of Assets Unit records the deposit of the declaration and stores it in a secure room. All individuals who fail to submit their declarations on time are contacted and provided one last opportunity to file. The Office of the Ombudsman then recommends that line agencies impose administrative sanctions against those who continue to refuse to declare their assets.

Verifying a targeted sample of declarations

The Declaration of Assets Unit also prepares a yearly list of individuals (by position) whose declarations will be audited based on varying criteria, such as the rank of the individual or the sensitive nature of their job. The unit will also randomly select a few more declarations for auditing.

If, during the audit, a discrepancy is identified, the unit will contact the filer to request an explanation or clarification. Unless the discrepancy is major, the filer will be provided the opportunity to correct his or her declaration. If, however, the auditor believes the discrepancy suggests there is underlying criminal behavior being hidden, a full corruption investigation may be launched.

Facilitating the use of declarations in corruption investigations

Income and asset declarations are also stored in the archives, ready to be used by the police or the Office of the Prosecutor General during criminal or corruption investigations. Although neither the Office of the Ombudsman nor the Office of the Prosecutor General had exact figures at the time this report was being prepared, both reported that income and asset declarations are systematically used as one of the investigatory tools in corruption investigations.

---

policy remit. This means that the Office of the Ombudsman has the power to request subpoenas to obtain information in cases of suspected corruption, which includes investigating the accuracy of income and asset declarations and the sources of the assets listed on those declarations.

If, in the course of the verification audit, small discrepancies are revealed, the Office of the Ombudsman will provide the individual with the opportunity to correct his or her declaration. However, if evidence of major (not defined) unaccounted assets is uncovered, the office will launch a corruption investigation using the power of the *police judiciaire*. Subsequently, three things may happen:

- If sufficient evidence is uncovered to pursue a criminal prosecution for an underlying corrupt act, the case will be referred to the prosecutor's office.
- If no underlying crime can be found, the ombudsman may instead ask the prosecutor's office to pursue a criminal case based solely on the filer's failure to declare all assets as required by law.
- If the investigation is inconclusive regarding the presence of these other assets, the case may be dropped.

As described, the Office of the Ombudsman relies on the Office of the Prosecutor General to prosecute any crimes it investigates. The Office of the Ombudsman has requested that Parliament grant it the power to prosecute corruption cases itself, rather than have to rely on the prosecutor general. This argument derives from the belief of the Office of the Ombudsman that the prosecutor general has neither the specialized expertise in corruption necessary for these cases nor as much interest as the ombudsman in pursuing cases not derived through normal police channels. However, the Office of the Prosecutor General has pointed out that the Office of the Ombudsman has referred an average of only one case per year.

The debate regarding the wisdom and efficacy of granting prosecutorial powers to the Office of the Ombudsman is significant. On the one hand, the Office of the Ombudsman wishes to remain as independent as possible and to have as many tools as possible at its disposal to fight corruption. On the other hand, granting prosecutorial powers to the Office of the Ombudsman may prompt other agencies to seek similar powers. The granting of the power of the *police judiciaire* to many agencies followed a similar pattern. Concerns were raised during numerous interviews for this study that providing prosecutorial powers to the Office of the Ombudsman could lead to a proliferation of prosecuting bodies and, therefore, undermine the Office of the Prosecutor General, which in turn could undermine development of the judicial system.

Interagency Collaboration

The Office of the Ombudsman reports that it has received excellent cooperation from other government agencies and that it regularly coordinates its activities with other ministries. With respect to the verification process, the Office of the

Ombudsman has not reported any difficulty obtaining relevant records from other government agencies. The office did, however, face resistance from some banks in the early years after its creation. But with clear statutory authority to obtain banking records, the office reports that it has since developed a working relationship with all banks in the country to obtain necessary records pursuant to legal oversight.

Public Access to Declarations

As noted in the legal framework section above, income and asset declarations are not publicly available, pursuant to Law No. 25 of 2003. Therefore Rwanda has tried to build its capacity to verify the accuracy of declarations, as described above. There is debate about making income and asset declarations publicly available, and some see this as the next step as the IAD system matures.

Reporting and Outreach

The Office of the Ombudsman produces a comprehensive yearly report of its activities, including key indicators for the IAD system, which it submits to Parliament and makes publicly available. In addition, the Asset Declaration Unit of the office has revised the IAD form each year as it attempts to ensure that the form is capturing relevant and useful information while presenting the least burden possible to filers. Although these changes may produce some confusion for filers from year to year, the revision process is an indication that the Office of the Ombudsman is actively monitoring declarations to determine the optimal form for its filers and to maximize the system's ability to monitor wealth accumulation in order to prevent, identify, and prosecute instances of illegally obtained assets.

Summary of Key Findings

The Rwandan income and asset disclosure system is a targeted and robust system that emphasizes the detection and prevention of illicit enrichment. The Office of the Ombudsman is responsible for the entire IAD system and closely monitors submission compliance while also auditing 6 percent of submitted declarations each year. Although declarations are not publicly available, the Office of the Ombudsman, police, and the Office of the Prosecutor General regularly use the income and asset declarations of covered individuals during investigations into corruption and other criminal behavior.

In addition, the office uses a mixture of strategies to determine which declarations to audit. It randomly audits a small portion of all declarations; chooses certain high-risk positions (such as procurement officers) to audit; chooses certain agencies, or units within agencies, to target each year; and audits the declaration of any individual who has been accused of wrongdoing. This strategy has maximized limited resources in order to provide the greatest deterrent effect possible. The IAD system in Rwanda has registered some notable achievements, including raising its submission compliance rate to 91 percent, as of the completion of this study, and having declarations used successfully during the prosecution of high-ranking officials for corruption-related offenses. With additional resources and training, the Office of the Ombudsman may be able to improve its performance even further, to facilitate ever greater rates of prevention and prosecution of corruption.

Although there have been rapid improvements during the seven years since its inception, the IAD system still registered only a 91 percent compliance rate by 2010. In response, the Office of the Ombudsman is aggressively recommending the imposition of administrative sanctions against anyone who fails to properly file a declaration. However, the office must rely on individual agencies levying the recommended sanctions against the individual, thereby raising questions about its ability to adequately enforce IAD requirements.

The Office of the Ombudsman has gradually increased its enforcement efforts since the creation of the IAD system. Rather than mete out sanctions for filing failures in the first year of operation, the office chose to issue warnings to individuals who failed to submit their declarations or who were found to have incorrectly filled out their declarations. By the third year, however, the office began pursuing administrative sanctions for noncompliance, and it now refers cases to the Office of the Prosecutor General. Furthermore, the Office of the Ombudsman has leveraged its limited resources to audit the highest-risk filers while also introducing an element of randomness to provide the greatest deterrent possible against providing false information on a declaration.

Note

1. The *police judiciaire* has the functions and responsibilities equivalent to a criminal investigation department.

Reference

StAR Initiative. 2012. *Public Office, Private Interests: Accountability through Income and Asset Disclosure.* Stolen Asset Recovery (StAR) Series. Washington, DC: World Bank.

CHAPTER 10

Slovenia

Stephanie E. Trapnell

Overview

Slovenia has established credible threats of detection and of sanctions in its income and asset disclosure (IAD) system (see box 10.1) by capitalizing on stable interagency collaboration in its verification and enforcement functions. The Commission for the Prevention of Corruption is legally allowed to demand information from external entities as part of the verification process, and has been granted greater enforcement authority for violations. Moreover, the involvement of several other agencies—such as the police and agency inspectorates—complements the work of the commission with respect to investigations and sanctions.

Effective leadership has been crucial to the survival of the commission as the principal driver of anticorruption efforts, a mandate that includes income and asset disclosure, conflict of interest prevention, and other prevention programs. Under the management of the current director, who has been in his position since the inception of the new anticorruption framework of 2004, the commission has been able to withstand several attempts by Parliament to eliminate it.

Not only is the IAD requirement consistently enforced, but also the commission played a significant role in drafting a new law that establishes new sanctions, assigns greater enforcement capability, and provides for public access to income and asset declaration content.

Background

The current Commission for the Prevention of Corruption was established in 2004 with the mandate to devise and manage anticorruption efforts in Slovenia, which included assuming responsibility for the IAD system. In fact, financial

This report is based on desk research and the findings of a visit to Slovenia in June 2010 undertaken on behalf of the Stolen Asset Recovery (StAR) Initiative and the Governance & Public Sector Management Unit of the World Bank to examine the country's IAD system. Special thanks for assistance in the preparation of this report go to Drago Kos of the Council of Europe/Group of States against Corruption (GRECO), Barbara Fűrst and Sergeja Oštir of the Slovenia Commission for the Prevention of Corruption, and Francesca Recanatini of the World Bank.

Box 10.1 Snapshot of the Income and Asset Disclosure System in Slovenia

Although minimal financial disclosure provisions had existed in Slovenia since 1992, it was not until 2004—following the creation of the Commission for the Prevention of Corruption—that a fully developed IAD and conflict-of-interest system was instituted. In June 2010, a new Integrity and Prevention of Corruption Act came into effect, with significant contributions from the commission staff, expanding the mandate of the commission and enhancing its ability to regulate anticorruption efforts.

Key elements of the system include:

- **Focus on both illicit enrichment and conflict of interest.** Financial disclosure serves twopurposes in the Slovenian system. Potential or actual conflicts of interest are identified by reviewing the contents of the declarations for incompatibilities between public office and private interests, while illicit enrichment is addressed through the verification of declaration content.
- **Centralized submission and monitoring.** The IAD and conflict-of-interest functions are centralized within the Conflict of Interest Unit in the Commission for the Prevention of Corruption. All submissions are received and reviewed by the five permanent staff. In 2009, there were 6,259 filers and the compliance rate was nearly 100 percent. A 2010 law raised the number of those who are required to file to approximately 14,000.
- **Random selection of declarations for verification.** Declarations are chosen for content verification through a random selection process. The number of declarations selected depends on the number of staff available to verify content and, therefore, may vary from year to year. In 2009, 33 percent of all declarations were selected to undergo verification, with a staff-to-declaration ratio of 1 to 413.
- **Interagency collaboration that allows for extensive content verification.** The content verification process consists of a comparison between the information on the declaration form and information from official databases. Information provided in declaration forms is checked against tax records, land registries, vehicle registries, livestock records, and corporate records of ownership and shares. This verification process normally lasts three to four months.
- **Sanctions enforced for noncompliance.** A significant change in the legal framework in 2010 revised the scope of penalties for the nonfiling of an income and asset declaration. Instead of automatic termination, the commission may require the withholding of salary up to a certain amount. The previous penalty of automatic termination had been nullified by the Constitutional Court for being too harsh, which had left nonfiling violations unpunishable.
- **Public access to declaration content.** Information on income, assets, and liabilities reported in income and asset declarations is made public. Personal identifying information, such as tax registration and national identification number, is confidential, as is information about activities and prior employment.

disclosure had been introduced nearly a decade earlier, soon after Slovenia gained independence from Yugoslavia. The Incompatibility of Performing Public Functions with Activities for Profit Act (1992) included both conflict-of-interest provisions and IAD requirements, with oversight provided by a parliamentary commission. Public officials were required to disclose income and assets every two years to this parliamentary commission, and all data were publicly available. However, there were no sanctions for violations of filing requirements, and a woefully understaffed and institutionally weak commission was not able to verify the contents of the declaration forms.[1]

The government of Slovenia began to take anticorruption efforts much more seriously in 2000, when it was cited by the Council of Europe for having neither a comprehensive anticorruption strategy nor a specialized agency to coordinate anticorruption efforts. In response, the government established both an interministerial anticorruption group and, by decree, the Office for the Prevention of Corruption in the Office of the Prime Minister. By February 2004, a new Law on the Prevention of Corruption was passed, which established the present-day Commission for the Prevention of Corruption. This commission is an independent constitutional body that reports only to Parliament and is tasked with, among other things, the management of a much more robust IAD system.

That same year—2004—saw a change of government that shifted support away from the independent anticorruption agency. By February 2006, Parliament had pushed through a new law that eliminated the need for a separate agency in favor of a commission composed of deputies from the National Assembly that would assume the responsibilities of an independent commission.[2] However, the Constitutional Court suspended that law in April 2006 and declared it unconstitutional in a March 2007 decision, ruling that the separation of powers outlined in the Constitution was not upheld with the new anticorruption framework devised by Parliament.[3] The provisions of the Prevention of Corruption Act (2004) continued to apply until unconstitutional provisions were amended or removed. A change in government in late 2006 swung favor back in support of a separate agency, and the amendments stalled in Parliament. The Commission for the Prevention of Corruption maintained its operations and continues to do so.

In June 2010, a new Integrity and Prevention of Corruption Act came into effect, expanding the mandate of the commission and enhancing its ability to regulate anticorruption efforts. The major changes to the anticorruption framework that address IAD are significant. They include:

- Sanctions for noncompliance with the anticorruption law (Article 77)
- A shift in the nature of the penalty for nonfiling of IAD forms: instead of automatic termination, the commission may require withholding of salary up to a certain amount (Article 44)—an automatic termination penalty had been nullified by the Constitutional Court for being too harsh, which had left nonfiling violations unpunishable
- Public availability of IAD data (Article 46)—public access had been included in an earlier law but was nullified by the Constitutional Court, which had ensured that declaration content remained confidential until the 2010 law

The new law increases the scope of the commission's mandate and grants it extensive powers with respect to administrative sanctions and fines. Although the size of the commission's staff has doubled since 2010, it is expected that additional personnel and resources will be needed to meet the goals set by the 2010 law.

Figure 10.1 displays Slovenia's anticorruption institutional timeline.

The IAD Legal Framework in Slovenia

The legal framework of IAD in Slovenia is regulated by the Integrity and Prevention of Corruption Act of 2010, which replaced the 2004 Prevention of Corruption Act.

Coverage of Officials

The coverage of public officials subject to disclosure requirements has been expanded from the 2004 Prevention of Corruption Act, in which only individuals included in the category of functionary were obliged to submit forms (see table 10.1 for a list of functionaries). According to Article 41 of the 2010 Integrity and Prevention of Corruption Act, in addition to professional functionaries, nonprofessional mayors and deputy mayors, senior civil servants, managers, and individuals responsible for public procurement are required to disclose income, assets, and liabilities.

Individuals responsible for public procurement include persons appointed by contracting authorities to expert committees for awarding public contracts, as well as persons deciding, approving, and proposing contents of the tender documentation, assessing bids, and proposing the bidder in the case of tender procedures.

Content of Declarations

The content of the income and asset declaration (see table 10.2) corresponds directly to Article 42 of the 2010 Integrity and Prevention of Corruption Act, which requires personal data, information on the position held, private business interests, income, debts, and assets.

Filing Frequency

Officials are required to file an income and asset declaration no later than one month after entering or leaving office, as per Article 41 of the 2010 Integrity and Prevention of Corruption Act. Although there is no annual filing requirement, Article 43 of that Act requires officials to report changes in function, activity, or ownership of private business interests, and any change in income, assets, cash, or debts that exceed €10,000 in value. This ad-hoc disclosure upon changes in assets must be received by the commission by January 31 for the previous year.

The commission may also compel an individual who has already left a position to file an additional declaration within one year of employment termination if there is reason to suspect that the financial circumstances reported on the disclosure deviate from actual circumstances.

Should there be grounds to suspect that a declarant is transferring property or income to family members for the purposes of evading detection, the commission

Figure 10.1 Anticorruption Institutional Timeline, Slovenia

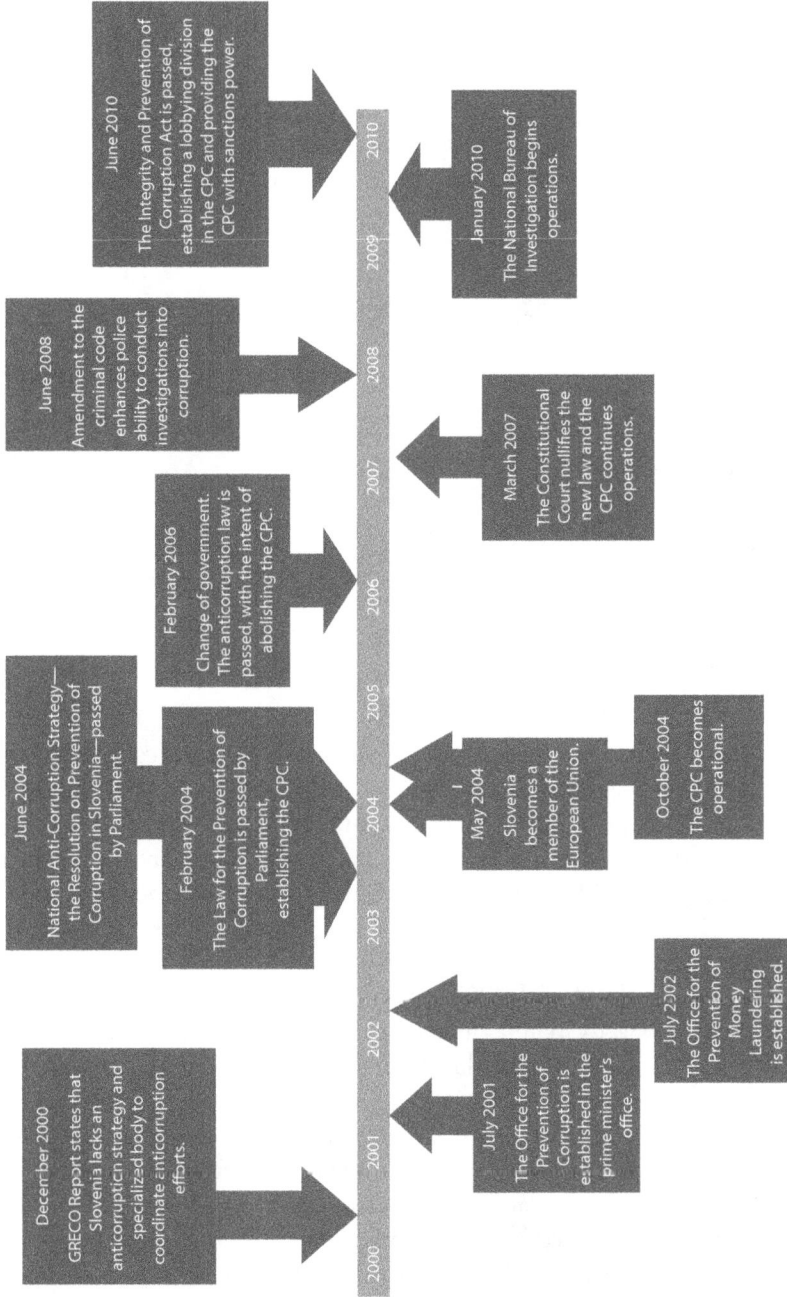

December 2000

GRECO Report states that Slovenia lacks an anticorruption strategy and specialized body to coordinate anticorruption efforts.

July 2001

The Office for the Prevention of Corruption is established in the prime minister's office.

July 2002

The Office for the Prevention of Money Laundering is established.

June 2004

National Anti-Corruption Strategy—the Resolution on Prevention of Corruption in Slovenia—passed by Parliament.

February 2004

The Law for the Prevention of Corruption is passed by Parliament, establishing the CPC.

February 2006

Change of government. The anticorruption law is passed, with the intent of abolishing the CPC.

May 2004

Slovenia becomes a member of the European Union.

October 2004

The CPC becomes operational.

March 2007

The Constitutional Court nullifies the new law and the CPC continues operations.

June 2008

Amendment to the criminal code enhances police ability to conduct investigations into corruption.

June 2010

The Integrity and Prevention of Corruption Act is passed, establishing a lobbying division in the CPC and providing the CPC with sanctions power.

January 2010

The National Bureau of Investigation begins operations.

Note: CPC = Commission for the Prevention of Corruption.

191

Table 10.1 Positions Covered by IAD Filing Obligations, Slovenia

Functionaries	Senior civil servants	Managers
Members of the National Assembly	Directors-general	Managers of public agencies
Members of the National Council	Secretaries-general of ministries	Managers of public funds
President of the republic	Heads of ministerial departments	Managers of public institutes
Prime minister	Heads of government offices	Managers of commercial public institutions
Ministers	Heads of administrative units	Managers of other entities of public law funded by the government budget
State secretaries	Directors or secretaries of municipalities	Managers of local authorities and public utility companies and enterprises in which the government or local authorities hold controlling interest
Members of the Constitutional Court		
Judges		
Public prosecutors		
Members of the European Parliament		
Governor of the Bank of Slovenia		
Functionaries in other government bodies, local authorities, the Bank of Slovenia, and the European Parliament		

Source: Integrity and Prevention of Corruption Act of 2010, Slovenia.

may require him or her to submit information on income and cash, liabilities, and assets of family members. As defined by Article 4 of the 2010 Integrity and Prevention of Corruption Act, family members include spouses, children, adopted children, parents, adoptive parents, brothers, sisters, and individuals living in the household or in extramarital cohabitation with the declarant.

Sanctions

According to Article 44 of the 2010 Integrity and Prevention of Corruption Act, if an individual fails to submit an income and asset declaration, the commission is required to contact the individual directly. By law, the individual has an additional 15 to 30 days to provide the required data after being contacted by the commission. If an individual fails to submit a declaration after the additional time has passed, his or her salary may be docked every month by an amount equal to 10 percent of their base salary.[4] Employers are compelled by law to implement these sanctions, as directed by the commission.

Beyond the administrative blocking of salary, the 2010 Integrity and Prevention of Corruption Act also prescribes misdemeanor fines of €400 to €1,200 for filing failures. The commission may levy fines within this range for failing to submit an income and asset declaration, refusing to provide additional information when requested, or submitting false data on an income and asset declaration.

Table 10.2 Contents of the IAD Form, Slovenia

	Disclosure requirement	Publicly available
Personal data		
Name	✓	✓
Identification number	✓	
Tax registration number	✓	
Position		
Information about the employment position	✓	✓
Work performed immediately prior to taking office	✓	
Other functions or activities	✓	
Private business interests		
Ownership	✓	✓
Shares and management rights in a company, a private institution, or other private activities with a description of activities and company or organization name	✓	✓
Shares and rights held in indirect ownership	✓	✓
Income and cash		
Annual taxable income	✓	✓
Cash in hand or at banks, savings banks, and credit services with a total value of the individual account exceeding €10,000	✓	✓
Type and value of securities, provided that the total value exceeds €10,000	✓	✓
Liabilities		
Debts, obligations, and commitments and loans the value of which exceeds €10,000	✓	✓
Assets		
Real estate with land registry data	✓	✓
Movable property the value of which exceeds €10,000	✓	✓

Source: Integrity and Prevention of Corruption Act of 2010, Slovenia.

Should an individual fail to provide sufficient clarification regarding the irregularities on his or her income and asset declaration, the commission is required to inform the authority with responsibility for oversight of elections or appointments (depending on the position of the individual). This authority may terminate or dismiss the individual and must inform the commission if such action is taken. In addition, the commission may refer the case to anti-money-laundering, tax, or financial control authorities if the commission suspects that the assets or income may be hidden or disposed of before action can be taken.

Submission Compliance and Verification

The commission is responsible for both submission compliance and verification of income and asset declarations. Verification is conducted by validating statements on the declaration with information contained in government agencies, such as land and vehicle registries, livestock rosters, and the tax department. Individuals have 15 days to clarify irregularities discovered through the

Income and Asset Disclosure • http://dx.doi.org/10.1596/978-0-8213-9796-1

verification process or to provide evidentiary data regarding statements on the income and asset declaration.

Public Access to Declarations

According to Article 46 of the 2010 Integrity and Prevention of Corruption Act, information on income, assets, and liabilities reported in income and asset declarations is made public. Personal identifying information, such as tax registration and national identification numbers, is confidential, as is information about activities and prior employment.

One important qualification regarding public disclosure concerns the timing of acquisition. The law excludes from the public disclosure requirement those assets or income acquired prior to taking office. This exception has no impact on content verification, since officials must declare all assets on the declaration, but it ensures that the first declaration of a public official will remain confidential. Data on the wealth of officials working in procurement and on the National Review Commission are also not subject to publication.

Mandate and Structure of the IAD Agency

The Commission for the Prevention of Corruption is responsible for managing the IAD system in Slovenia. The agencies involved in enforcing the IAD system include the State Prosecutor's Office, the police, agency inspectorates, the National Bureau of Investigation, and the Office for the Prevention of Money Laundering. In 2010, a reorganization of departments that coincided with the selection of a new commissioner was initiated.

Instead of four separate departments (Prevention, Integrity, Conflict of Interest, and Lobbying), the commission is now arranged in two functional units: the Investigative and Oversight Bureau and the Center for Prevention and Integrity of the Public. The Investigative and Oversight Bureau handles both investigations and oversight within its remit, including financial disclosures, conflicts of interest, lobbyist registration, whistleblower protection, and interagency coordination with law enforcement and prosecutorial bodies. The Center for Prevention and Integrity of the Public deals with preventative measures, including the implementation of the National Anti-Corruption Action Plan, the development of Integrity Plans for public sector entities, review of draft anticorruption legislation, and coordination with civil society and research institutions.

Figure 10.2 provides an organizational chart of Slovenia's Commission for the Prevention of Corruption.

Resources and Procedures of the IAD System

Facilities and Use of Technology

The commission is housed on one floor of an office building fairly close to the center of the city (Ljubljana). The overall area of the premises is 1,100 square

Figure 10.2 Organizational Chart of the Commission for the Prevention of Corruption, Slovenia

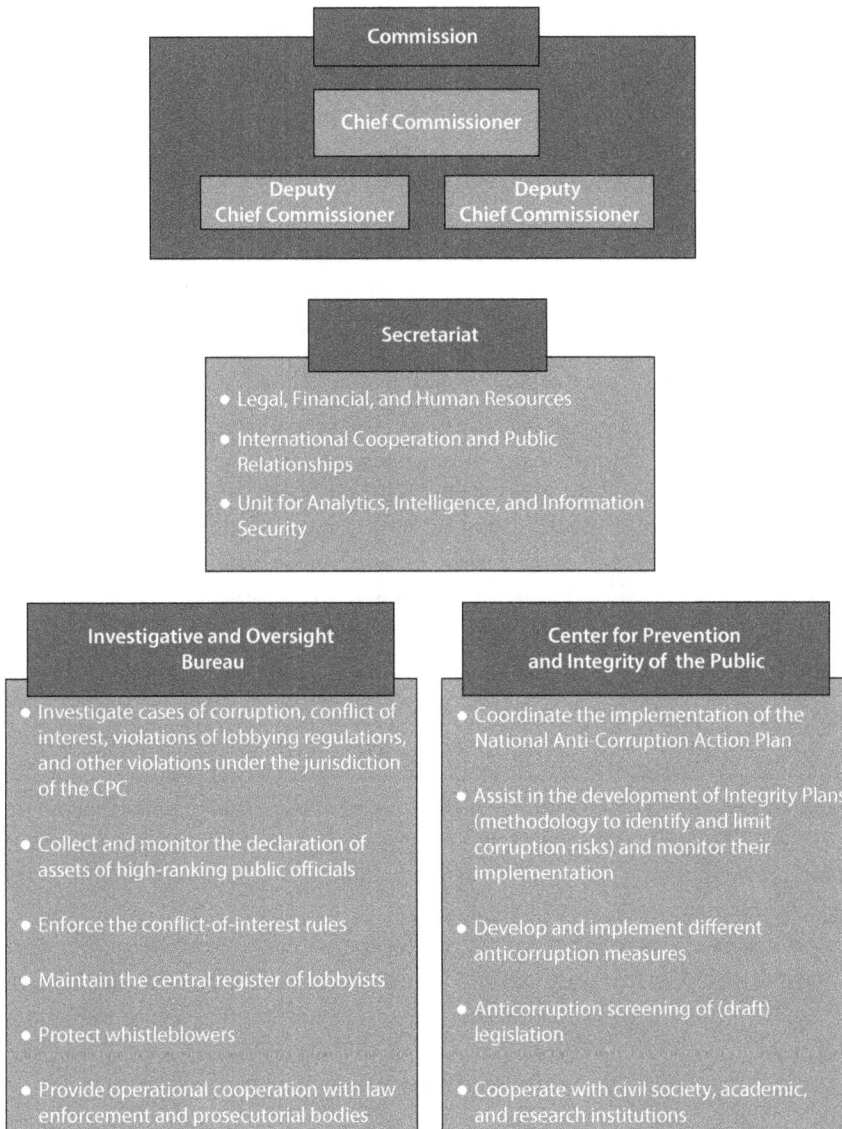

meters, and staff share offices. Computers are assigned to all staff, and server hardware and software were less than two years old in 2010. The Commission for the Prevention of Corruption transitioned to online submission of income and asset disclosure information in 2011. Public officials are now required to submit wealth information via the online form on the commission's website. Prior to online submission, declarations were submitted in hard copy and all data were maintained in locked cabinets in a locked room, using a filing system based on unique, randomly assigned case numbers.

Human Resources

There are five permanent staff in the Conflict of Interest Division—head, assistant head, and three advisers (politically appointed)—and one intern. The commission employs a staff of 25; however, because of funding issues, only 65 percent of the positions were filled as of June 2010. In 2009, the conflict-of-interest staff managed income and asset declarations and conflicts of interest for 6,259 filers, making the ratio of staff to filers 1 to 1,138. However, the 2010 Integrity and Prevention of Corruption Act requires disclosure from approximately 14,000 officials, which will likely lead to a need for additional personnel.

- **Recruitment:** All civil servants are hired through a competitive process overseen by a hiring commission, while members (chairs, deputies, and advisers) are appointed by the president based on their qualifications for the positions. For example, one of the commission deputies has experience in the Court of Auditors, and thus assists with financial matters in cases.
- **Qualifications:** Eighty-two percent of nonadministrative staff at the commission have at least four years of postsecondary education. All staff are expected to have a working knowledge of computer programs upon hiring.
- **Training:** By law, all staff are required to receive training on privacy laws. Informal training is conducted by senior staff on regulations and procedures, if necessary. There is also an intranet forum that allows staff to share information across divisions and hierarchies. Staff may attend external training if relevant, as was the case when staff were granted permission by management to attend external training on a new procurement law deemed pertinent to their scope of work.
- **Performance evaluations:** Annual performance evaluations are conducted in line with civil service regulations. There has been little turnover since the commission's inception; loyalty to the organization has been considerable, given the small staff size and the threat of dismantlement from previous governments. Since 2004, the commission staff has more than doubled.

Budget

The proposed budget for all anticorruption activities is submitted by the Commission for the Prevention of Corruption directly to the Ministry of Finance based on the number of staff, whose wages are set according to the Slovenian public wage system.[5] Parliament approves and dispenses funding directly to the commission. Table 10.3 presents an example of budget allocation.

The commission budget has increased steadily since its inception in 2004, which has allowed the commission to enlarge the scope of its operations correspondingly in order to meet its regulatory mandate (see figure 10.3).

Table 10.3 Expenditures of the Commission for the Prevention of Corruption, Slovenia, 2009

Category of expenditure	Amount of expenditure
Salaries of permanent staff	€562,406
Materials	€431,017
Investments (for example, durable goods, training)	€55,657
Total	€1,049,080

Source: Commission for the Prevention of Corruption, Slovenia.

Figure 10.3 Annual Budget of the Commission for the Prevention of Corruption, Slovenia, 2007–10

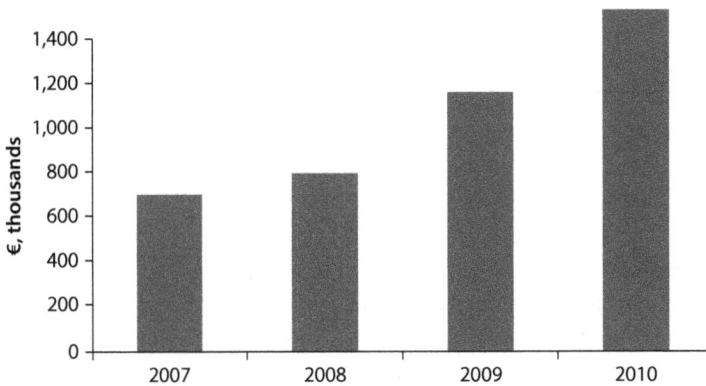

Source: Commission for the Prevention of Corruption, Slovenia.

Regulatory Function

Pursuant to law, the Commission for the Prevention of Corruption will issue administrative (technical) regulations to implement specific provisions. The primary means of communicating the commission's position on corruption cases is through opinions that are posted online for public access, with details of the case removed for privacy purposes. Frequently asked questions regarding laws are also posted online.

According to the 2010 Integrity and Prevention of Corruption Act, the commission is officially responsible for the following regulatory functions:

- Issuing public opinions, positions, recommendations, and explanations on issues of anticorruption, keeping specific case information confidential
- Implementing the Resolution on Prevention of Corruption in the Republic of Slovenia, and drafting amendments to the resolution
- Approving agency plans regarding actions outlined in the resolution
- Implementing obligations derived from international agreements
- Cooperating with responsible government bodies in the drafting of legislation relating to the prevention of corruption and monitoring implementation of legislation

• Submitting initiatives to the National Assembly and the government for amendments to the laws and other regulations falling within the scope of its powers

Managing Submission Compliance

All institutions are obliged to identify IAD declarants within their organizations and to send lists of declarants to the Commission for the Prevention of Corruption within 30 days of any changes. In fact, the commission is not obligated to inform declarants of their filing requirements and deadlines, but in order to obtain complete information, the commission does request each obligated declarant to fulfill his or her duty. Declarants are also consulted if they do not file an IAD form on time or when there are questions about the accuracy of the information submitted on the declaration.

Declaration forms are available for download and in hard copy, but must be submitted on paper directly to the commission. Once received by the commission, basic personal information (nonfinancial) is entered into an Excel file, and each declarant is randomly assigned a number for security and recordkeeping purposes. This process normally takes one to two weeks.

Content Verification

Once personal information is stored electronically, a review is performed on the incompatibility of employment functions (for example, if an individual holds two positions that may not be held simultaneously, such as local mayor and a ministerial post). A review is then performed on the incompatibility of private interests, such as shares, business ownership, outside employment, and public or government office. Finally, a random audit of declarations is performed to identify which cases reveal a disproportionate increase in wealth or a discrepancy between the contents of the declarations and information contained in external registries.

The number of declarations included in the random audit is calculated each year based on the number of staff available. For 2009, 33 percent of declarations were audited in this manner, making the ratio of staff to verified declarations 1 to 413. The commission has designed internal procedures for the verification process, which involves comparing the information on the declaration with information from official databases. Information provided in declarations is checked against tax records, land registries, vehicle registries, livestock records, and corporate records of ownership and shares.[6] This entire verification process normally takes three to four months.

If there are irregularities present, the commission will ask for clarification from the declarant. If further administrative investigation is required, the commission will inform the office where the declarant is employed, since this office may be required to perform its own investigation (inspection) based on public mandate. If criminal activity is suspected, the case is referred to the relevant agency for criminal investigation.

Box 10.2 summarizes the IAD procedures performed by Slovenia's Commission for the Prevention of Corruption.

Income and Asset Disclosure • http://dx.doi.org/10.1596/978-0-8213-9796-1

Box 10.2 IAD Procedures Performed by Slovenia's Commission for the Prevention of Corruption

Slovenia's Commission for the Prevention of Corruption is responsible for managing the submission and verification of income and asset declarations, which includes administrative investigations into disproportionate increases in wealth. Once received by the commission, all income and asset declarations are subject to the following process:

- Basic personal information from the declarations (name, address, identification number, and so forth) is entered into an electronic spreadsheet.
- A check on incompatibility of functions is performed.
- A check on business limitations (shares, ownership, and so forth) is performed.
- A random annual audit of a sample of income and asset declarations to check for irregularities is performed.

If the commission finds a disproportionate increase in wealth, the declarant is asked to explain the discrepancy. If the explanation is not satisfactory, the commission will recommend discharge or removal from office, a sanction that must be implemented by the employing agency. In the case of suspicious findings or the threat of immediate disposal of assets, the commission may refer the case to the relevant criminal investigatory body.

Administrative cases regarding employees are also referred to the appropriate agency inspectorate, should the nature and scope of the case be relevant to the agency mandate.

Investigatory Function

By law, the Commission for the Prevention of Corruption has been granted wide administrative investigatory powers and can impose administrative sanctions for violations of anticorruption provisions, which include IAD requirements. These powers include the authority to demand information from any agency, public or private, for the purposes of verification or investigation into complaints of corruption, and also the authority to impose fines on individuals who do not cooperate. Law enforcement agencies, such as the police or the National Bureau of Investigation, are referred cases only when administrative options are exhausted and criminal penalties are at stake, or when suspicious findings suggest an immediate threat to public funds.

Interagency Collaboration

Under the 2010 Integrity and Prevention of Corruption Act, external agencies are required to provide information, including content audits of declaration forms, to the commission within 15 days of a request for an administrative investigation. Information is transmitted electronically between agencies; the average turnaround time for requests is one week.

The commission must explain the legal grounds for obtaining data and the purpose for which the data will be used. If the agency refuses to cooperate, the commission will refer the case to law enforcement or supervisory bodies for further enforcement. Until recent changes in the management of the ministry, the commission faced considerable difficulty working with the Ministry of the Interior, which includes the police service. Although the commission has now established a memorandum of understanding with the police, there is still difficulty in gaining cooperation with the prosecutor's office with respect to the implementation of criminal policy in line with anticorruption regulations.

The State Prosecutor's Office, the police, the National Bureau of Investigation, and the Office for the Prevention of Money Laundering are jointly tasked with criminal investigations initiated when the commission refers cases with suspicious findings.

The National Assembly has primary oversight over the commission and requires an annual report on the contents and scope of its work; the decisions, findings, and opinions issued by the commission; and an assessment of the current state of corruption and potential for its prevention. However, Parliament continues to demand more information from the commission than is required by law, including the names of complainants, which the commission has repeatedly denied. Despite public proclamations of support for the anticorruption agenda and its implementation by the commission, Parliament also purportedly blocks investigations that are related to ministries.

Public Access to Declarations

Since public availability has only recently been granted—in the 2010 Integrity and Prevention of Corruption Act—as of the writing of this report, it was slated to be initiated during the current round of submission. As per the decision by the Constitutional Court in 2007, there was no public access to the data provided in the declarations. However, high-profile public officials occasionally granted permission for the commission to provide the media with the content of their declarations.

Reporting and Outreach

Data are released annually on disclosure compliance and content audits in annual reports; these data note the number of declarants who were subject to noncompliance sanctions, which are typically fewer than 10 per year. In addition, data on content verification are provided, but no instances have been found of disproportionate increases in wealth or discrepancies intentionally made by declarants. Most discrepancies are the result of recordkeeping failures by external registries. In addition to training sessions for public officials, there is considerable outreach to the public and interaction with the media regarding anticorruption efforts.

Summary of Key Findings

Because of its wide administrative investigatory powers and its enforcement authority, the Slovenian income and asset disclosure system presents both a credible threat of detection and a credible threat of sanction for noncompliance and false disclosure. There is a high probability that violators will be caught, since the random audit covers at least one-third of declarations and the commission can demand information from external entities as part of the verification process. Law enforcement and other relevant agencies may be involved in the verification process if information is not provided within 15 days from a request to provide the information. A significant change made in the legal framework in 2010 allows the commission to apply administrative sanctions and fines on violators, while a memorandum of understanding between the commission and the police force provides a basis for collaboration on potential criminal charges.

Even though public access to IAD content was expected to be instituted in 2010, conflict-of-interest incompatibility checks and IAD content audits should continue to be rigorous. Without access to external databases or technical investigative methods, civil society is left to "lifestyle audits" to establish violations of conflict of interest, IAD requirements, and anticorruption regulations. There is also very little history of investigative journalism in Slovenia, a circumstance that hinders attempts to conduct inquiries into the conduct and undertakings of public entities or officials.

As substantiated by many commission staff, effective leadership is vital to the success of the agency. The first chair of the commission was instrumental in facilitating Slovenia's ratification of the United Nations Convention against Corruption, in increasing the resources available to the commission, and in protecting the mandate of the commission against parliamentary initiatives.[7] At the time of preparing this report, new leadership was expected to be tasked not only with maintaining the profile of the commission, but also with implementing the provisions of the 2010 Integrity and Prevention of Corruption Act, which substantially enlarge the scope of the commission's activities.

Notes

1. The commission was not allowed to verify data with external agencies, such as land and vehicle registries.
2. The Incompatibility of the Exercise of Public Office with Profit-Making Activities Act (ZNOJF-1).
3. Decision U-I-57/06, dated March 29, 2007, the Constitutional Court of Slovenia, *Official Gazette* RS, Nos. 100/05, 46/06, and 33/07, Ljubljana.
4. Nonprofessional mayors, deputy mayors, and lobbyists are exempt from this penalty.
5. IAD functions are not isolated from the overall commission budget.
6. By law, bank accounts cannot be accessed by the commission.
7. Mr. Drago Kos is the President of GRECO and the former chair of the Commission for the Prevention of Corruption.

References

Decision U-I-57/06, dated 29/3-2007, the Constitutional Court of Slovenia. *Official Gazette* RS, Nos. 100/05, 46/06, and 33/07, Ljubljana.

Kos, D. 2005. Establishment and Functioning of the Anti-Corruption Prevention Body (UNCAC, Article 6): The Case of Slovenia. http://www.unodc.org/documents/corruption/Best%20Practices/Slovenia.pdf

OECD (Organisation for Economic Co-operation and Development). 2007. *Specialised Anti-Corruption Institutions: Review of Models.* Paris: OECD.

———. 2010. *Steps Taken to Implement and Enforce the OECD Convention on Combating Bribery of Foreign Public Officials in International Business Transactions: Slovenia.* Paris: OECD.

Slovenian Commission for the Prevention of Corruption. 2009. *Annual Report on the Work of the Commission for the Prevention of Corruption in 2008.* Ljubljana.

Stroligo, K. 1999. "Slovenia: Ethics and Good Governance." *Journal of Financial Crime* 7 (2): 186–90.

CHAPTER 11

United States

Daniel W. Barnes and Tammar Berger

Overview

The primary purpose of the income and asset disclosure (IAD) system in the United States (see box 11.1) is the detection and prevention of potential conflicts of interest. The system is not directly designed to combat illicit enrichment. The required financial disclosures are instead intended to show transparency and independence of public officials and public employees in their decision making and to increase public trust and confidence in the integrity of government.

With one of the oldest systems in the world, the United States presents an important, though relatively unique, case. The current financial disclosure requirements for public officials in the United States at the federal level were established by the Ethics in Government Act of 1978,[1] which sets disclosure requirements for the executive, legislative, and judicial branches of the federal government. The act gives the Office of Government Ethics (OGE) jurisdiction over supervising and monitoring the implementation of and compliance with ethical standards of the executive branch. The legislative and judicial branches are each responsible for their own ethics programs. Each legislative chamber has its own ethics committee—the Senate Select Committee on Ethics and the House Committee on Standards of Official Conduct. The judicial branch ethical programs are under the purview of the Judicial Conference Committee on Codes of Conduct.

Although the OGE is the lead agency responsible for regulating the IAD system of the executive branch of the U.S. government, the overall system is actually highly decentralized. Every agency of the government has a designated agency ethics official (DAEO) (and staff) responsible for implementing an IAD system within his or her agency. The OGE issues detailed regulations and advice

This report is based on desk research and interviews undertaken in July 2010 on behalf of the Stolen Asset Recovery (StAR) Initiative and the Governance & Public Sector Management Unit of the World Bank. The Governance & Public Sector Management Unit and the StAR Initiative would like to thank Joseph Gangloff, Jane Ley, and Wendy Pond of the Office of Government Ethics; Barbara Fredericks and Pamela Smith of the Department of Commerce; and Elizabeth Kellar of the International City/County Management Association for their valuable contributions to the development of this case study.

Box 11.1 Snapshot of the Income and Asset Disclosure System in the United States

Financial disclosure requirements for public officials in the United States at the federal level were established by the Ethics in Government Act of 1978. The Office of Government Ethics (OGE) is the agency responsible for overseeing the IAD system of the executive branch of the government; the legislative and judicial branches are responsible for their own ethics and IAD programs. IAD systems at the state level are regulated by the individual states, each of which is independent in its decision to have a financial disclosure requirement. The IAD system for the executive branch of the federal government in the United States is well established, with high overall compliance with financial disclosure requirements. There are approximately 24,000 public financial declaration filers in the executive branch of the U.S. government and approximately 325,000 filers of confidential financial reports throughout the federal government. Approximately 5,800 executive branch employees administer the federal ethics program. The OGE reports that 99 percent of public filers who were required to declare their income and assets submitted their declarations in 2008.

Key elements of the system include:

- **A design calculated to detect and prevent potential conflicts of interest.** Financial disclosure is intended to enhance and to demonstrate transparency in government and the independence of officials in public office. The system is designed to support public trust and confidence in the integrity of the government.
- **Separate bodies for submission compliance and investigations.** Neither the OGE nor the 134 designated agency ethics officials in the agencies in which officials are employed verifies the accuracy of disclosures. Disclosures are reviewed for completeness and for actual or potential conflicts of interest. If there is a complaint or a clear illegality is detected on a disclosure form, the OGE or the designated agency ethics officials refers the case to the Office of the Inspector General, the Federal Bureau of Investigation, or the Public Integrity Section of the Department of Justice.
- **A centrally managed oversight system with decentralized functions.** Officials submit their financial disclosures to the agency in which they work. Each agency is the primary recipient and reviewer of its employees' disclosures. The OGE receives and reviews the financial disclosures of the president, vice president, and OGE director, and is also a secondary review agency for the financial disclosures of presidential appointees requiring confirmation and of designated agency ethics officials.
- **A user-friendly electronic and paper submission process.** Agencies have the choice of using an electronic or hardcopy filing system. About 20 federal agencies use electronic filing. The OGE retains a hard copy of all the financial disclosures it certifies (which is a subset of disclosures).
- **Public access to income and asset declarations.** Each agency and the OGE (for presidential nominees who require Senate confirmation) is responsible for making public income and asset declarations available upon request by the public within 30 days of submission of the final report. Confidential financial declarations for employees in less senior positions but who are more at risk for conflicts of interest are not available to the public.
- **Sanctions for filing failures.** Criminal, civil, and administrative actions can apply for filing false information or for failing to submit required information. Reports that are deemed incomplete are subject to requests for additional information. A late filing fee of US$200 is assessed if a report is more than 30 days late.

that dictate many of the procedures used by each agency, but each DAEO can tailor the confidential IAD system to his or her specific agency. Although the OGE's role is largely advisory, it is responsible for receiving and analyzing the income and asset declarations of the president and vice president of the United States and the OGE director. It is also the secondary review agency for certain financial disclosures from high-ranking officials from other agencies.

Because of the system's emphasis on identifying and preventing conflicts of interest, declarers are not required to identify the exact value of their assets. Instead, declarations are focused on the source and type of income or asset held by the individual; therefore the U.S. federal disclosure system does not require any type of verification of the information contained in the financial disclosure forms. Instead, the DAEO offices or the OGE analyze the contents of the declarations to determine whether a potential or actual conflict of interest exists based on the income and assets owned by the filer and the responsibilities of their job. The declarations are also reviewed for completeness; entries are taken at face value unless there is a patent omission or ambiguity, or the reviewer has independent knowledge of matters outside the report.

Although there is no systematic verification of the accuracy of declarations, individuals who falsify the forms are subject to criminal, civil, and administrative penalties (18 U.S.C. § 1001 and 5 U.S.C. App. § 104). However, only upon a complaint or readily apparent illegality does the case get referred to the Inspector General's Office of the employee's individual agency, the Federal Bureau of Investigation, or the Public Integrity Section of the Department of Justice for further action. Neither the DAEOs nor the OGE have investigatory or prosecutorial authority, so all investigations are referred to the appropriate law enforcement authorities.

The U.S. IAD system makes the income and asset declarations of only certain high-ranking officials publicly available. The declarations of lower-level employees remain confidential, but they are still reviewed by the DAEOs to identify potential or actual conflicts of interest.

Below the national level, state systems are often similar to the federal framework in that they aim to prevent potential conflicts of interest rather than specifically combat illicit enrichment. However, states are independent from the federal government in their decision to have financial disclosure requirements, and many states have comprehensive ethics programs, ethics commissions designed to improve and ensure the integrity of government, or both. These programs often use income and asset declarations as one of their tools. Currently, 40 of the 50 states have some type of ethics program. However, among the 10 states that do not have ethics programs or commissions, there are states that have a financial disclosure system for state public officials, legislators, candidates for public offices, and lobbyists. Forty-six states require some form of financial disclosure from some class of public officials of the executive branch,[2] and 47 states require some form of financial disclosure from members of their legislatures.[3]

Below the state level, many counties and cities have also created ethics commissions, instituted financial disclosure systems, or both, adding a layer of complexity to understanding ethics and IAD systems in the United States. Indeed, some counties and cities have more comprehensive and well-established programs than their own state programs. These subnational programs, however, lie beyond the purview of this report and are mentioned only to demonstrate the complexity and range of systems to be found throughout the United States.

Background

In the United States, particular attention has always been paid to public ethics, stemming directly from the ideals reflected in the U.S. Constitution. Corruption, along with treason, are the only crimes expressly mentioned in the U.S. Constitution, which says, "The President, Vice President and all civil Officers of the United States, shall be removed from Office on Impeachment for, and Conviction of, Treason, Bribery, or other high Crimes and Misdemeanors."[4] Indeed, the first Code of Conduct for Federal Employees dates back to 1829 and contains provisions that are still relevant today, the most noteworthy of which are provisions prohibiting certain elected officials from accepting gifts.[5]

Notwithstanding these prominent considerations, concerns about the lack of specific standards of conduct and requirements for financial disclosure for government officials,[6] and about the potential impact outside income might have on government officials' decision making, began to surface only in the 1940s. For example, in 1946, Senator Wayne Morse of Oregon introduced a resolution requiring senators to disclose sources of outside income. The senator's resolution, though never adopted, was based on the notion that officials' behavior should be above suspicion and that the disclosure of income would dispel rumors of impropriety. Moreover, in 1951, President Harry Truman sent a message about the ethical standards expected of federal employees in the form of a letter to Congress in which he outlined a framework of ethical conduct for federal employees, including the need for people working in the president's office, members of Congress, and other federal employees to make their financial affairs public.

Although an executive order signed by President Johnson in 1965 established a confidential financial disclosure program in the executive branch,[7] it was not until the 1970s—in the wake of the Watergate scandal involving presidential malfeasance—that public outrage and invigorated public interest in increased transparency and accountability in government provided the necessary impetus for anticorruption legislation. The far-reaching and well-publicized scandal, and the important legislation that followed, helped thrust income and asset disclosure into the mainstream of American public discourse.[8] The U.S. Congress enacted the Government Sunshine Act of 1976 and the Ethics in Government Act of 1978 as part of a push for more transparency in government, with the latter directing a spotlight on IAD systems as tools to help prevent conflicts of interest.[9] Thus the aforementioned legislation was part of a much broader effort to detect and prevent corruption, including creating the first domestic inspectors general, the Office of Special Counsel (to protect whistleblowers), the Federal Election Commission (to regulate election spending), the Office of Personnel Management,[10] and the Merit Systems Protection Board.

At the time of enactment of the Ethics in Government Act, several states already had public financial disclosure laws;[11] the act drew in part on these laws. For the sake of transparency and openness, it sought to change the existing disclosure system for federal officials, which had previously relied only on internal reporting within each agency. The Ethics in Government Act also established which offices are responsible for the collection and reporting of financial disclosures within each branch of government (legislative, judiciary, executive). The law identifies the Clerk of the House of Representatives and the Secretary of the Senate as the appropriate offices for the House and Senate, respectively, and the Judicial Conference for the Judiciary.[12] In relation to the executive, the OGE—a small agency within the executive branch—was established by the act to provide unity and direct policies dealing with conflicts of interest and behavior for the executive branch. The OGE was originally an agency within the Office of Personnel Management, but through the Office of Government Ethics Reauthorization Act of 1988 was made a free-standing agency.[13] The OGE, with its headquarters in Washington, DC, has legal responsibility for "interpreting and implementing certain criminal and civil provisions of the law."[14]

The resulting body of federal law and regulation concerning asset disclosure is structured in response to the concern "that an impairment of impartial judgment can occur in even the most well-meaning men when their personal economic interests are affected by the business they transact on behalf of the government."[15] The government has moved away from "managing conflicts of interest through primarily reactive criminal prosecutions,"[16] as was the case prior to the 1960s, to "a proactive training, education and counseling program focused upon the criminal, civil and administrative standards and the detection and resolution of potential conflicts of interests from financial disclosure reports."[17] The current program is "supported by an effective enforcement system with a range of penalties."[18]

As originally envisioned by Congress, the public financial disclosure requirement is intended to act as a tool for identifying and resolving potential conflicts of interest, and to:

- Increase public confidence in the government
- Demonstrate the high level of integrity of the vast majority of government officials
- Deter conflicts of interest from arising because official activities would be subject to public scrutiny
- Deter persons whose personal finances would not bear up to public scrutiny from entering public service

- Better enable the public to judge the performance of public officials in light of their outside financial interests[19]

Although financial disclosure in the United States has evolved significantly in the last half century, it was not without some pushback. The most notable challenge concerns the balance between public access to information and the protection of privacy rights for individual public officials subject to disclosure requirements.[20] However, as will be seen below, the argument in favor of public access won the day and now plays a major role in the system.

Literature produced by the OGE is helpful in gaining an understanding of the characteristics and complexities of the American disclosure system. As noted, each of the three branches of the U.S. government has its own ethics programs created to manage conflicts of interest, with common elements, including:

- Enforceable standards
- Public and/or confidential financial disclosure systems[21]
- Systematic training and counseling services
- Effective enforcement mechanisms[22]

The U.S. system is also notable for its level of decentralization and for the role of the OGE.[23] The OGE "is responsible for providing overall regulatory direction to the executive branch program for managing conflicts of interest."[24] The office is also responsible for "interpreting and implementing certain criminal and civil provisions of the law."[25]

Much of the relevant literature focuses on the executive branch because it "has the most extensive program."[26] Ultimate responsibility for the administration and enforcement of the ethics program for each executive branch agency falls on the shoulders of the head of that agency. However, "each of dozens of agencies is required to have a designated agency ethics official who is responsible for the administration of the day-to-day activities of managing conflicts of interest."[27] Such "day-to-day" activities include counseling and training employees and reviewing financial disclosure reports. Regional and remote offices, such as postal offices and military bases, often host individuals who have, as part of their responsibilities, the "local" face of that agency's ethics program and who are responsible for managing conflicts of interest. In all, approximately 5,800 employees of the executive branch work in some capacity to administer the ethics program.[28]

Certain individual agencies have created an electronic platform for training public servants in the executive branch on conflict-of-interest standards. Upon completion, the program sends a notification of completion to the agency's ethics official in order to track compliance. As part of regular oversight, and in order to assess the effectiveness of its programs, the OGE has implemented employee surveys to "assess employee knowledge of executive branch rules of ethical conduct, employee awareness of agency ethics program resources, effectiveness of agency ethics education and training, and general agency ethical culture."[29]

The U.S. legislative branch is governed by a similar regulatory structure of its IAD program. Members of Congress are not required to make an actual disclosure when a conflict of interest arises, but rather are forced to abstain from taking any action. "For example, members of the United States Congress ... cannot vote if they have a direct pecuniary interest."[30] However, this requirement has been narrowly interpreted as arising "only when the member's interests are directly affected and not as one of a class affected."[31] For instance, a wheat farmer elected to Congress to represent a constituency of wheat farmers would not be barred from voting on legislation that provided benefits for all wheat farmers; however, the representative would be forced to abstain should those benefits accrue only to his or her farm.[32] In addition, "the declarations of members of Congress are available for public inspection within days of lodgment (upon written application). The declarations are also published in a consolidated form by 1 August each year."[33] In addition to governing disclosures and conflicts of interest, the U.S. law strictly "limits campaign donations for congressional elections."[34]

In addition to OGE guidance, Executive Order 12674 (1989), as amended by Executive Order 12731 (1990), states 14 general principles that define the obligations of public servants.[35] In summary, these principles state that public officials and public servants shall not use public office for private gain, shall act impartially and not give preferential treatment to anyone, and must strive to avoid any action that would create an appearance that the law or ethical standards are being violated.[36]

Box 11.2 provides a timeline of the evolution of the IAD legal framework in the United States.

The IAD Legal Framework in the United States

Financial disclosure laws in the United States at the federal level are aimed primarily at the detection and prevention of conflicts of interest.[37] The laws are detailed and comprehensive in scope and extend far beyond the financial disclosure of income and assets. The laws also address the issues of outside activities of senior officials,[38] postemployment restrictions,[39] and remedies for financial conflicts of interest.[40]

As mentioned, the financial disclosure requirements for public officials are established by the Ethics in Government Act of 1978. The act prescribes disclosure requirements for the executive, legislative, and judicial branches of the federal government. The duty to supervise and monitor the implementation of and compliance with ethical standards of the executive branch stipulated by the act is carried out by the OGE. The legislative branch is responsible for its own ethics programs. Each legislative chamber has its own ethics committee—the Senate Select Committee on Ethics and the House Committee on Standards of Official Conduct. The judicial branch ethical programs fall under the purview of the Judicial Conference Committee on Codes of Conduct.

In addition to the statutory language adopted by Congress, the OGE has issued regulations clarifying the specific requirements of the IAD system of

Income and Asset Disclosure · http://dx.doi.org/10.1596/978-0-8213-9796-1

Box 11.2 Timeline of the Evolution of the IAD Legal Framework in the United States

1951 – Financial Disclosure Law Recommended by President Harry S. Truman, September 27, 1951, *Congressional Record*, vol. 123, part 24 (September 27, 1977), pp. 31313–31314. President Truman's message to Congress supporting public disclosure of personal finances by senior members of all three branches of government.

1958 – Code of Ethics for Government Service, 72 Stat. B12, H.Con.Res. 175. 85th Cong., House proceeding, *Congressional Record*, vol. 103, part 12 (August 28, 1957), p. 16297, addressing the issue of conflicts of interest.

1965 – Executive Order 11222, signed into law by President Lyndon B. Johnson on May 8, 1965, prescribing standards of ethical conduct for government officers and employees and establishing a confidential financial disclosure system for heads of agencies and certain White House staff.

1978 – Ethics in Government Act, S. Rept. 95–170, 95th Cong., 1st Sess. 117 (1977), establishing public financial disclosure for senior officials of the federal government.

1979 – *Duplantier v. United States,* 606 F.2d 654 (5th Cir. 1979). The Court of Appeals reasoned that the Ethics in Government Act should remain valid if it "substantially furthered government interests." The court explained that the public's interest in accountability and integrity of public officials outweighed judicial officials' privacy interest in regard to their financial privacy.

1988 – Office of Government Ethics Reauthorization Act, Pub. L. 100–598, 102 Stat. 3031 (1988).

1989 – Ethics Reform Act, Pub. L. 101–194, 202, 103 Stat. 1716, at 1724 (1989).

1989 – Executive Order 12674, signed into law by President George H. W. Bush providing the framework for the ethical behavior required of all federal employees in the effort to ensure public confidence in the integrity of the federal government. (Later modified by Executive Order 12731.)

1996 – Office of Government Ethics Authorization Act, Pub. L. 104–179, 110 Stat. 1566.

2009 – *United States v. Carbo,* 572 F.3d 112, 119 (3d Cir. 2009). The Court of Appeals broadened liability for failure to disclose financial interests to private citizens associated with public officials.

---

the executive branch of the U.S. government. These regulations are found in the Code of Federal Regulations, 5 C.F.R. Part 2634—Executive Branch Financial Disclosure, Qualified Trusts, and Certificates of Divestiture (1992), which provides the requirements and procedures for the executive branch IAD system. The regulations governing the IAD system are complex, detailed, and technical.

Coverage of Officials

The Ethics in Government Act and 5 C.F.R. Part 2634 establish two types of IAD requirements: public disclosure and confidential disclosure. The public financial disclosure system applies to high-ranking government officials, and the confidential financial disclosure system covers lower-ranking officials and employees who hold positions that are more at risk for conflicts of interest.

Section 101 of Title I of the Ethics in Government Act and 5 C.F.R. Part 2634.202 list executive branch officials who are required to file publicly available income and asset declarations. This list includes, among others, the president, vice president, and secretaries of agencies (ministers). As noted, members of Congress also declare their income and assets, but those declarations are regulated by internal rules of the House of Representatives and the Senate.

Among the other public filers are senior executive branch officers and employees above the GS-15 level,[41] certain special government employees,[42] certain political appointees, high-ranking members of the military and other uniformed services (those whose pay grade is at or higher than 0–7 under 37 U.S.C. 201, which corresponds to all generals and admirals), the director of the OGE, and each government agency's primary DAEO. Income and asset declarations are also required of presidential nominees who require Senate confirmation. In addition, presidential and vice-presidential candidates and individuals running for Congress are required to file income and asset declarations when they file for candidacy. Interestingly, the declarations of congressional candidates are filed with the Federal Election Commission, an agency of the executive branch. The Federal Election Commission, however, determines who has become a candidate, which is a trigger for filing the form.

Spouses and dependent children of public filers are not required to file separate financial disclosure reports; however, sources of earned income (above a minimum threshold), honorariums, investment income, assets, gifts, reimbursements (when not received totally independent of a relationship with the filer), liabilities, and transactions for spouses and dependent children must be disclosed on the public official's financial disclosure form.

In addition to the list of public filers appointed by the president—which total approximately 1,200 individuals—less-senior executive branch employees, whose government duties involve the exercise of significant discretion in certain sensitive areas, report their financial interests and outside business activities to their employing agencies to facilitate the review for possible conflicts of interest. These declarations (totaling approximately 24,000 across the entire executive branch of the government) assist an agency in administering its ethics program and counseling its employees, while also making these declarations available to the public.

In summary, the law and federal regulations explicitly define the list of public filers and requires the disclosure of assets, income, and outside positions.

Content of Declarations

Filers of publicly available income and asset declarations are required to disclose their financial interests and those of their spouse and minor children on OGE Form 278 (table 11.1).

Importantly, the public declaration system in the United States does not require the declaration of specific values of the assets and investment income of

Table 11.1 Required Contents of Income and Asset Declarations, United States

Assets

Interests in property held in a trade or business or for investment or the production of income
(real estate, stocks, bonds, securities, futures contracts, beneficial interest in trusts or estates,
pensions and annuities, mutual funds, farms, and so forth) that meet reporting thresholds; reported
by categories of values

Sources and amounts of income

Sources, type, and amount by category of value of investment income meeting a threshold amount

Sources and exact amounts of earned income (other than from U.S. government employment),
including honorariums

Transactions

Purchases, sales, and exchanges of real property and securities that meet reporting thresholds

Liabilities

Creditor, amount by category, and terms of liabilities meeting a threshold amount reached at any point
during the reporting period (major exceptions include mortgage on personal residence, certain
family loans, and some revolving credit obligations)

Gifts and reimbursements

Gifts and reimbursements that meet reporting thresholds

Positions held outside of government

Positions as an officer, director, trustee, partner, proprietor, representative, employee, or consultant

Agreements and arrangements with respect to past or future employment

Parties to and terms of any agreement or arrangement with respect to future employment, leaves of
absence, payments from and/or continuing participation in a benefit plan of a previous employer

Major clients (first-time filers only)

Identity of each source of income over a threshold amount generated by the performance of personal
services for that source

Source: U.S. Office of Government Ethics, OGE Form 278, 5 C.F.R. Part 2634 OMB No. 3209 – 0001.

the items listed above (although it does require exact amounts for earned income). Instead, the filing form contains value ranges, such as US$0 to US$1,001 and US$1,001 to US$15,000, with the highest range being for items whose value exceeds US$50 million. Not requiring specific values is consistent with the IAD system's focus on identifying and preventing potential conflicts of interest rather than monitoring illegal wealth accumulation.

The confidential reporting system requires employees to provide only information relevant to the administration and application of criminal conflict-of-interest laws, administrative standards of conduct, and agency-specific statutory and program-related restrictions.[43] Though similar to the public disclosure form, the declaration form designed for confidential reporting (OGE Form 450) differs from the public disclosure form (OGE 278) mainly in that Form 450 does not require categories of asset values and income amounts to be reported, nor does it require financial interests (including salary, consulting fees, honorariums, equity interests, interests in real or personal property, dividends, royalties, rent, capital gains, intellectual property income, money market mutual funds, or U.S. obligations and government securities) to be reported. Instead, the form requires only the declaration of the asset itself, rather than its specific value. The biggest difference, however, is that OGE

Form 450 is confidential and not available to the public. There are approximately 325,000 filers of confidential financial reports throughout the federal government.

Filing Frequency

The Ethics in Government Act and 5 C.F.R. Part 2634 set specific deadlines for submitting income and asset declarations. Public filers are required to file annual declarations (OGE Form 278) by May 15 if they held an office for at least 60 days in the preceding calendar year. Presidential nominees who require Senate confirmation are required to submit the declaration within five days of the public announcement of their nomination. New employees are required to file public financial disclosure reports within 30 days of assuming an office that is covered by the disclosure requirements. Upon termination of employment, the public filer is required to file a final public financial report within 30 days. In each case, it is possible to obtain an extension of up to 90 days.

For confidential filers (OGE Form 450), the deadline for annual filing is February 15.[44] Based on information provided by the filers, if there has been no change in the financial situation of the individual from the previous reporting year, a shorter form is used; using the short form (OGE Form 450-A), the filer recertifies the contents of the previous form and states that there have been no changes in his or her financial status.

Sanctions

Section 104 of Title I of the Ethics in Government Act, 5 C.F.R. 2634.701 and 704, and 18 U.S.C. 1001 enumerate sanctions for filing failures. Criminal, civil, and administrative actions may be taken against a filer who submits false information or fails to submit required information. Reports deemed incomplete are subject to requests for additional information. A late-filing fee of US$200 is assessed if a report is more than 30 days late.

A civil monetary penalty of up to US$50,000 may be assessed against nonfilers or individuals who knowingly and willfully submit false information in their financial disclosure reports. Administratively imposed disciplinary sanctions may also be applied to nonfilers or individuals who fail to submit required information. An individual may also be subject to criminal sanctions (including imprisonment) for knowingly and willfully providing false information in a financial disclosure report or for failing to file.[45]

Submission Compliance and Content Verification

All public filers, including Senior Executive Service employees, submit their income and asset declarations to the DAEO where the individual is employed. The president and vice president file their declarations with the director of the OGE. Presidential and vice-presidential candidates file income and asset declarations with the Federal Election Commission, which reviews them and then sends copies of the reports to the director of the OGE. The OGE reviews and certifies these reports.

Income and Asset Disclosure • http://dx.doi.org/10.1596/978-0-8213-9796-1

Public financial disclosure reports of presidential nominees for positions that require Senate confirmation are reviewed prior to confirmation hearings by the White House Counsel's Office, by the agencies in which the nominees will serve, and by the OGE. The OGE certifies the final reports before they are transmitted to the Senate. The information in the reports is carefully analyzed for potential conflicts, and appropriate remedial measures are agreed to in a formal ethics agreement between the appointee and the government. Both the agency DAEO and the OGE track a presidential appointee's compliance with any ethics agreement that the appointee made during the confirmation process. These agreements may concern the financial interests of the appointee and of the appointee's spouse or dependent children. An appointee is required to certify, with documentation to the OGE, that such agreements have been satisfied within 90 days of confirmation.[46]

Neither the separate agencies nor the OGE has authority to independently check the bank accounts, tax records, or brokerage accounts of the public filers. Explicit criteria in the law are used to confirm the completeness of each financial disclosure report, but no agency is responsible for verifying the report's accuracy. Once the reviewing official of the report identifies a potential conflict between the filer's duties and the disclosed financial interests, and since the purpose of disclosure is to detect potential conflicts of interest and prevent them, the reviewer consults with the filer and possibly the filer's supervisor. Several remedies are made available to avoid an actual violation of laws or regulations. Those remedies include recusal or disqualification, waiver, divestiture, and creation of a qualified trust. If a review discloses an actual or potential violation of a law or regulation—such as the outside earned income restrictions or a law prohibiting ownership of a particular asset—other steps may be taken, including referral for investigation.

Public Access to Declarations

Each agency is responsible for making the public income and asset declarations available, upon request by a member of the public, within 30 days of submission of the final report. The request must be made in writing. Agencies may use OGE Form 201 as an application form for requests to furnish a public financial disclosure report. The application includes:

- The requesting person's name, occupation, and address
- The name and address of any other person or organization on whose behalf the inspection or copy is requested
- Provisions stating that the requesting person is aware of certain prohibitions against obtaining or using the report (including commercial uses)[47]

A reasonable fee, established by agency regulation, may be levied to cover the cost of reproduction or mailing of public financial disclosure reports. Financial disclosure reports are maintained for six years after submission, except in cases of ongoing investigation.

State Systems (in Brief)

As noted, each state is free to decide for itself whether to have an IAD system for state officials and employees. The federal IAD system is entirely distinct from the state systems. Some states have laws and regulations and quite comprehensive ethics programs, including well-established financial disclosure processes; others have no requirements. Generally speaking, the purpose of financial disclosures at the state level is to identify and prevent conflicts of interest, just as it is at the national level. Currently, 40 states have some type of ethics program, but among these, not all require financial disclosure. In 10 states there are no ethics commissions, but some of those states do have financial disclosure requirements for public officials, legislators, lobbyists, candidates for office, and others.[48] Forty-six of the 50 states require some form of financial disclosure from some class of public officials in the executive branch,[49] and 47 states require some form of financial disclosure from members of their legislatures.[50]

Box 11.3 provides a brief description of the IAD system in one state, Maryland, and one county within that state, Montgomery County, as one example of the range of systems that exist in the United States.

Mandate and Structure of the IAD Agency

The OGE plays a leadership role in preventing conflicts of interest in the executive branch of the U.S. federal government and in detecting and resolving potential conflicts of interests that occur. The OGE aims to raise public confidence in the integrity and impartiality of members of the executive branch.[51]

The OGE is divided into six programs and agency support offices:

- The Office of the Director
- The Office of the General Counsel and Legal Policy
- The Office of International Assistance and Governance Initiatives
- The Office of Agency Programs
- The Office of Administration
- Information Resources Management (figure 11.1).

The OGE director is appointed by the president and confirmed by the Senate. The director advises the White House and executive branch presidential appointees on government ethics matters; provides guidance on ethics to executive branch departments and agencies; and oversees and coordinates all OGE rules, regulations, formal advisory opinions, and major policy decisions.[52]

Following is a description of the responsibilities of each relevant OGE division.

The Office of the General Counsel and Legal Policy develops regulations and legislative proposals pertaining to conflict-of-interest statutes and standards of ethical conduct applicable to executive branch officers and employees, and

---

Box 11.3 Financial Disclosure at the State and County Levels in Maryland

Financial Disclosure at the State Level in Maryland

In the State of Maryland, the State Ethics Commission administers the financial disclosure program for state elected officials, state agency managers, regulators, purchasing staff, and some of the appointed members of boards and commissions. More than 8,000 state officials must file annual financial disclosure statements. The filers are required to disclose real estate interests, equity interests, and other relationships such as employment, debts, and gifts.

The purpose of financial disclosure is to show the integrity and impartiality of the officials and their independence of judgment. The deadline for annual filing is April 30. New filers must file within 30 days of assuming an office that requires financial disclosure. Persons leaving office are required to file a termination statement within 60 days of leaving that position.

The financial disclosure forms are available to the public. However, individuals wishing to examine or copy a statement must appear in person to register their names and home addresses as well as the name of persons whose statements they wish to examine or copy. A person who has a statement on file is entitled, upon request, to be notified of the name and address of anyone inspecting his or her statement.

Financial Disclosure in Montgomery County, Maryland

The Montgomery County Ethics Law (Montgomery County Code Chapter 19A. Ethics) requires county employees and those serving on county boards, committees, commissions, and other public employees to file financial disclosure statements. The law and a supplementing Executive Regulation and Council Resolution specify, by employment position, who must file a financial disclosure form. These regulations also specify whether the disclosure is public, limited public, or confidential.

There are over 1,900 filers in Montgomery County. The filers are required to disclose all economic interests in real property or any business, all sources of income from economic interests that meet the threshold, all gifts received by the filer or members of the filer's immediate family, debts and liabilities, and other relationships such as directorships and trusteeships.

The deadline for annual filing is April 15. The employee or volunteer is required to file a financial disclosure report within 15 days after he or she begins employment or service in a position. In addition, employees or volunteers required to file disclosures must file a termination disclosure just prior to terminating their employment. A final paycheck will not be issued until the employee has filed the required financial disclosure statement. The public financial disclosure forms are available to the public upon request.

Sources: http://ethics.gov.state.md.us/bluepamphlet.htm; and http://ethics.gov.state.md.us/Ethics%20Law.pdf.

---

pertaining to executive branch public and confidential financial disclosure requirements. In addition, this office provides advice and counseling to agency ethics officials through formal and informal advisory opinions, policy memoranda, and consultations. This office also manages the OGE's review and certification of financial disclosure reports filed by persons nominated by the president for positions requiring Senate confirmation.[53]

Figure 11.1 Organizational Chart of the Office of Government Ethics, United States

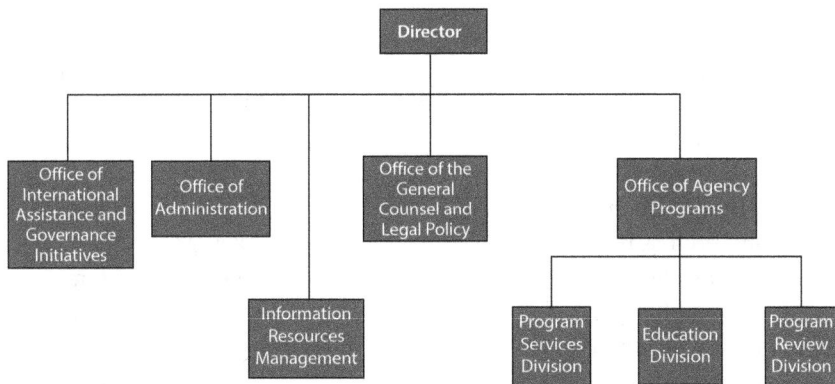

Source: Office of Government Ethics, the United States.

The Office of International Assistance and Governance Initiatives focuses on sharing with other countries technical information and practical experiences in establishing standards of conduct, issuing rules and regulations on conflict of interest restrictions, establishing the framework for financial disclosure systems, developing training and education programs, and providing assistance in understanding the relationship of the OGE ethics program to other governmental systems designed to promote transparency and institutional integrity. The goal of the OGE's international technical assistance and cooperation program is to assist other nations in developing and improving programs intended to prevent corruption and promote integrity within government.[54]

The Office of Agency Programs has three divisions that monitor and provide services to federal agency ethics programs. These are the Program Services Division, the Program Review Division, and the Education Division. The three divisions coordinate their services to assist agencies in carrying out their programs.

- *The Program Services Division (PSD)* provides liaison and program support services to each executive branch department and agency ethics office through the Desk Officer Program. Each department and agency is assigned an OGE desk officer who is responsible for providing assistance in maintaining effective ethics programs and providing advice and guidance on the standards of conduct for employees of the executive branch.

    In addition, the PSD manages the annual and termination public financial disclosure reporting system for approximately 1,100 presidential appointees confirmed by the Senate (presidential appointment with Senate confirmation, or PAS, positions) and 133 designated agency ethics officials. After individual agencies review these reports based on their own guidelines, they are returned to the OGE and the PSD for final review and certification. An additional 25,000 high-level officials are required to file an OGE 278 (the public

Income and Asset Disclosure • http://dx.doi.org/10.1596/978-0-8213-9796-1

financial disclosure report form) with their agencies for certification at the agency only. Within the OGE, the PSD has primary responsibility for tracking, collecting, reviewing, and certifying these public reports. The staff also review public financial disclosure reports filed by presidential appointees confirmed by the Senate at the time of their nomination, and track and ensure compliance with ethics agreements made by these presidential appointees during their confirmation process.

The PSD also handles administrative aspects of the financial disclosure program, such as responding to agency requests for exemptions.[55]

- *The Program Review Division (PRD)* conducts on-site ethics program reviews of agency and department headquarters and regional offices to determine whether an agency has an effective ethics program tailored to its mission. Program reviews entail a thorough analysis of the agency's implementation of all basic requirements of an ethics program, as well as more unique elements of a program that may arise because of the specific mission of the agency. Among individual ethics program elements that PRD examines are public and confidential financial disclosure, outside activities, and postemployment.
- *The Education Division* develops and provides ethics training courses and materials for executive branch departments and agencies. This division trains agency ethics officials and creates tools that ethics officials can use when training their agency employees.[56]

Although the OGE is the lead agency responsible for regulating the IAD system of the executive branch of the U.S. government, the system is actually highly decentralized. As noted, every agency of the executive branch has a DAEO (and staff) responsible for implementing an IAD system within the agency. The OGE issues detailed regulations and advice that dictate many of the procedures used by the agency, but—for the confidential disclosure portion of their system, and subject to OGE approval—each DAEO can tailor the IAD system to his or her particular agency. Although the OGE's role is largely advisory, it is responsible for receiving and analyzing the income and asset declarations of the president and vice president of the United States and the OGE director. It is also the secondary review agency for certain financial disclosures of high-ranking officials from other agencies.

Resources and Procedures of the IAD System

Because of the decentralized and complex nature of the IAD system in the United States, a comprehensive review of the functioning of every individual DAEO was impossible. Instead, detailed interviews with OGE personnel were used to construct a picture of how the U.S. system functions broadly. The same set of in-practice indicators used across each case study in this volume was used in the United States, but was applied primarily to the OGE. However, because the OGE closely monitors the IAD systems administered by every DAEO, its staff was able to provide information and data regarding the operation of these individual systems as well as its own operation. The details of the system are described below.

Facilities and Use of Technology

Both the OGE and the individual agency DAEO offices have sufficient facilities to perform their assigned functions. Although detailed information regarding the exact size of the OGE facility was not available, the building accommodates all staff, files, and technology requirements. In addition to containing offices for all staff, the OGE headquarters has secure facilities for the storage of all income and asset declarations submitted to it. The OGE reports that the same is true for every individual agency with a designated ethics official. These agencies maintain secure storage facilities for all declarations submitted to them.

The OGE and the DAEO offices in individual agencies employ sophisticated information technology systems to manage the IAD system in the executive branch of the U.S. government. All employees have computers, and the vast majority of their work requires their use. Computer hardware at the OGE was upgraded in 2009, and both hardware and software were less than 10 years old at most agencies.

The OGE receives the official, signed hard copies of the income and asset declarations. The individual agencies vary in their use of electronic submission, with some agencies allowing electronic submission and others still requiring hardcopy submission. Regardless of the method of submission, however, the OGE and the individual agencies must manually review the declarations to determine whether any potential conflicts of interest exist.

Human Resources

Ninety-three percent of the OGE professional nonadministrative staff has at least four years of postsecondary education. No statistics are kept specifically on staff turnover, but the OGE believes the number is quite low. Personnel receive general training in administrative processes and relevant laws and regulations covering asset disclosure upon hiring. As needed, staff get computer hardware or software training. All agency staff receive periodic performance evaluations.

At the individual agency level, other than for an attorney position, there are no postsecondary education requirements. Further, the reviewing staff receive training approximately twice a month, the public filers are trained every year, and confidential filers get training every three years. Competitive recruitment is used to staff ethics offices within the agencies, as per Office of Personnel Management regulations.[57] Newly hired personnel are required to know how to use computer software such as word processing programs, e-mail, and spreadsheet programs.

Budget

The cost of the aggregate IAD system of the executive branch of the U.S. government is difficult to compile because of the decentralized nature of the system. However, the OGE reports that funding is generally adequate to ensure that DAEOs have the ability to monitor submission compliance, enforce sanctions, and analyze declarations for conflicts of interest. There is, of course, variation in the staffing, budget, and level of commitment to the IAD process across agencies, but the OGE uses its regulatory power to ensure compliance with the requirements of the Ethics in Government Act of 1978.

The OGE's 2008 budget was about US$13.4 million.[58] The budget, itself, is a helpful indicator of the resources available to an IAD system. However, another metric sometimes discussed is the ratio of declarations to staff member. The U.S. system relies on manual reviews of declarations to determine whether a conflict of interest exists, making this ratio particularly important. However, as will be seen, the raw ratio can vary widely depending on the specific reviewing responsibilities of the staff involved, rendering comparisons of these ratios across countries difficult to interpret.

Regardless, it is interesting to examine the example of one agency, the U.S. Department of Commerce, which had 617 annual public filers, 136 new entrants, and 120 termination reports in 2008. There are 14 staff persons handling the annual filings and two attorneys working almost exclusively on new entrant reports. This results in an approximate ratio of 53 declarations per staff member and 68 declarations per attorney. In 2008, there were 7,100 confidential financial disclosure filers and seven staff persons working on such confidential disclosures (representing a ratio of 1,014 declarations per staff member). Most of the confidential reports are short forms that certify that no changes have taken place in the filer's financial situation since the prior year's report.

Regulatory Function

The OGE is the body that, by law, has ultimate regulatory authority over the entire executive branch IAD system. The agency is legally allowed to issue regulations. Specifically, the Office of the General Counsel and Legal Policy within the OGE develops regulations and legislative proposals on conflict-of-interest statutes and standards of ethical conduct. All staff members have clearly written job descriptions that are communicated to employees. Operating manuals are comprehensive and available to staff.

Since the OGE's financial disclosure program is established, there are no new implementing regulations being issued on a yearly basis. However, at least every three years the gifts and travel reimbursement reporting thresholds are adjusted by amended regulations. The OGE regularly issues "DAEOgrams," which are memoranda from the OGE to the executive branch DAEOs providing guidance on how to interpret and comply with modifications to conflict-of-interest regulations, standards of conduct regulations, or financial disclosure policies and procedures. Of the DAEOgrams mentioned above, approximately 40 percent deal with statutory interpretation concerns and approximately 60 percent deal with procedural issues of the IAD system.

In addition, the OGE's Office of the General Counsel issues opinions in response to questions the OGE receives about conflict-of-interest laws and regulations, standards of conduct, and financial disclosure requirements in the executive branch. These are informal advisory opinions that are now so extensive (more than 1,200) that they form a body of detailed guidance that can prove useful for filers and agencies alike. These advisory opinions are not, strictly speaking, legally precedential. In practice, similar factual cases are likely to be decided in the same manner, and thus these cases do offer insight into interpretation of the law and regulations. However, from a legal perspective, the OGE is not making "common law" with these advisory opinions. Instead, administrative law judges will apply the law de novo to each case presented before them. These advisory opinions from OGE are an effective means of offering informal (though highly reasoned) advice to filers and DAEOs regarding specific questions of interpretation about how to comply with the IAD system regulations.

Managing Submission Compliance

The OGE is the primary recipient of the financial disclosure reports of the president, vice president, and the OGE director; it is also the secondary review agency for the financial disclosures of the most senior officials of all the agencies. Each agency is designated as the primary recipient and reviewer of its employees' disclosures. Filers of public financial disclosures are identified by position and level of pay, while filers of confidential financial disclosures are midlevel employees who hold positions that pose a higher risk of conflicts of interest. The risk level is based on an agency's determination using criteria issued by the OGE.

Approximately 25,000 high-level officials are required to file form OGE 278 with their agencies for certification by the agency. The OGE manages the nominee and new entrant annual and termination public financial disclosure reporting system for approximately 1,100 presidential appointees confirmed by the Senate (PAS positions) and 133 DAEOs.

The filing forms clearly reflect the statutory requirements. The forms are available in both hard copy and electronically, although PAS forms are submitted to the OGE in hard copy. Individual agencies have either electronic or hardcopy submission processes in place. Each agency is responsible for managing and annually updating the internal filers list. Obligated parties receive official notices regarding submissions, amendments, and consultations. This is required by the regulations, and each agency is responsible for its filers.

All income and asset declarations are subject to review. Reports are not "audited"; they are reviewed for completeness, internal consistency, and actual or potential conflicts of interest.

Content Verification

Neither the OGE nor the agencies audit or verify the financial disclosures for accuracy. The reports are reviewed for completeness and actual or potential conflicts of interest. As we have repeatedly noted, the purpose of the IAD system in the United States is to detect and prevent potential conflicts of interest; thus the system is designed to check only for completeness and to identify potential conflicts of interest. In fact, the legislative history of the Ethics in Government Act specifically says that these disclosures will not be audited.

Investigatory Function and Interagency Collaboration

Neither the OGE nor the ethics offices within the agencies have an investigatory function. If there is a complaint regarding inaccuracy or the withholding of information on the filing form that appears to be something more than an unintentional error (which employees are first encouraged to correct), the case gets referred to the inspector general of the individual agency or to the Federal Bureau of Investigation. Neither the OGE nor DAEO offices in individual agencies have access to nonpublic information held by other government agencies (such as tax records) for verification of the accuracy of information reported on the income and asset declarations.

The absence of investigative and prosecutorial authority within the OGE has not diminished the effectiveness of the system; other federal investigative resources and the prosecutors' offices are sufficiently reliable and adequately resourced that they pursue these cases when they are forwarded to them by the OGE.

Although the OGE and individual agencies do not review income and asset declarations for the specific purpose of finding evidence of a crime, these declarations are regularly used in the prosecution of corruption-related crimes and other criminal offenses by public officials. In fact, the OGE conducts an annual survey of prosecutions involving the conflict-of-interest criminal statutes (18 U.S.C. §§ 202–209). The information is provided to the OGE by the Executive Office for United States Attorneys at the Department of Justice. U.S. Attorneys' offices and the Public Integrity Section of the Department of Justice's Criminal Division handle these prosecutions. Table 11.2 shows the breakdown of the cases prosecuted that involve financial disclosure failures.[59]

Public Access

The OGE (for presidential appointees) and the employing agency (for OGE personnel) are responsible for ensuring public access to a copy of income and asset declarations. The OGE usually provides the income and asset declarations on the same day they are requested. Copies of declarations are not posted on the Internet by the OGE or agencies, and instead are available only in hard copy. The law currently requires an individual request for a copy of the form. By law, the public asset declarations have to be available to the public, upon request, within 30 days after being received by the agency.

Table 11.2 Cases Involving Financial Disclosure Failures, United States, 2006–07

Year	Total prosecutions involving conflicts of interest	Total financial disclosure offenses	Failure-to-disclose cases	Making-false-statement cases	Falsely certifying confidential statement	Failure to file termination report	Cases involving financial disclosure failures in combination with other offenses
2006	12	5	1	1	1	0	2
2007	19	6	1	1	1	1	2

Source: Public Integrity Section, Department of Justice, the United States.

Federal law prohibits the commercial use of (profiting from) IAD forms or the data contained therein. However, there is no restriction on copying and disseminating the forms or the data contained in them as long as there is no commercial gain in doing so. In practice, the media, nongovernmental organizations, and private citizens access the declarations of certain public officials and actively disseminate the information contained in them. Indeed, in 2008, the OGE received 79 separate requests from the public for copies of 421 individual declarations. These numbers are higher than normal, though, because 2008 was a transition year to a new presidential administration.

Reporting and Outreach

The OGE submits to Congress an annual *Performance Accountability Report*, which is available on the OGE's website. The report includes:

- Accomplishments related to the initiatives undertaken by the OGE to meet its main priorities as set forth in its strategic plan
- Assessment and determination that the OGE's systems for accounting and internal control are in compliance with the provisions of the Federal Managers' Financial Integrity Act
- An auditing report on the OGE's financial statements, certifying that no material weaknesses were found related to the OGE's compliance and internal controls over financial reporting

The main priorities for FY2008 and FY2009 were to:

- Assist in the transition to a new administration
- Engage agency leadership in developing and supporting an ethical culture
- Use technology to improve the delivery of ethics services, information, and materials

The OGE made substantial progress during FY2008 in all three areas. The metrics show that the actual results for performance targets were higher than projected for this period.[60]

As can be seen by the comprehensiveness of its annual report, the OGE maintains an extremely high level of capacity to monitor and regulate the IAD system for the executive branch of the U.S. government. Not only does it have a detailed organizational chart of the agency, listing the specific functions and responsibilities of its various departments, but it maintains a highly skilled staff that produce detailed regulations and advisory opinions that help guide both filers and DAEOs.

The OGE is primarily charged with advisory responsibility, but the individual agencies provide preliminary advice to their employees on ethics issues and financial disclosures. The OGE's response rate to requests for advice on financial disclosures is 100 percent. The OGE tries to respond within 24 hours, but response time depends on the complexity of the question.

Income and Asset Disclosure • http://dx.doi.org/10.1596/978-0-8213-9796-1

Summary of Key Findings

The income and asset disclosure system in the United States is a well-established and comprehensive system, with emphasis on the trust and confidence of the public toward the integrity and impartiality of the government. The federal system has a well-regulated and functioning framework in place, with the Office of Government Ethics in charge of supervision and oversight of the overall ethics programs, including financial disclosure processes.

At the state level, the situation is different, because there are no mandatory requirements for states to have financial disclosure systems. Therefore, some states have extensive ethics programs with well-established financial disclosure mechanisms, while other states have only limited financial disclosure requirements.

Major Achievements

The decentralized nature of the IAD system for the executive branch of the U.S. federal government makes it both tailored to the specific needs of individual agencies and more difficult to monitor closely. However, the United States has devoted significant resources to ensuring that income and asset declarations are closely analyzed in order to identify and prevent potential conflicts of interest. By adopting a proactive and collaborative approach with filers, the U.S. system helps officials avoid conflicts. In addition, the OGE reports that 99 percent of public filers who were required to declare their income and assets submitted their declarations in 2008.

Continuing Challenges

The lack of electronic filing at most agencies is an obstacle to filing, particularly since all filers have regular access to computers at their jobs. Currently, only 31 agencies or entities have electronic filing available for their employees at the federal level. Though it requires significant financial resources and political will to establish electronic filing, the advantages of an electronic system are considerable. For example, electronic filing saves time and storage space and, most important, enables the ethics officials to more easily detect flaws or incomplete applications and to quickly conduct comparative analyses of data to identify conflicts of interest. This also allows agencies to do more comprehensive forensic analyses to look for anomalies or vulnerabilities.

In addition, the OGE itself has recommended that the filing form be simplified and tailored more specifically to the task it is meant to achieve: identifying and preventing potential conflicts of interest.[61] Indeed, in this context, the primary information needed is simply the source of income and what the asset is, rather than its approximate value placed in an arbitrary value band. Because of the sometimes unnecessary detail required, OGE officials have, on occasion, discouraged the adoption of a similar IAD form by other countries. The rest of the system, however, provides a valuable example of a high-capacity, comprehensive, and well-functioning conflict-of-interest model.

Furthermore, the United States does not conduct verification audits of the contents of declarations. Instead, there is a clear emphasis on working with filers to help them identify potential trouble areas where their financial interests may conflict with their public duties. As a result, the U.S. system has chosen to forswear auditing these declarations, even though this approach may undermine the system's ability to identify inaccuracies on the forms or to identify underlying corrupt behavior.

However, the United States has explicitly chosen to frame its IAD system as a collaborative process with filers—one in which the IAD system is there to help filers avoid the possibility of inadvertently placing themselves in a conflict-of-interest situation. In part, this decision was enabled by a strong Federal Bureau of Investigation, which actively investigates any credible allegations of corruption; the Inspector General's Offices, which investigate potential corruption within their agencies; and the Public Integrity Section of the Department of Justice, which actively prosecutes credible cases of corruption in the public sector.

Key Lessons

The U.S. IAD system operates smoothly and has a high rate of compliance among public officials. The disclosure forms are designed as a tool for counseling, but in many corruption cases (criminal, civil, or administrative) asset declarations are used as prima facie evidence. There are many cases prosecuted involving different conflict-of-interest criminal statutes, and usually these include some offense combined with falsifying the financial disclosure report. As such, the IAD system is being used effectively to fight corruption and to reduce conflicts of interest.

Notes

1. Previously existing disclosure systems varied widely in terms of application. For example, during the Kennedy administration, there were certain disclosure requirements for the White House staff and some senior officials. During the Johnson administration, the IAD system was expanded to include heads of agencies and members of commissions.

2. Center for Public Integrity, Governors Disclosure Ranking; http://www.publicintegrity .org/accountability/waste-fraud-and-abuse/states-disclosure.

3. Personal Financial Disclosure for Legislators, National Conference of State Legislatures; http://www.ncsl.org/legislatures-elections/ethicshome/financial-disclosure-for-legislators-income.aspx.

4. Constitution of the United States of America, Art. II, sec 4. The Constitution also has a gifts prohibition. Art. I, sec. 9: "No title of nobility shall be granted by the United States: and no person holding any office of profit or trust under them, shall, without the consent of the Congress, accept of any present, emolument, office, or title, of any kind whatever, from any king, prince, or foreign state."

5. The Foreign Gifts and Decorations Act (5 U.S.C. Section 7342) provides this gift-acceptance authority; http://www.law.cornell.edu/uscode/text/5/7342; Gifts from

Outside Sources. There are certain exceptions to this prohibition, one of which includes acceptance of gifts in value of US$20 or less and with a limit of US$50 for one calendar year from the same source. In addition, the financial disclosure laws require the reporting of all financial interests of public officials and their spouses and minor children, including gifts and reimbursements that meet the reporting threshold, their assets, earned income, liabilities, postemployment agreements and benefit arrangements, and outside employment. Some of the cases in the United States that involve criminal prosecutions involve gifts and nondisclosure of those gifts in the financial disclosure reports. For more details and a summary of cases, see http://www .oge.gov/Topics/Enforcement/Conflict-of-interest-Prosecution-Surveys/.

6. Amer 2008, p. 3; Straus 2011.

7. Executive Order 11222 – Prescribing standards of ethical conduct for Government officers and employees, May 8, 1965.

8. Rohr 1998, p. 46.

9. See OGE 2004, pp. 1–7; http://www.niehs.nih.gov/about/od/ethics/disclosure/ a_reviewers_reference.pdf; Rohr 1998, p. 46.

10. Originally the Civil Service Commission.

11. See http://www.publicintegrity.org/accountability/waste-fraud-and-abuse/states-disclosure/rankings.

12. 5 U.S.C. 504(c)(1); 5 U.S.C. App. §103 (Ethics in Government Act of 1978).

13. Office of Government Ethics Reauthorization Act of 1988, Public Law 100-598, 5 U.S.C. app. IV.

14. Raile 2004, p. 14.

15. *United States v. Mississippi Valley Generating Co.* 364 U.S. 520, 549 (1960).

16. Ley 2001, p. 8.

17. Ley 2001, p. 8.

18. Ley 2001, p. 8.

19. OGE 2006, pp. 28 and 30.

20. The U.S. legal system has largely determined the validity of financial disclosure requirements for public officials on a case-by-case basis, using a balance-test approach. As reflected in *Duplantier v. United States* (606 F.2d 654 (5th Cir. 1979)) and *United States v. Carbo* (572 F.3d 112, 119 (3d Cir. 2009)), the right to financial privacy for public officials is not absolute and has been refined through diligent consideration of a number of relevant interests. Courts aim to uphold the broadly defined constitutional rights to individual privacy. The balancing-test approach employed in *Duplantier* is effective for determining whether mandating asset disclosure intrudes upon a public official's right to privacy.

21. Only the executive branch has confidential financial disclosure.

22. Ley 2001, p. 3.

23. Raile 2004, p. 14.

24. Raile 2004, p. 14.

25. Raile 2004, p. 14.

26. Ley 2001, p. 1.

27. Currently, there are 125 DAEOs; Raile 2004, p. 14.

28. Raile 2004, p. 14.

29. Raile 2004, p. 15.

30. Carney 1998.

31. Carney 1998, Section 3b, 1.

32. Carney 1998, Section 3b, 1.

33. Carney 1998, Section 3b, 7.

34. Carney 1998, Section 3b, 7.

35. Executive Order 12674, President George H. W. Bush, 1989; http://www.usoge.gov/laws_regs/exec_orders/eo12674.pdf. Executive Order 12731, President George H. W. Bush, 1990; http://www.usoge.gov/laws_regs/exec_orders/eo12731.pdf.

36. http://www.oge.gov/Education/Education-Resources-for-Federal-Employees/14-General-Principles-Card/; General Principles. See also Gilman 20015, p. 18.

37. OGE 2009.

38. A definition of *outside activities* can be found at http://www.oge.gov/Topics/Outside-Employment-and-Activities/Outside-Employment---Activities/.

39. A definition of *postemployment* can be found at http://www.oge.gov/Topics/Post-Government-Employment/Post-Government-Employment/.

40. A definition of *remedies for financial conflicts of interest* can be found at http://www.oge.gov/OGE-Advisories/Legal-Advisories/92x12--Remedies-for-Resolving-Conflicts-of-Interest/.

41. "...or if other than under the General Schedule, the rate of basic pay fixed at a rate equal to or greater than 120% of the minimum rate of basic pay for GS-15 of the General Schedule" ("Duty To File Public Financial Disclosure Report," Memorandum Opinion for the Counsel to the President, December 19, 2002).

42. "...the term 'special Government employee' shall mean an officer or employee of the executive or legislative branch of the United States Government, of any independent agency of the United States or of the District of Columbia, who is retained, designated, appointed, or employed to perform, with or without compensation, for not to exceed one hundred and thirty days during any period of three hundred and sixty-five consecutive days, temporary duties either on a full-time or intermittent basis, a part-time United States commissioner, a part-time United States magistrate judge, or, regardless of the number of days of appointment, an independent counsel appointed under chapter 40 of title 28 and any person appointed by that independent counsel under section 594 (c) of title 28. 18 USC 202 - Sec. 202." Note: Not all special government employees necessarily file publicly. Special government employees "fall under the same criteria for filing SF 278s as other regular Government employees. If they meet the pay conditions for public filing and work more than 60 days in a calendar year, then they must file new entrant, annual, or termination SF 278s, as appropriate" (OGE 2004, pp. 2–5).

43. 5 C.F.R. Part 2634.901.

44. 5 C.F.R. Part 2634.903.

45. A significant case in this area is the Villalpando case. Villalpando was found guilty of obstruction of justice and tax evasion, and became the only U.S. Treasurer (appointed under the George H. W. Bush administration) to be sent to prison. Villalpando was charged with three felonies: tax evasion, conspiracy to make false statements regarding her finances on her financial disclosure forms, and obstruction of a grand jury. She pled

guilty to all three counts and was sentenced to four months' imprisonment, three years' probation, 200 hours of community service, and a US$150 tax evasion fee.

46. See 5 U.S.C. app. 4 §§ 101-111: Public financial disclosure requirements.

47. 5 C.F.R. Part 2634.603.

48. See http://www.ncsl.org/LegislaturesElections/Ethics/StateEthicsCommission Jurisdiction/tabid/15361/Default.aspx#md for a table listing state requirements.

49. Center for Public Integrity, Governors Disclosure Ranking; http://www.publicintegrity .org/accountability/waste-fraud-and-abuse/states-disclosure/rankings.

50. Available at Personal Financial Disclosure for Legislators, National Conference of State Legislatures; http://www.ncsl.org/?tabid=15329.

51. See http://162.140.97.1/about/background_mission.aspx.

52. Organization and Functions: http://162.140.97.1/about/organization_functions .aspx. See 5 C.F.R. Part 2600.103.

53. See Organization and Functions; http://162.140.97.1/about/organization_functions .aspx. See 5 C.F.R. Part 2600.103.

54. http://www.usoge.gov/international/international.aspx.

55. The individual agencies are responsible for granting extensions and collecting the late filing fee (5 C.F.R. part 2634.201(f)).

56. See Agency Program Services; http://162.140.97.1/about/agency_program_services .aspx.

57. The Office of Personnel Management is the centralized human resource agency of the federal government and closely regulates the vast majority of federal government hiring.

58. Gilman 2005, p. 8.

59. For more details and a summary of cases, see http://www.oge.gov/Topics/Enforcement/ Conflict-of-interest-Prosecution-Surveys/.

60. OGE 2008.

61. OGE 2005.

References

Amer, M. 2008. "Enforcement of Congressional Rules of Conduct: An Historical Overview," Congressional Research Service Report for Congress, Congressional Research Service, Washington, DC, November 18.

Carney, G. 1998. "Conflict of Interest: Legislators, Ministers, and Public Officials." Transparency International Working Paper, Section 3B,1, Transparency International, Berlin.

Gilman, S. 2005. *Ethics Codes and Codes of Conduct as Tools for Promoting an Ethical and Professional Public Service: Comparative Successes and Lessons*. Washington, DC: World Bank.

Ley, J. S. 2001. "Managing Conflicts of Interest at the U.S. Federal Level (with Emphasis on the Executive Branch). Paper presented at the Organisation for Economic Co-operation and Development–Organization of American States Forum on Ensuring Accountability and Transparency in the Public Sector, Brasilia, Brazil, December 5–6.

OGE (Office of Government Ethics). 2004. *Public Financial Disclosure: A Reviewer's Reference*, Second Edition. Washington, DC: OGE.

———. 2005. *Report to Congress Evaluating the Financial Disclosure Process for Employees of the Executive Branch and Recommending Improvements to It*. Washington, DC: OGE.

———. 2006. *Report to the President and to Congressional Committees on the Conflict of Interest Laws Relating to Executive Branch Employment*. Washington, DC: OGE.

———. 2008. "Financial Statements and Independent Auditor's Report." Fiscal Year 2008 Performance Accountability Report, Washington, DC, November.

———. 2009. *Report: Elements of a Successful Financial Disclosure Program*. Washington, DC, March, OGE.

Raile, E. 2004. "Managing Conflicts of Interest in the Americas: A Comparative Review." Paper presented at the Organisation for Economic Co-operation and Development–Inter-American Development Bank Forum on Implementing Conflict of Interest Policies in the Public Service, Rio de Janeiro, Brazil, May 5–6.

Rohr, J. A. 1998. *Public Service, Ethics, and Constitutional Practice*. Lawrence, KS: University of Kansas Press.

Straus, J. R. 2011. "Enforcement of Congressional Rules of Conduct: An Historical Overview." Congressional Research Service Report for Congress, Congressional Research Service, Washington, DC, June 14. http://www.fas.org/sgp/crs/misc/RL30764.pdf.

Methodology and Indicators Used for this Volume

The case studies presented in this volume are based on the findings of a World Bank and Stolen Asset and Recovery (StAR) Initiative team, desk research, and the analysis of data gathered as part of the World Bank's Public Accountability Mechanisms (PAM) Initiative. The findings use data on the legal frameworks for income and asset disclosure (IAD) systems in 88 countries (table A.1). Detailed country studies were conducted in 11 countries: Argentina; Croatia; Guatemala; Hong Kong SAR, China; Indonesia; Jordan; the Kyrgyz Republic; Mongolia; Rwanda; Slovenia; and the United States. Country studies were conducted by means of in-depth interviews with practitioners, academics, and representatives of civil society in each of these countries. The companion volume to these case studies is *Public Office, Private Interests: Accountability through Income and Asset Disclosure*, which examines the objectives, design features, and implementation approaches that can contribute to the effectiveness of an IAD system in a variety of contexts.

The PAM Initiative

To meet the demand for more effective monitoring of the policies and institutions that contribute to governance outcomes, the PAM Initiative is a work in progress that provides information on the transparency of governments and the accountability of public officials.[1] The initiative is focused on four types of public official: heads of state, ministers and cabinet members, members of Parliament, and civil servants as defined by the individual countries. Spouses and children of each category of public official are also included. The field of inquiry covers five types of transparency and accountability regimes:

- Income and asset disclosure
- Conflict of interest

Table A.1 Economies for which IAD and COI Legal Framework Data Have Been Collected as Part of the AGI Initiative

	Countries		
High-income (14)	Czech Republic	Italy	Slovak Republic
	Estonia	Japan	Slovenia
	France	Norway	United Kingdom
	Germany	Poland	United States
	Hungary	Russian Federation	
Europe and Central Asia (19)	Albania	Kazakhstan	Serbia
	Armenia	Kyrgyz Republic	Tajikistan
	Azerbaijan	Latvia	Turkey
	Bosnia and Herzegovina	Lithuania	Ukraine
	Bulgaria	Macedonia, FYR	Uzbekistan
	Croatia	Moldova	
	Georgia	Romania	
East Asia and the Pacific (14)	Cambodia	Palau	Timor-Leste
	Fiji	Papua New Guinea	Tonga
	Indonesia	Philippines	Vanuatu
	Lao PDR	Solomon Islands	Vietnam
	Mongolia	Taiwan, China	
Latin America and the Caribbean (6)	Bolivia	Guyana	Argentina
	Dominican Republic	Honduras	Mexico
Middle East and North Africa (2)	Jordan	Morocco	
South Asia (5)	Bangladesh	Nepal	Sri Lanka
	India	Pakistan	
Africa (28)	Angola	Guinea	Nigeria
	Benin	Kenya	Senegal
	Botswana	Madagascar	Sierra Leone
	Burkina Faso	Malawi	South Africa
	Burundi	Mali	Tanzania
	Congo, Dem. Rep.	Mauritania	Uganda
	Congo, Rep.	Mauritius	Zambia
	Ethiopia	Mozambique	Zimbabwe
	Gambia	Namibia	
	Ghana	Niger	

Note: COI = conflict of interest.

- Freedom of information
- Immunity protections
- Ethics training

The PAM Initiative publishes detailed and regularly updated data on efforts to enhance the transparency and accountability systems in a sample of 88 countries worldwide.[2] It also involves the creation of a pool of relevant indicators that can be used in monitoring the implementation of reform efforts. For both of these goals, the PAM Initiative develops Actionable Governance Indicators that provide insight into how governance subsystems function and which actions may produce better outcomes.

Actionable Governance Indicators (AGIs)

AGIs measure the direct impacts of institutional reform efforts on how particular governance subsystems function. These *actionable* indicators are narrowly circumscribed and clearly defined, and focus on relatively specific aspects of governance rather than broad dimensions. They provide greater clarity regarding the actions that governments can take to achieve better results on assessments of certain areas of governance. They include:

- *Institutional arrangements* (aka "rules of the game"), which are the formal and informal rules governing the actions of agents involved in the operation of a given governance system. These rules (1) assign responsibilities and authority across relevant agents or actors; (2) specify permitted, required, and forbidden activities by those agents or actors; and (3) establish procedures governing the activities and behavior of those agents or actors. These rules create (better or worse) incentives for agents to perform their roles.

- *Organizational capacity features*, which are characteristics of the resources employed by the relevant agents or actors assigned responsibilities under the legal framework. Such indicators typically capture (1) the magnitudes of particular resources (money, personnel, equipment, facilities and buildings, and so forth), and (2) the quality of those resources (for example, types of technology employed, quality of staff, and so forth).

- *Governance system performance*, which captures information on the practices of the agents assigned particular asset declaration implementation responsibilities. The variance of the organizational behavior and practices sheds light on whether practices are likely to advance the underlying objectives of the asset declaration legal framework (figure A.1).

Legislative AGIs

In the PAM Initiative, legislative indicators capture information on the formal institutional arrangements or rules of an accountability mechanism. These indicators are fact-based assessments of legislation and related laws, decrees, and codes of conduct that are externally reviewed by country technical experts. They are based on the content analyses prepared by lawyers regarding the country legal frameworks. These legislative indicators capture data on the characteristics of legal frameworks of accountability within countries.

Selection of Primary Sources

Data sources for legislative indicators consist of laws, decrees, or codes of conduct that relate to the mechanism under study.

Figure A.1 Actionable Governance Indicators

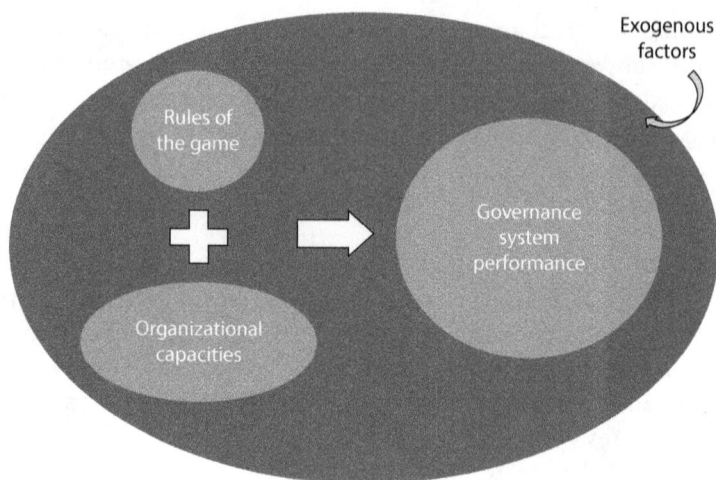

Source: PAM initiative.

Analysis of Legal Frameworks

Primary source documents (for example, laws, decrees, codes) are used to complete the analysis, in the original language if possible. All relevant legislation is included in the analysis, even if it is not specifically part of the mechanism framework; that is, if the civil service law contains some sanctions for noncompliance, it is included in the analysis. No secondary sources are used in the analysis of country legal frameworks (see table A.2).

Reliability Checks

Data for each mechanism were collected using primary sources and were peer reviewed by the team. Both the data and the summaries of each characteristic were then sent to an external reviewer in the relevant country for feedback. This reviewer is expected to have either in-depth legal knowledge of the mechanism being examined in a specific country or expertise in a related field. Once feedback was received, the changes were incorporated into the data set for the country. To minimize both reliability and validity problems, data were also sent to World Bank country offices for feedback.

Implementation AGIs

Implementation indicators are focused on all three categories: (1) informal institutional arrangements or rules, (2) organizational capacity, and (3) performance of a governance system (that is, its accountability mechanism). They are fact-based assessments of implementation processes, with data gathered by

Table A.2 Legal Framework Indicators for IAD

1	**Legal framework**
2	Laws regulating income and asset disclosure
3	Constitutional requirement
4	**Coverage of public officials**
5	Head(s) of state
6	Ministers/cabinet
7	Members of parliament (MPs)
8	Civil servants
9	Spouses and children
10	**Scope of declarations content**
11	*Head(s) of state*
12	Assets, liabilities, and income items covered are explicitly defined
13	Real estate must be disclosed
14	Movable assets must be disclosed
15	Cash must be disclosed
16	Loans and debts must be disclosed
17	Earned income must be disclosed
18	Unearned income must be disclosed
19	*Ministers/cabinet members*
20	Assets, liabilities, and income items covered are explicitly defined
21	Real estate must be disclosed
22	Movable assets must be disclosed
23	Cash must be disclosed
24	Loans and debts must be disclosed
25	Earned income must be disclosed
26	Unearned income must be disclosed
27	*Members of Parliament (MPs)*
28	Assets, liabilities, and income items covered are explicitly defined
29	Real estate must be disclosed
30	Movable assets must be disclosed
31	Cash must be disclosed
32	Loans and debts must be disclosed
33	Earned income must be disclosed
34	Unearned income must be disclosed
35	*Civil servants*
36	Assets, liabilities, and income items covered are explicitly defined
37	Real estate must be disclosed
38	Movable assets must be disclosed
39	Cash must be disclosed
40	Loans and debts must be disclosed
41	Earned income must be disclosed
42	Unearned income must be disclosed
43	*Spouses and children*
44	Assets, liabilities, and income items covered are explicitly defined
45	Real estate must be disclosed
46	Movable assets must be disclosed

table continues next page

Table A.2 Legal Framework Indicators for IAD *(continued)*

47	Cash must be disclosed
48	Loans and debts must be disclosed
49	Earned income must be disclosed
50	Unearned income must be disclosed
51	**Filing frequency**
52	*Head(s) of state*
53	Filing required upon taking office
54	Filing required upon leaving office
55	Filing required annually
56	Filing required within 3 years of leaving office
57	Filing required upon change in assets
58	Verifiable declaration (not oral)
59	*Ministers/cabinet members*
60	Filing required upon taking office
61	Filing required upon leaving office
62	Filing required annually
63	Filing required within 3 years of leaving office
64	Filing required upon change in assets
65	Verifiable declaration (not oral)
66	*Members of Parliament (MPs)*
67	Filing required upon taking office
68	Filing required upon leaving office
69	Filing required annually
70	Filing required within 3 years of leaving office
71	Filing required upon change in assets
72	Verifiable declaration (not oral)
73	*Civil servants*
74	Filing required upon taking office
75	Filing required upon leaving office
76	Filing required annually
77	Filing required within 3 years of leaving office
78	Filing required upon change in assets
79	Verifiable declaration (not oral)
80	**Sanctions**
81	*Head(s) of state*
82	Sanctions stipulated for late filing
83	Fines stipulated for late filing
84	Administrative sanctions stipulated for late filing
85	Criminal sanctions stipulated for late filing
86	Sanctions stipulated for incomplete submission
87	Fines stipulated for incomplete submission
88	Administrative sanctions stipulated for incomplete submission
89	Criminal sanctions stipulated for incomplete submission
90	Sanctions stipulated for nonfiling
91	Fines stipulated for nonfiling
92	Administrative sanctions stipulated for nonfiling

table continues next page

Table A.2 **Legal Framework Indicators for IAD** *(continued)*

93	Criminal sanctions stipulated for nonfiling
94	Sanctions stipulated for providing false information
95	Fines stipulated for providing false information
96	Administrative sanctions stipulated for providing false information
97	Criminal sanctions stipulated for providing false information
98	*Ministers/cabinet members*
99	Sanctions stipulated for late filing
100	Fines stipulated for late filing
101	Administrative sanctions stipulated for late filing
102	Criminal sanctions stipulated for late filing
103	Sanctions stipulated for incomplete submission
104	Fines stipulated for incomplete submission
105	Administrative sanctions stipulated for incomplete submission
106	Criminal sanctions stipulated for incomplete submission
107	Sanctions stipulated for nonfiling
108	Fines stipulated for nonfiling
109	Administrative sanctions stipulated for nonfiling
110	Criminal sanctions stipulated for nonfiling
111	Sanctions stipulated for providing false information
112	Fines stipulated for providing false information
113	Administrative sanctions stipulated for providing false information
114	Criminal sanctions stipulated for providing false information
115	*Members of Parliament (MPs)*
116	Sanctions stipulated for late filing
117	Fines stipulated for late filing
118	Administrative sanctions stipulated for late filing
119	Criminal sanctions stipulated for late filing
120	Sanctions stipulated for incomplete submission
121	Fines stipulated for incomplete submission
122	Administrative sanctions stipulated for incomplete submission
123	Criminal sanctions stipulated for incomplete submission
124	Sanctions stipulated for nonfiling
125	Fines stipulated for nonfiling
126	Administrative sanctions stipulated for nonfiling
127	Criminal sanctions stipulated for nonfiling
128	Sanctions stipulated for providing false information
129	Fines stipulated for providing false information
130	Administrative sanctions stipulated for providing false information
131	Criminal sanctions stipulated for providing false information
132	*Civil servants*
133	Sanctions stipulated for late filing
134	Fines stipulated for late filing
135	Administrative sanctions stipulated for late filing
136	Criminal sanctions stipulated for late filing
137	Sanctions stipulated for incomplete submission
138	Fines stipulated for incomplete submission

table continues next page

Table A.2 Legal Framework Indicators for IAD *(continued)*

139	Administrative sanctions stipulated for incomplete submission
140	Criminal sanctions stipulated for incomplete submission
141	Sanctions stipulated for nonfiling
142	Fines stipulated for nonfiling
143	Administrative sanctions stipulated for nonfiling
144	Criminal sanctions stipulated for nonfiling
145	Sanctions stipulated for providing false information
146	Fines stipulated for providing false information
147	Administrative sanctions stipulated for providing false information
148	Criminal sanctions stipulated for providing false information
149	**Monitoring and oversight**
150	*Head(s) of state*
151	Enforcement body explicitly identified
152	Depository body explicitly identified
153	Some agency assigned responsibility for verifying submission
154	Some agency assigned responsibility for verifying accuracy
155	*Ministers/cabinet members*
156	Enforcement body explicitly identified
157	Depository body explicitly identified
158	Some agency assigned responsibility for verifying submission
159	Some agency assigned responsibility for verifying accuracy
160	*Members of Parliament (MPs)*
161	Enforcement body explicitly identified
162	Depository body explicitly identified
163	Some agency assigned responsibility for verifying submission
164	Some agency assigned responsibility for verifying accuracy
165	*Civil servants*
166	Enforcement body explicitly identified
167	Depository body explicitly identified
168	Some agency assigned responsibility for verifying submission
169	Some agency assigned responsibility for verifying accuracy
170	**Public access to declarations**
171	*Head(s) of state*
172	Public availability
173	Timely posting
174	Clearly identified location
175	Reasonable fees for access
176	Length of records maintenance is specified
177	*Ministers/cabinet members*
178	Public availability
179	Timely posting
180	Clearly identified location
181	Reasonable fees for access
182	Length of records maintenance is specified
183	*Members of Parliament (MPs)*
184	Public availability

table continues next page

Table A.2 Legal Framework Indicators for IAD *(continued)*

185	Timely posting
186	Clearly identified location
187	Reasonable fees for access
188	Length of records maintenance is specified
189	*Civil servants*
190	Public availability
191	Timely posting
192	Clearly identified location
193	Reasonable fees for access
194	Length of records maintenance is specified
195	*Spouses and children*
196	Public availability
197	Timely posting
198	Clearly identified location
199	Reasonable fees for access
200	Length of records maintenance is specified

Source: PAM Dataset 2009.

governments, World Bank country teams, and civil society organizations. The broad functional categories for the mechanisms are as follows:

- *Management and accountability* arrangements, capacities, and practices of the agents responsible for ensuring implementation of each mechanism. Such management and accountability indicators capture characteristics of the accountability, financial, and human resource management systems of the agents responsible for implementing a given public accountability mechanism (for example, income and asset disclosure).

- *Enforcement* arrangements, capacities, and practices of the agents responsible for ensuring implementation of each mechanism. Such enforcement indicators capture information on the production technologies employed to implement or enforce the requirements of a particular mechanism. Examples of the sorts of features to be captured might include regulatory capacities and practices, activities aimed at ensuring compliance with the mechanism rules and procedures, verification and investigations practices, interagency collaboration efforts, advisory activities, and the monitoring and reporting of results.

- *Immediate impact* indicators capture the extent to which particular, well-specified, immediate objectives of the accountability mechanism are being achieved. These intermediate outcome indicators do not capture performance in the sense of ultimate outcomes, such as reduced corruption, reduced state capture, or more ethical behavior of civil servants. Instead, these immediate impact indicators aim to capture compliance with the legal framework (by the officials covered by the legislation); the signaling of government commitment to enforcement of legal provisions; and the extent to which the information covered by that legislation is being accessed by citizens or organized groups of citizens (that is, evidence that access to that information has, in practice, been improved).

Data on implementation efforts were collected through collaboration with country governments, World Bank country offices, and civil society organizations. In most cases, data were collected through interviews with relevant government officials and civil society representatives and through site visits to government offices. Additional communication with relevant officials was conducted for clarification of data (see table A.3).

Table A.3 Implementation Indicators for IAD and COI, Declaration Required

Section 1: Management and Accountability

1.1	*Facilities*	
	Is a physical space designated for IAD/COI activities?	R
	What is the ratio of desks to personnel?	C
	Is the computer hardware less than 10 years old? (desktop, laptops, and/or monitors, etc.)	C
	Is the computer software less than 5 years old? (word processing, spreadsheet, and/or e-mail software, etc.)	C
	What is the ratio of computers to personnel?	C
	Is basic office equipment (computers, Internet access, photocopy machines, and/or printers) available for IAD/COI purposes?	C
	How often is Internet access available? (always, sometimes, rarely, never)	C
	Was outdated or broken office equipment replaced?	P
	Was outdated or broken computer hardware replaced?	P
	Was outdated or nonfunctional computer software replaced?	P
	Were all new permanent employees provided a computer and workstation?	P
1.2	*Data management*	
	Which agency is obligated to store the hard copies of completed declarations?	R
	Is there a procedure for storing the content of declarations electronically?	R
	Is oversight of the IAD/COI data management system assigned to a particular individual?	R
	Please identify the person who is responsible for data management.	R
	Is a physical space available for storing the hard copies of completed declarations?	C
	Is the physical space for storage of completed declarations capable of storing all hard copies securely?	C
	Are IAD/COI personnel aware of record-keeping procedures?	C
	Were declarations and related documents stored in the designated space?	P
	If not, please explain why.	P
	Was information from declarations stored electronically, hard copy, or both? (please select below)	
	Personal background information of declarant	P
	Financial information of declarant	P
	Aggregate data for individuals	P
	Aggregate data for groups of public officials	P
	Did oversight of the records policy ensure that documents are properly kept?	P
	If not, please explain why.	P

table continues next page

Table A.3 Implementation Indicators for IAD and COI, Declaration Required (continued)

1.3	*Human resources*	
	Which staff member in the IAD oversight agency is responsible for overall IAD management?	R
	Which staff member is responsible for management of IAD/COI issues in line agencies?	R
	Is there an accurate organigram of IAD/COI staff in the oversight agency?	R
	Are IAD/COI operating manuals available to staff in the oversight agency?	R
	Are IAD/COI operating manuals available to staff in the line agencies?	R
	How many individuals are responsible for IAD/COI tasks in the oversight agency?	C
	How many individuals are responsible for IAD/COI tasks in the line agencies?	C
	How many individuals responsible for IAD/COI obligations are contract employees?	C
	How are IAD/COI-related positions filled? (competitive recruitment, political appointments, both)	C
	What is the percentage of nonadministrative IAD/COI staff having at least 4 years of post-secondary education?	C
	Did personnel receive training in IAD/COI principles and/or regulations?	P
	Did personnel receive performance evaluations?	P
	How many staff have left their positions in the last five years?	P
1.4	*Financial management*	
	Is the oversight agency required to submit a budget proposal for its IAD/COI-related activities, or to include specific IAD/COI line items in its budget proposal?	R
	Does the oversight agency have a statutorily-defined budget for IAD/COI activities?	R
	Does the oversight agency receive IAD/COI funding from an oversight agency or directly from Treasury?	R
	What is the budget for IAD/COI-related activities?	C
	What is the wage bill for IAD/COI (IAD/COI-dedicated budget/IAD/COI personnel)?	C
	How are IAD/COI-related funds allocated? (e.g., at the beginning of the fiscal year, in tranches throughout the year, based on performance, etc.)	C
	Did the agency assess its budgetary needs to fulfill its IAD/COI obligations as part of the annual budget cycle?	P
	Were the following costs calculated as part of the annual budget cycle?	
	Salaries/wages	P
	Facilities and equipment	P
	Training and capacity	P
	Public awareness/promotion	
1.5	*Policy and regulatory management*	
	Is the oversight agency responsible for issuing implementing regulations?	R
	Are the line agencies responsible for issuing implementing regulations?	R
	Do IAD/COI policy and guidelines exist?	R
	Is there a procedure for communicating IAD/COI policy and guidelines to obligated parties?	R
	How does the national archives policy affect IAD/COI policy at the agency level?	R
	Does the agency have the resources to disseminate plans, policies, or guidelines to all public officials?	C
	If not, please explain why	C
	Does the agency have the resources to disseminate plans, policies, or guidelines to the general public?	C
	If not, please explain why	C
	Do senior-level agency officials participate in strategic planning processes for IAD/COI?	P
	Did the agency's strategic planning process incorporate IAD/COI-specific goals, objectives, and outcomes?	P
	Did the agency create internal regulations to fulfill its IAD/COI obligations?	P
	If yes, please describe the nature of these internal regulations.	P
	How did the agency make internal regulations available to the public?	
	Agency website	P

table continues next page

Table A.3 Implementation Indicators for IAD and COI, Declaration Required *(continued)*

Media (radio, television, newspapers)	P
Brochures, pamphlets, or other printed materials	P
Other (please specify)	P
Were IAD/COI plans, policies, and guidelines revised?	P
If yes, please explain why the IAD/COI plans, policies, or guidelines were last revised.	P
Did the agency disseminate plans, policies, or guidelines to all public officials?	P
How did the agency disseminate these plans, policies, or guidelines to public officials? (please select below)	
Agency website	P
Media (radio, television, newspapers)	P
Brochures, pamphlets, or other printed materials	P
Other (please specify)	P
Did the agency disseminate plans, policies, or guidelines to the public?	P
How did the agency disseminate these plans, policies, or guidelines to the public? (please select below)	
Agency website	P
Media (radio, television, newspapers)	P
Brochures, pamphlets, or other printed materials	P
Other (please specify)	P
Section 2: Implementation	
2.1 *Submission compliance*	
Who is obligated to file declarations?	
President	R
Members of Parliament (deputies, members, senators, lords, etc.)	R
Ministers	R
Senior civil servants	R
Judges	R
Other (please list)	R
What type of information must be disclosed on the filing form?	
Assets (real estate, vehicles, jewelry, etc.)	R
Earned income (wages from primary and secondary employment, etc.)	R
Cash (domestic or foreign bank accounts, cash in hand, etc.)	R
Investments (shares in companies, stocks, bonds, etc.)	R
Other (please specify)	R
How frequently are obligated parties required to file declarations?	
Upon starting employment	R
Upon leaving employment	R
Annually	R
Within 1–3 years after leaving employment	R
Upon change of assets	R
Other (please specify)	R
What agency is assigned responsibility for receiving IAD/COI forms?	R
Is there a procedure requiring the creation and maintenance of a register of filers?	R
Is the administrative structure of the submission process centralized or delegated to line ministries?	R
Is there a procedure for receiving IAD/COI forms?	R
Does the procedure for receiving IAD/COI forms require a check for completeness upon submission?	R
Are IAD/COI personnel aware of the procedures for receiving declarations?	C

table continues next page

Table A.3 Implementation Indicators for IAD and COI, Declaration Required (*continued*)

What is the ratio of personnel to declarations regarding the check for completeness?	C
If line agencies are responsible for checking declarations for completeness, how many employees are responsible per agency?	C
Does the agency have the resources to maintain an updated register of obligated parties?	C
If not, please explain why.	C
Which of the following methods are available to public officials for submission of IAD/COI forms? (please select below)	
In-person delivery of hard copy	C
Delivery of hard copy by mail	C
Electronic submission via e-mail	C
Electronic submission via online form	C
Other (please specify)	C
Is software available for the submission process?	C
How does software assist IAD/COI personnel in the submission of declarations? (please select below)	
To receive information in an online form	C
To store personal information (name, address, identification number, etc.)	C
To store financial information	C
Was the procedure for receiving declarations followed?	P
If not, please explain why	P
How was the declaration form made available? (electronically or hard copy or both)	
Downloadable form on website	P
Online form (cannot be downloaded)	P
Via e-mail	P
Hard copy	P
Was the register of obligated parties updated?	P
If not, please explain why.	P
Did obligated parties receive official notices regarding submissions?	P
Did obligated parties receive official notices regarding investigations?	P
How many working days were required to check all declarations for completeness?	P
What was the average number of working days required to check one declaration for completeness? (number of working days needed to check all declarations for completeness / number of declarations)	P

2.1.1   *Sanctions*

Which agency has the authority to apply sanctions on public officials for filing failures? (late submission or complete failure to file a declaration)	R
If the IAD/COI oversight or line agency is not authorized to apply sanctions, are they authorized to recommend sanctions?	R
Is the agency authorized to apply/recommend administrative sanctions for filing failures? (late submission or complete failure to file a declaration)	R
What kind of administrative sanctions is the agency authorized to apply for filing failures? (late submission or complete failure to file a declaration)	
Banned from practice or office	R
Dismissals	R
Suspensions	R
Warnings/censure	R
Is the agency authorized to apply/recommend fines for filing failures? (late submission or complete failure to file a declaration)	R
What is the minimum fine that the agency is authorized to apply/recommend for filing failures? (late submission or complete failure to file a declaration)	R

table continues next page

Table A.3 Implementation Indicators for IAD and COI, Declaration Required *(continued)*

	What is the maximum fine that the agency is authorized to apply/recommend for filing failures? (late submission or complete failure to file a declaration)	R
	Is the agency authorized to apply/recommend criminal sanctions for filing failures? (late submission or complete failure to file a declaration)	R
	What was the percentage of cases subject to administrative sanctions for filing failures in which the sanction was enforced?	P
	What was the total amount in fines that were collected for filing failures?	P
	What was the percentage of cases subject to fines for filing failures in which the sanction was enforced?	P
	What was the percentage of cases subject to criminal sanctions for filing failures in which the sanction was enforced?	P
2.2	*Content verification*	
	What is the focus of the disclosure system? (conflict of interest, Illicit enrichment, dual)	R
	Are IAD/COI personnel aware of procedures for verifying the content of declarations?	C
	What is the ratio of personnel to declarations regarding the content verification?	C
	If content verification/incompabilities review is performed by the line agencies, how many employees are responsible per line agency?	C
	What is the ratio of IAD/COI personnel to total number of declarations received?	C
	What is the ratio of IAD/COI personnel to the number of declarations subject to content verification or incompatibilities review?	C
	Is software available for content verification or incompatibilities review?	C
	How does software assist IAD/COI personnel in content verification or incompatibilities review? (please select below)	
	To store information (personal or financial)	C
	To analyze data from the declaration	C
	To compare data from external sources to data in the declaration	C
2.2.1	*Conflict-of-interest function*	
	Is there a procedure for reviewing declarations for incompatibilities between public function and private interests?	R
	What agency is assigned responsibility for reviewing declarations for incompatibilities?	R
	Is the agency authorized to review all declarations or a sample of declarations for incompatibilities?	R
	What is the policy for selection of declarations for incompatibilities review? (please select below)	R
	All declarations	
	Targeted verification (risk-based selection)	R
	Tiered verification (only high-ranking officials)	R
	Random verification	R
	Upon complaint	R
	Does the agency have the authority to access information on public officials from the following institutions? (please select below)	
	Banks	R
	Tax agency	R
	Land registry	R
	Vehicle registry	R
	Private sector corporate entities	R
	Which agency is authorized to advise remediation for identified conflicts of interest?	R
	What are the types of remediation that the agency is authorized to advise (please select below)	
	Divestiture of the investments/interests that pose a conflict of interest	R
	Cessation of further acquisition or divestiture of the investments/interests	R

table continues next page

Table A.3 Implementation Indicators for IAD and COI, Declaration Required *(continued)*

Freezing any investment transaction for a specified period of time	R
Placement of the investment in a blind trust (without the requirement to first divest from current investments)	R
Cessation from handling cases with the potential for a conflict of interest with the individual's investment	R
Assignment of duties that may give rise to a conflict of interest situation to another officer	R
Was the procedure followed for reviewing declarations for incompatibilities between public function and private interests?	P
If not, please explain why.	P
How many declarations were reviewed for incompatibilities?	P
What is the percentage of all declarations received that were reviewed for incompatibilities?	P
In how many instances were the following types of remediation advised? (please insert figures below)	
Divestiture of the investments/interests that pose a conflict of interest	P
Cessation of further acquisition or divestiture of the investments/interests	P
Freezing any investment transaction for a specified period of time	P
Placement of the investment in a blind trust (without the requirement to first divest from current investments)	P
Cessation from handling cases with the potential for a conflict of interest with the individual's investment	P
Assignment of duties that may give rise to a conflict of interest situation to another officer	P
How many working days were needed to review all selected declarations for incompatibilities?	P
What was the average number of working days required to review for incompatibilities per declaration? number of working days needed to verify all declarations chosen for incompatibilities review / number of declarations chosen for incompatibilities review)	P

2.2.2   *Sanctions*

Which agency has the authority to apply sanctions on public officials for failure to adhere to remediation obligations?	R
If the IAD/COI oversight or line agency is not authorized to apply sanctions, is that agency authorized to recommend sanctions for failure to adhere to remediation obligations?	R
Is the agency authorized to apply/recommend administrative sanctions for filing failures? (late submission or complete failure to file a declaration)	R
What kind of administrative sanctions is the agency authorized to apply for failure to adhere to remediation obligations? (please select below)	
Banned from practice or office	R
Dismissals	R
Suspensions	R
Warnings/Censure	R
Is the agency authorized to apply fines for failure to adhere to remediation obligations?	R
What is the minimum fine that the agency is authorized to apply for failure to adhere to remediation obligations?	R
What is the maximum fine that the agency is authorized to apply for failure to adhere to remediation obligations?	R
Is the agency authorized to apply criminal sanctions for failure to adhere to remediation obligations?	R
What was the percentage of cases subject to administrative sanctions for failure to adhere to remediation obligations in which the sanction was enforced?	P
What was the total amount in fines that was collected for failure to adhere to remediation obligations?	P
What was the percentage of cases subject to fines for failure to adhere to remediation obligations in which the sanction was enforced?	P
What was the percentage of cases subject to criminal sanctions for failure to adhere to remediation obligations in which the sanction was enforced?	P

table continues next page

Income and Asset Disclosure • http://dx.doi.org/10.1596/978-0-8213-9796-1

Table A.3 Implementation Indicators for IAD and COI, Declaration Required *(continued)*

2.2.3	*Illicit enrichment function*	
	Is content verification mandated by law?	R
	What agency is assigned responsibility for verifying the content of declarations?	R
	Is there a procedure for verifying the content of declarations?	R
	What is the policy for selection of declarations for verification? (please select below)	
	Targeted verification (risk-based selection)	R
	Tiered verification (only high-ranking officials)	R
	Random verification	R
	Upon complaint	R
	What is the method of content verification? (please select below)	
	Check for internal consistency within one form	R
	Compare over time 2 or more forms from the same filer	R
	Cross-check declarations with external records (registries, banks, tax agency, etc.)	R
	Conduct lifestyle checks	R
	Does the agency have the authority to access information on public officials from the following institutions? (please select below)	
	Banks	R
	Tax agency	R
	Land registry	R
	Vehicle registry	R
	Private sector corporate entities	R
	Was the procedure followed for verifying the content of declarations?	P
	If not, please explain why.	P
	How many declarations were subjected to content verification?	P
	What is the percentage of declarations that were subjected to content verification?	P
	In how many instances were filers asked for additional information or documents for clarification purposes?	P
	How many working days were needed to verify the content of declarations?	P
	What was the average number of working days required for content verification per declaration? number of working days needed to verify all declarations chosen for verification / number of declarations chosen for verification)	P
2.2.4	*Sanctions*	
	Which agency has the authority to apply sanctions on public officials for false disclosure on a declaration?	R
	If the IAD/COI oversight or line agency is not authorized to apply sanctions, is that agency authorized to recommend sanctions for false disclosure?	R
	Is the agency authorized to apply administrative sanctions for false disclosure on a declaration?	R
	What kind of administrative sanctions is the agency authorized to apply for false disclosure on a declaration? (please select below)	
	Banned from practice or office	R
	Dismissals	R
	Suspensions	R
	Warnings/censure	R
	Is the agency authorized to apply fines for false disclosure on a declaration?	R
	What is the minimum fine that the agency is authorized to apply for false disclosure on a declaration?	R
	What is the maximum fine that the agency is authorized to apply for false disclosure on a declaration?	R
	Is the agency authorized to apply criminal sanctions for false disclosure on a declaration?	R
	What was the percentage of cases subject to administrative sanctions for false disclosure in which the sanction was enforced?	P

table continues next page

Table A.3 Implementation Indicators for IAD and COI, Declaration Required *(continued)*

	What was the total amount in fines that was collected for false disclosure?	P
	What was the percentage of cases subject to fines for false disclosure in which the sanction was enforced?	P
	What was the percentage of cases subject to criminal sanctions for false disclosure in which the sanction was enforced?	P
2.3	*Investigations*	
	Which agency has the authority to conduct investigations in the event of suspicious findings?	R
	Which staff member is responsible for management of investigations?	R
	Are IAD/COI personnel aware of procedures for either applying sanctions or referring cases to other agencies for sanctions?	C
	Are IAD/COI personnel aware of procedures for conducting investigations?	C
	How many employees are responsible for conducting investigations?	C
	What is the ratio of IAD/COI personnel to the number of investigations?	C
	Was the procedure for conducting investigations followed?	C
	If not, please explain why.	P
	How many cases were subject to investigation?	P
	How many cases were forwarded to the police/prosecutor for further action?	P
	How many cases that were forwarded to the police/prosecutor have been resolved?	P
2.4	*Information access*	
	Is the agency authorized to release declaration content to the public?	R
	For which ranks/categories of public official is the agency authorized to release declaration content? (please select below)	
	All filers	R
	High-ranking public officials	R
	Senior civil servants	R
	Members of Parliament	R
	Head of state	R
	Is there a communications policy for the agency regarding the publication of IAD/COI procedures, policies, and statistics to citizens?	R
	Is there a policy requiring proactive disclosure of IAD/COI content?	R
	Which of the following information must be proactively released?	
	Disclosure IAD/COI compliance statistics	R
	Names of individuals that violated IAD/COI compliance requirements	R
	Content verification data	R
	Names of individuals investigated for nondisclosure or false disclosure of IAD/COI information	R
	Efficiency data on IAD/COI performance	R
	Are IAD/COI personnel aware of procedures for proactively disclosing information?	C
	Are the following methods available to the agency for purposes of proactively disclosing information? (please select below)	
	Agency website	C
	Media (radio, television, newspapers)	C
	Brochures, pamphlets or other printed materials	C
	Other (please specify)	C
	What was the average number of days between the time a request was made for IAD data and the time the data was provided?	P
	What was the average number of days between the time a declaration is filed and the time it is made publicly available?	P
	Were disclosure compliance statistics released to the public?	P

table continues next page

Table A.3 Implementation Indicators for IAD and COI, Declaration Required *(continued)*

How were disclosure compliance statistics released to the public?	
Agency website	P
Media (radio, television, newspapers)	P
Published materials in hard copy (e.g., Annual Report, *Official Gazette*, etc.)	P
Other (please specify)	P
Upon request	P
Were names of individuals that violated compliance requirements released to the public?	P
How were the names of individuals that violated compliance requirements released to the public?	
Agency website	P
Media (radio, television, newspapers)	P
Published materials in hard copy (e.g., Annual Report, *Official Gazette*, etc.)	P
Other (please specify)	P
Upon request	P
Was aggregate data on content verification/incompatibilities review released to the public?	P
How was aggregate data on content verification/incompatibilities review released to the public?	
Agency website	P
Media (radio, television, newspapers)	P
Published materials in hard copy (e.g., Annual Report, *Official Gazette*, etc.)	P
Other (please specify)	P
Upon request	P
Was IAD/COI efficiency data from oversight agency or line agencies released to the public?	P
How was IAD/COI efficiency data from oversight agency or line agencies released to the public?	
Agency website	P
Media (radio, television, newspapers)	P
Published materials in hard copy (e.g., Annual Report, *Official Gazette*, etc.)	P
Other (please specify)	P
Upon request	P
Were the names of individuals investigated for nondisclosure or false disclosure of IAD/COI information released to the public?	P
How were the names of individuals investigated for nondisclosure or false disclosure of IAD/COI information released to the public?	
Agency website	P
Media (radio, television, newspapers)	P
Published materials in hard copy (e.g., Annual Report, *Official Gazette*, etc.)	P
Other (please specify)	P
Upon request	P

Section 3: Immediate Impacts

3.1 *Filing compliance*

What is the total number of declarations received?	IM
What was the percentage of declarations received on time?	IM
What was the percentage of filing failures? (late submission or complete failure to file a declaration)	IM
What was the percentage of incomplete declarations received?	IM
What was the final submission compliance rate? (percentage of declarations received from all obligated parties)	IM
What is the percentage of all filers that were *prima facie* subject to administrative sanctions for filing failures? (late submission or complete failure to file a declaration)	IM

table continues next page

Table A.3 Implementation Indicators for IAD and COI, Declaration Required *(continued)*

	What is the percentage of all filers that were *prima facie* subject to fines for filing failures? (late submission or complete failure to file a declaration)	IM
	What is the percentage of all filers that were *prima facie* subject to criminal sanctions for filing failures? (late submission or complete failure to file a declaration)	IM
3.2	*Disclosure integrity*	
	What is the percentage of declarations in which the filer failed to adhere to COI remediation obligations?	IM
	What is the percentage of declarations in which suspicious findings were identified?	IM
3.3	*Public engagement*	
	What is the average number of requests for declaration data per month?	IM
	If IAD/COI data is proactively made available online, what is the average number of visits to the webpage per month?	IM
	What is the average number of complaints filed with the IAD/COI agency per month, regarding the content of declarations?	IM

Sources: PAM Unit; authors' compilation.
Note: IAD/COI = income and asset disclosure/conflict of interest; R = rules (legal and policy framework and/or institutional arrangements): baseline assessment; C = organizational capacities (resources): baseline assessment and/or annual evaluation; P = organizational performance: annual and/or demand-based evaluation; IM = immediate impact.

Products

The PAM Initiative generates several interrelated products for assessing the quality of each of the above institutional mechanisms. Simplified quantitative data are available through the AGI Data Portal at https://www.agidata.org. More detailed qualitative data are available at https://www.agidata.org/pam, along with the following laws, links, and statistics:[3]

- *Library of laws* contain the relevant primary legislation; all legal citations are also made available with the data.
- *List of contributors* consist of local technical experts in each area of public accountability who provide guidance and reliability checks on the legislative data.
- *Country contexts* are provided through historic timelines, descriptions of country economic and political environments, and specification of legal systems (civil, common, customary, and so forth).
- *Links to country-specific institutions* are responsible for the enforcement of accountability mechanisms.
- *AGIs* capture data on (1) the characteristics of the legal framework governing each institution, (2) the capabilities and performance of organizations responsible for implementing the legislation, and (3) the immediate impacts on behavior of targeted agents. These data will be available in *summaries* of the data associated with each characteristic, with citations to the appropriate legislation, if relevant.
- *Descriptive statistics* showcase patterns across countries, regions, and globally, with respect to legislative indicators.

Notes

1. This is part of a larger project to develop such Actionable Governance Indicators, which is described in this appendix.

2. This is part of a larger project to develop such Actionable Governance Indicators, which is described in this appendix.

3. Internal World Bank users may access these websites at http://agidata and https://www.agidata.info/pam. Additional materials are made available to World Bank employees only.

APPENDIX B

Key Characteristics of Selected IAD Systems

Economy	Type of system	Type of agency	Frequency of filing	Total number of filers (year)	Centralized or delegated submission process	Uses of ICT in procedures	Public access to compliance information	Verification procedures	Public access to IAD content	Sanctions for noncompliance
Argentina	Dual objective system	Department in Ministry of Justice (MoJ)	Entry, exit, annually	36,000 (2008)	Delegated: Top 5 percent file centrally Other 95 percent file with HR offices	Electronic submission, verification, and data storage	All compliance data published on MoJ website	Yes: formal review (100 percent) Targeted verification (approx. 7 percent)	Yes ("public annex" only) by request and in person	Criminal penalties apply for nonsubmission and false declarations
Croatia	Conflict of interest	Parliamentary Commission	Entry, exit, ad hoc	1,800 (2008)	Centralized: All declarations submitted to the Commission	Paper submission; data transfer for online publication and storage	Noncompliance may be published in *Official Gazette*	No	Yes (aggregate data) online and in person	Fines for late filing; publication/ reprimand in *Official Gazette*; dismissal for false filing
Guatemala	Illicit enrichment	Integrity Department within Comptroller's Office (CGC)	Entry, exit, ad hoc	12,000 (2009)	Centralized: All declarations submitted to the CGC	Paper submission; data transfer for online publication and storage	*Official Gazette*	Targeted verification of declarations upon leaving office	No	Fines for late or nonfiling; irregularities referred for investigation
Hong Kong SAR, China	Conflict of interest	Civil Service Bureau	Entry + annually	—	Delegated	Limited data storage	Official reports	No: analysis for conflicts of interest only	Yes	Administrative sanctions for filing failures, criminal for false filing
Indonesia	Illicit enrichment	Specialized Corruption Eradication Commission	Entry, exit, ad hoc, and on request by Corruption Eradication Commission	116,451 (2009)	Partially delegated	Form available online; submitted in hard copy; electronic verification and storage	*Official Gazette* and online	Yes: Formal review (100 percent) Verification of accuracy (1 to 5 percent)	Yes (summary available in *Official Gazette*)	(Unspecified) administrative sanctions for late or nonfiling
Jordan	Illicit enrichment	Department in MoJ	Entry + exit + semiannually	4,117 (2009)	Centralized	Paper submission; electronic registry of filers	No	No: verification only upon an investigation triggered by a complaint	No	Criminal sanctions for late, non-, and/or false filing

table continues next page

Economy	Type of system	Type of agency	Frequency of filing	Total number of filers (year)	Centralized or delegated submission process	Uses of ICT in procedures	Public access to compliance information	Verification procedures	Public access to IAD content	Sanctions for noncompliance
Kyrgyz Republic	Dual objective system	Civil Service Agency (CSA) (renamed State Personnel Service)	Entry + exit + annually	18,000 (2008)	High public officials submit to CSA; civil servants submit to their agencies	Paper submission	Official bulletin, CSA website	No	Yes: only summaries	No: for high public officials / Yes: for civil servants
Mongolia	Illicit enrichment	Independent Anti-Corruption Commission	Entry + annual + ad hoc	52,800 (2009)	Delegated	Paper submission; electronic storage and limited electronic verification	Annual Report + press articles	Verification upon complaint filed against individual	Yes	Administrative sanctions only
Rwanda	Illicit enrichment	Ombudsman (Anti-Corruption Authority)	Entry + exit + annually	5,000 (2011)	Centralized	Limited verification and storage / Electronic filing coming	Annual Report	Targeted verification and limited random audits	No	Administrative sanctions for deadline failure / Criminal for lying
Slovenia	Dual objective system	Independent Anti-Corruption Agency (Commission for the Prevention of Corruption, CPC)	Entry + exit + annually + ad hoc	14,000 (2010)	Centralized	Basic personal information stored electronically	Annual Report + CPC website + media reports	Random audits using external databases (approx. 33%)	Online, but limited to income and assets acquired during an official's mandate	Fines for noncompliance and false disclosure; Removal from office upon finding of unsubstantiated increase in wealth
United States	Conflict of interest	Ethics Agency (Office of Government Ethics)	Entry + exit + annually	~24,000 public filers (2010)	Delegated	Electronic submission available for some agencies	Annual Report	No: analysis for conflicts of interest only	Yes	Administrative sanctions for filing failures / Criminal sanctions for lying

Note: IAD = income and asset disclosure; ICT = information and communication technology; — = not available.

People and Agencies Consulted in the Research for the Case Studies

Economy	Name	Title	Organization/institution
Argentina	Gerardo Serrano	Director de Planificación de Política de Transparencia	Anticorruption Office, Ministry of Justice
	Nestor Baragli	Subdirector de Planificación de Política de Transparencia	Anticorruption Office, Ministry of Justice
	Claudia Sosa	Director, Investigations Department	Anticorruption Office, Ministry of Justice
	Martin Montero	Investigations Department	Anticorruption Office, Ministry of Justice
	Patricio O'Reilly	Coordinator of Investigations, Investigations Department	Anticorruption Office, Ministry of Justice
	Maximiliano Flamma	Coordinator of Intake, Investigations Department	Anticorruption Office, Ministry of Justice
	Luis Arocena	Investigator	Anticorruption Office, Ministry of Justice
	Haydee Tramontana	Head, Income and Asset Declarations Administration Department	Anticorruption Office, Ministry of Justice
	Manuel Garrido	Director	Centro para la Implementación de Políticas para la Equidad y el Crecimiento (CIPPEC)
Croatia	Zeljko Jovanovic	President	National Council for Monitoring the Implementation of the National Anti-Corruption Program, Croatian Parliament
	Mate Kacan	President	Commission for the Prevention of Conflicts of Interest
	Adranka Kolarevic		Office of the Parliamentary Commission for the Prevention of Conflicts of Interest
	Zorislav Antun Petrovic		Office of the Parliamentary Commission for the Prevention of Conflicts of Interest
	Vlaho Bogišic		Office of the Parliamentary Commission for the Prevention of Conflicts of Interest
	Duro Sessa	Justice	State Judicial Council
	Vesna Siklic Odak		Central State Office for Administration
	Dinko Cvitan	Head of the Office	State Attorney's Office, Office for the Suppression of Corruption and Organised Crime
	Natasa Durovic	Deputy Head of the Office	State Attorney's Office, Office for the Suppression of Corruption and Organised Crime
	Fulvio Bianconi	Attaché, Customs, Taxation and Anti-Corruption Policy	Delegation of the European Union to the Republic of Croatia
	Zorislav Antun Petrovic	President	Transparency International, Croatia
	Sandra Pernar	Program Coordinator	GONG (NGO for Electoral System, Participatory Democracy, Civil Society and International Cooperation)
	Dubravka Prelec	Project Coordinator/Key Expert	British Council
	Mirna Santro	Governance Projects Manager	British Council
	Alan Uzelac	Professor	University of Zagreb
Guatemala	Walfred Orlando Rodriguez Tórtola	Director, Dirección de Probidad	Contraloría General de Cuentas de la República de Guatemala
	Alex Pellecer		Contraloría General de Cuentas de la República de Guatemala
	Luz Ofelia Aquino		Contraloría General de Cuentas de la República de Guatemala

table continues next page

Economy	Name	Title	Organization/institution
Hong Kong SAR, China	Candy Ma Siu-hung	Chief Executive Officer	Civil Service Bureau of the Hong Kong Special Administrative Region
	Bessie Liang		Civil Service Bureau of the Hong Kong Special Administrative Region
	Ian McWalters	Deputy Director of Public Prosecutions	Department of Justice, Prosecutions Division, Commercial Crime Unit
	Francis C. S. Lee	Director of Investigation	Independent Commission Against Corruption
	Daniel So	Principal Investigator, Operations Department	Independent Commission Against Corruption
	Rebecca Li	Assistant Director, Operations Department	Independent Commission Against Corruption
	Michael Burley	Chief Investigator, Operations Department	Independent Commission Against Corruption
	Winky Hsu	Principal Investigator, Operations Department	Independent Commission Against Corruption
	Melissa Tang	Chief Investigator, Operations Department, Financial Investigations Unit	Independent Commission Against Corruption
	Samuel Hui	Assistant Director, Corruption Prevention Department	Independent Commission Against Corruption
	Eileen Lau	Chief Corruption Prevention Officer	Independent Commission Against Corruption
	Raymond Ng Kwok ming	Principal Corruption Prevention Officer	Independent Commission Against Corruption
	Vanessa So Cheung	Principal Education and Mass Communication Officer	Independent Commission Against Corruption
	Nelson Cheng	Superintendent	Hong Kong Police Force, Financial Investigations
	Bernard Law	Detective Senior Inspector	Hong Kong Police Force, Financial Investigations
Indonesia	Moch Jasin	Commissioner	Corruption Eradication Commission, KPK
	Bibit Samad Rianto	Commissioner	Corruption Eradication Commission, KPK
	Bambang Sapto Pratomosunu	Secretary General	Corruption Eradication Commission, KPK
	Eko Soesamto Tjiptadi	Deputy of Prevention	Corruption Eradication Commission, KPK
	Cahya Hardianto Harefa	Director	Directorate of Registration and Examination of Public Officials' Wealth Disclosure, KPK
	David Hartor o Hutauruk	Head of Business Analyst Section	Directorate of Registration and Examination of Public Officials' Wealth Disclosure, KPK
	Ardy Aulia	Head of Registration Section	Directorate of Registration and Examination of Public Officials' Wealth Disclosure, KPK
	M. Najib Wahito	Head of Examination Team	Directorate of Registration and Examination of Public Officials' Wealth Disclosure, KPK
	Khaidir Ramli	Head of Legal Bureau	Legal Bureau
	Firman Yudiansyah	Head of Training Section	Human Resources Bureau
	Nadia Sarah	Business Analyst Specialist	Directorate of Registration and Examination of Public Officials' Wealth Disclosure, KPK

table continues next page

Economy	Name	Title	Organization/institution
	Diaz Adiasma	Business Analyst Specialist	Directorate of Registration and Examination of Public Officials' Wealth Disclosure, KPK
	Yulia Anastasia Fu'ada	Business Analyst Specialist	Directorate of Registration and Examination of Public Officials' Wealth Disclosure, KPK
	Indra Mantong Batti	Legal Specialist	Legal Bureau
	Dian Novianthi	Human Resource Specialist (HR Planning & Development Section)	Human Resources Bureau
	Ninuk Dyah Wahyuni	Planning and Financial Specialist	Planning and Financial Bureau
	Ipi Maryati Kuding	Public Relations Specialist	Public Relations Bureau
	Miranda Hotmadia Tandjung	International Cooperation Specialist	Directorate of Fostering Network Between Commission and Institution
	Syafira Putri Larasati	International Cooperation Specialist	Directorate of Fostering Network Between Commission and Institution
Jordan	Dr. Nazem Aref	Head of the Income and Asset Disclosure Department	Income and Asset Disclosure Department
	Imad Neimat	Communication Officer	Income and Asset Disclosure Department
	Seren Hijazi	Chief Clerk	Income and Asset Disclosure Department
	Shaymaa Alhadidi	Secretary	Income and Asset Disclosure Department
	Mohmmad Addialeh	Legal Researcher	Income and Asset Disclosure Department
	Ammar Husseini	Head of the International Relations Department/Ministry of Justice	International Relations Department
	Dr. Abed Shakhanbeh	Chairman/Anti-Corruption Commission	Anti-Corruption Commission
	Kholoud Al-Oran	Head, Division of International Relations	Anti-Corruption Commission
	Dr. Hasan Al-Abdallat	First Prosecutor of Amman	Public Prosecution
	Krayyem Tarawneh	Cassation Court Judge, Head of the Judicial Inspection Department	Judiciary
	Dr. Salah Albashir	Former Minister of Justice and Foreign Affairs	
Kyrgyz Republic	Bakytbek Sagynbaev	State Secretary of the State Personnel Service	State Personnel Service
	Esen Sherbotoev	Lead Specialist of the IAD Unit	State Personnel Service
	Zulfiya Aitieva		Civil Service Agency
	Bekbolot Bekiev	Coordinator	Millennium Challenge Corporation Threshold Program
	Jackie Charlton	Senior Regional Governance Adviser for Central Asia	UK Department for International Development (DFID)

table continues next page

Economy	Name	Title	Organization/institution
Mongolia	Sangaragchaa	Commissioner General	Independent Authority Against Corruption of Mongolia
	Amarbat Erdenebat	Head of Investigation Department, Commissioner in Charge	Independent Authority Against Corruption of Mongolia
	Batzorig Badam	Head of Research & Analysis Service, Senior Commissioner	Independent Authority Against Corruption of Mongolia
	Badarch Gungaa	Head of Administration Department, Commissioner in Charge	Independent Authority Against Corruption of Mongolia
	Radnaased Sh	Legal Policy Adviser to the President of Mongolia	Office of the President of Mongolia
	Lkhagva ZAYA		German Technical Cooperation (GTZ)
	Bill Infante	Representative	Asia Foundation
	Davaasuren Baasankhuu	Program Officer	Asia Foundation
	Sanjaasuren Oyun	Member of Parliament of Mongolia	Parliament of Mongolia
	Khashkhuu Naranjargal	President	Globe International
	P. Erdenejargal	Executive Director	Open Society Forum
	Jay Carver		USAID Rule of Law Project in Mongolia
Rwanda	Anastase Shyaka	Executive Secretary	Rwanda Governance Advisory Council
	Tito Ruraremara	Chief Ombudsman	Office of the Ombudsman
	Seraphin N. Fumaziminsi	Director, Preventing & Fighting Corruption and Related Offenses Unit	Office of the Ombudsman
	Francois Byabarumwanzi	Member of Parliament	Chamber of Deputies of the Republic of Rwanda
	Jules Marius Ntete	Inspector General	Prosecutor General of the Republic of Rwanda
	Obadiah R. B raro	Deputy Auditor General	Office of the Auditor General of State Finances
	Rwego K. Albert	Program Manager	Transparency Rwanda
Slovenia	Sergeja Oštir	Head of the Conflict of Interest Division	Commission for Prevention of Corruption
	Sandra Blagcjević	Assistant Head of Integrity Division	Commission for Prevention of Corruption
	Bečir Kečanović	Assistant Chairman	Commission for Prevention of Corruption
	Vita Habjan	Assistant Head of Prevention Division	Commission for Prevention of Corruption
	Drago Kos	Chairman	Commission for Prevention of Corruption
	Barbara Fürst	Public Relations Officer	Commission for Prevention of Corruption
	Tina Divjak	Head of Activity	Legal Informational Centre for NGOs
	Goran Forbic		Centre for Information Service, Co-operation and Development of NGOs
	Simona Habič	President	Association for Ethics in Public Service
United States	Barbara Fredericks	Assistant General Counsel for Administration	U.S. Department of Commerce
	Joseph Gangloff	Deputy Director	U.S. Office of Government Ethics
	Jane Ley	Deputy Director for International Assistance and Governance Initiatives	U.S. Office of Government Ethics
	Wendy Pond	International Programs Specialist	U.S. Office of Government Ethics

Environmental Benefits Statement

The World Bank is committed to reducing its environmental footprint. In support of this commitment, the Office of the Publisher leverages electronic publishing options and print-on-demand technology, which is located in regional hubs worldwide. Together, these initiatives enable print runs to be lowered and shipping distances decreased, resulting in reduced paper consumption, chemical use, greenhouse gas emissions, and waste.

The Office of the Publisher follows the recommended standards for paper use set by the Green Press Initiative. Whenever possible, books are printed on 50% to 100% postconsumer recycled paper, and at least 50% of the fiber in our book paper is either unbleached or bleached using Totally Chlorine Free (TCF), Processed Chlorine Free (PCF), or Enhanced Elemental Chlorine Free (EECF) processes.

More information about the Bank's environmental philosophy can be found at http://crinfo.worldbank.org/crinfo/environmental_responsibility/index.html.

green press
INITIATIVE